# Matthew 1-2

## Commentary

by

Stephen Manley

Upward Flight Books™

**Matthew 1-2 Commentary**



Edited by Delphine Manley

ISBN: 978-0-578-01967-3



**Additional copies may be ordered from:**

Stephen Manley Evangelistic Association, Inc.
PO Box 2089
Lebanon, TN 37088-2089

www.crossstyle.org

# Matthew 1-2

## Commentary

by

Stephen Manley

Upward Flight Books™

**Matthew 1-2 Commentary**



Edited by Delphine Manley

ISBN: 978-0-578-01967-3



**Additional copies may be ordered from:**

Stephen Manley Evangelistic Association, Inc.
PO Box 2089
Lebanon, TN 37088-2089

www.crossstyle.org

# CONTENTS

**Part Three: Matthew 2:1-12**

***Seeking the King***



**Part Four: Matthew 2:13-16**

***Tragedy at Christmas***

**Part Five: Matthew 2:19-23**

***The Return Home***

# PART ONE

# Matthew 1:1-17

## The Cross – The Throne of the King

Cross Style in the Genealogy

# Matthew 1-7

# The King

Every era of history holds a wealth of information. The people of each era have something to teach us. If we can understand the events of their lives, we can understand the lessons we must learn. It is easy to speculate about the trends and traditions of these people and never get involved in their struggles. As sociologists and historians, we talk about people and their patterns, but we never experience the heat of their pressures. I fear we have a tendency to approach the Old Testament, and the period between the Old and the New Testaments, from a historical view, and never get into the sandals of the people. We can gather information by viewing their history and the trends of their times, but if we want to be accurate, it is absolutely necessary to feel what they felt and see what they saw. The pressures upon them must become our pressures. This is very important as we move into the opening statement of the Book of Matthew. Matthew was not writing in a vacuum. In the midst of the political and spiritual condition of the Jews, Matthew planted the Gospel story. For four hundred years the voice of the prophets had been silent. In four hundred years, no one had shouted, "The Word of the Lord came unto me." It seemed the revelation of God had ended abruptly. For four hundred years there were no burning bushes, no pillars of fire by night, nor clouds by day. The people in this time period had never seen a dark cloud descend upon a mountain to bring revelation to them. There was no evidence that God was even within the Holy of Holies in the temple. It was four hundred years of complete silence.

Judah emerged from the Babylonian captivity, never to be the same again. Ezra and Nehemiah led a group of Jews back to Jerusalem to rebuild the city and the temple. Prior to these events, the history of the Jewish nation was that of constant backsliding. They were forever slipping into idolatry. The Old Testament is a picture of the tragic cycle of revival, lukewarmness, backsliding into idolatry, followed by another cycle of revival, lukewarmness, backsliding into idolatry. It occurred again and again. But something happened in the life of this nation when the people came out of the Babylonian captivity. They never again entered into this tragic cycle.

In order to keep from repeating their previous cycle of backsliding, these people focused on the Scripture, the law of God, as if it alone were their salvation. During the four hundred years from Malachi to Matthew, a group called the Pharisees became a dominate part of the Jewish society. They took the law of God and added to it by interpretation. Their oral tradition of the law included six hundred and thirteen commandments. These oral commandments were more sacred to them than the actual Scriptures themselves. There were two hundred and forty-eight commandments which called for positive action. But there were three hundred and sixty-five negative commandments, one for every day of the year, which emphasized the "don't do that."

Another group, which formed the setting of the New Testament hour, was the Sadducees. They were the wealthy, political group who were dedicated to preserving the Jewish tradition, but they did it differently than the Pharisees. The two groups had great theological differences between them. Both the Sadducees and the Pharisees called the people back to their Jewish traditions and ceremonies, but the Sadducees wanted to reestablish their heritage in God Jehovah rather than the law. For a period of four hundred years, the Sadducees had studied the Old Testament Scriptures to establish the Jewish religious traditions.

There is yet another element we must throw into the mix. It is the tremendous persecution and political unrest the Jews experienced during this four hundred-year period. One nation after another had captured the Jews during this time, and when we come to Matthew's writing, the Jews were under the domination of Rome. In Matthew's record of the genealogy (Matthew 1:12-16), he records the ancestors of Christ following their return from the Babylonian captivity, but he lists no kings. Israel was without her own king during this four hundred-year period. Israel only knew domination and suppression during these days, yet they were inhabiting their own land.

They were a down trodden nation. They had only one hope of freedom. Jehovah God had promised them a King. His promise rang throughout the Old Testament. At the very beginning of the Old Testament (Genesis 3:15), it is recorded that a King would come in power, bruising the Devil's head and taking back what was lost through sin. Because of this King the ***scepter shall not depart from Judah, nor the ruler's staff from between His feet,*** (Genesis 49:10.) The prophets always spoke of this King's rule as everlasting, eternal and forever.

King David's lineage was central in the ancestry of the coming eternal King. Nathan, the prophet, said, ***"And your house and your kingdom shall endure before Me forever, your throne shall be established forever,*** (2 Samuel 7:16.) In the Psalms, David gives constant reference to the coming King. ***But as for Me, I have installed My King upon Zion, My holy mountain. I will surely tell of the decree of the Lord: He said to Me, "Thou art My Son, today I have begotten Thee. Ask of Me, and I will surely give the nations as Thine inheritance, and the very ends of the earth as Thy possession,"*** (Psalms 2:6-8). He continues his reference to the coming King as ***the King of glory*** and ***the Lord of hosts,*** (Psalms 24:10).

Isaiah tells us He would be born of a virgin (Isaiah7:14), and He would be despised, forsaken, stricken, pierced through, crushed, chastened, scourged, oppressed, and afflicted (Isaiah 53:3-7). Daniel speaks of Him as ***One like a Son of Man*** (Daniel 7:13). Yet Isaiah also tells us ***the government will rest on His shoulders; and His name will be called Wonderful Counselor, Mighty God, Eternal Father, Prince of Peace. There will be no end to the increase of His government or of peace*** (Isaiah9:6-7), and He will be called ***Immanuel,*** which means ***God with us,*** (Isaiah 7:14; Matthew 1:23). Through Micah, the Lord promised Bethlehem: ***From you One will go forth for Me to be ruler in Israel. His goings forth are from long ago, from the days of eternity*** (Micah 5:2). Zephaniah tells his people when this King comes He will be ***King of Israel, the Lord*** in their midst (Zephaniah

3:15). Zechariah tells us He will ***be just and endowed with salvation*** (Zechariah 9:9), and when He reigns, every family on earth will be able to ***go up to Jerusalem to worship the King, the Lord of hosts,*** (Zechariah 14:17).

Living in the pressure of these two great forces made life difficult for the Jews. The political upheaval from the domination of Rome and the spiritual pressure of living up to the law and traditions of the Sadducees and Pharisees, filled the life of the Jew with turmoil. This brought a burning passion to the heart of every Jew. They wanted a King. They looked for Him every day. The first words they uttered each morning were, "Could this be the day?" Their deepest desire for hope lay in their promise of a King.

Are you surprised when I tell you this is the message of the New Testament? Jesus is presented by the writers of each book as the King of Kings who has established a great Kingdom. In the twenty-seven books of the New Testament, the term Kingdom is used one hundred and forty-four times. The writers refer to Jesus as King at least thirty-five times. They use the term "to reign" ten times.

The Book of Matthew is the introduction to the New Testament. For twenty-eight chapters, Matthew focuses on one great truth. Jesus is King. As Matthew writes to the Jews, he presents argument after argument. He plays the role of a lawyer, presenting overwhelming evidence that Jesus alone qualifies to be the promised King for whom they are longing.

A general survey of the first seven chapters of the Book of Matthew will give us a sense of how Matthew introduces this subject. He begins with **THE GENEALOGY, HIS ANCESTRY** (1:1-17). Look at verse one! ***The book of the genealogy of Jesus Christ, the Son of David, the Son of Abraham;*** (1:1). Matthew traces the lineage of Jesus through the royal line of Israel, King David. He presents a descending line, from Abraham through David, through Joseph, to Jesus, who is called Christ. This is significant! Since the destruction of the Temple and Jerusalem in 70 AD, no genealogies exist that trace the ancestry of any Jew now living. That means no Jew of this day can establish his lineage through to the throne of David and verify it. Jesus was the last one who could verify this claim. He is King!

**THE GENESIS, HIS ARRIVAL** is found in the next section (1:18-25). This is about the amazing birth of this King. It was Isaiah who prophesied the King would come in this manner. ***Therefore the Lord Himself will give you a sign: Behold, the virgin shall conceive and bear a Son, and shall call His name Immanuel,*** (Isaiah 7:14). This King will know no earthly father, but will be born from above. He will be the God man with Divine blood flowing through His veins. He is God with us. That is why He is the adequate Messiah King. He will be recognized as such.

**THE GUEST, HIS ASTROLOGERS** (2:1-12) is found in chapter two. The wise men from the East have come with an army. They are men who search for new Kings. They have seen a star in the East, and they have followed it. This King is One worthy of their journey and their worship. They have come to bow at His feet and present Him with gifts. His Kingship is of such magnitude that they can spare nothing to find Him. He is not only King of the Jews, but King of the wise men from the East. They recognize Him as the King of the world.

Matthew then turns his narrative to a subject he will use again and again to present his argument. It is prophecy. He presents us with **THE GUIDELINES, HIS AUTHENTICATION** (2:13-23). It is here that Matthew highlights the prophecies surrounding the birth of the King and the attempt to destroy Him. When the true King comes, there can be no other. Lesser kings attempt to usurp His throne, but to no avail.

There is **THE GOING BEFORE, HIS ANNOUNCER** (3:1-2). John the Baptist, the forerunner, comes to prepare the way for the King. He is the herald who announces the arrival of the One for whom we are waiting. John himself is a fulfillment of prophecy, who has come to bring the revival necessary for the path of the Messiah. The forerunner will pave the path with his own blood. It will be over this path of blood the Messiah King will walk to establish His cross.

Matthew quickly moves to tell the story of the launching of the ministry of this great King. He takes us to Jesus' baptism by John the Baptist. It is here we see **THE GUARANTEE, HIS ADVOCATE** (3:13-17). This King is endorsed by the Father, through the Holy Spirit. This King is the representative of the Trinity. No one else could have the wisdom or the power to bring about the redemption necessary to establish the Kingdom. The dreams of God will be fulfilled through this King.

Do not think for one moment this will be smooth sailing! War has been declared. The enemy has launched a full frontal attack. **THE GUILE, HIS ATTACK** (4:1-11) is Matthew's next presentation. But how can this Christ be an adequate King? Can he win victories as a King? In the heat of the battle, we see His substance. In moments of temptation, He holds back nothing. He conquers every trick of the Devil with the truth of the Kingdom He is establishing. What a King!

It is in the beginning moments of His ministry where we see **THE GIFT, HIS ASSISTANCE** (4:12-25). Compassion seems to be the key word. This King does not live for Himself, but from the very beginning, He pours out His life for others. His focus is only for others.

What kind of King is He? What kind of Kingdom will He establish? The King opens his ministry with the great Sermon on the Mount. His manifesto, **THE GOSPEL, HIS ANNOUNCEMENT** (5-7) is the declaration of the content, style and concept of the Kingdom of God. We do not adequately understand it at first. We must see this King demonstrate His lifestyle. We must see Him wash dirty feet and love His enemies. We will be shaken by His death on the cross, knowing He did not have to die. We will be thrilled with His resurrection. Then we will see that He is King of this new Kingdom.

While the message of Matthew declared Jesus as King, with no way to dispute it, it has to become personal. What good is great Biblical truth if it is not applied to our personal lives? Is He King of your life? Matthew does not allow the mere acknowledgment of the truth of His Kingship, or even paying homage to Him as King with certain rituals. This Kingship demands more than lip service! He demands more than patterns, habits, and traditions which acknowledge His Kingship. He requires more from us than singing nice choruses which highlight His Kingship. That is not enough for the true King.

This King has established a new Kingdom. For Him to be King, we must step into the Kingdom. Geographic location and paying taxes is not as important as inner attitude and spirit. The King calls you to a total loss of your life to Him and His Kingdom. We must allow Jesus to totally dominate us in every scene and intent of life. The central issue of Kingship is always control. He must control, not as a dictator, but as One to whom we have given ourselves.

This truth unfolds in the Book of Matthew. When the supreme King comes, everything which has been in control becomes pressured and resists. Battles are fought. You can see it happening among the Jews in this book. For four hundred years the Jews have been aggressively reestablishing their Jewish traditions and ceremonies. Certainly they are not bad. God gave these traditions to them as a constant reminder of what was to come. But when the King appears and begins to challenge Jewish loyalty to the traditions, there is war. There had always been the tradition of offering sacrificial lambs. During the Passover Week over a quarter of a million lambs were killed, all pointing to the coming King. Jesus said they did not need to continue this tradition. He had come as The Lamb of God. But their tradition had been king, and they would not bow at the feet of The King.

What traditions and patterns control you and reign as king of your life? It is easy to be mastered by what we have always done. We spend years developing and establishing our personal system. It is the way we like things. But the King is now here! Will we allow Him to change our personal patterns or will we crucify Him again?

The Jews have spent four hundred years developing their oral laws. These were more sacred to them than even the Scriptures. They were so controlled by these laws, when the King came and challenged them, there was war. They had developed laws concerning their Sabbath day, but Jesus reminded them He was King over the Sabbath day. He, in fact, made the Sabbath day (Matthew 12:8). They were not to be controlled by their laws, but by Him.

The issue is not about good and bad. The issue is about control. When even a good thing controls you, it takes the place of The King. Your loyalty is to be to Him alone! He wants to reign from within you. We are to experience the flow of His life and Spirit. We must know His mind and share His heart. We must vibrate with His passion. We must become His Kingdom, His territory. He must reign with our flesh. We are to become His body, allowing Him to live through us. He is to be our KING!

# Matthew 1:1

## The Book of Genealogy

***The book of the genealogy of Jesus Christ, the Son of David, the Son of Abraham,*** (1:1). These are usual words in the English language, but the discovery of these words in their original Greek greatly impacted me. The first word in the original Greek is ***Biblios.*** It is translated into the English as book and sometimes record. It is the Greek word for Bible. It has the sense of Divine truth or sacred writing. I was about to receive a very important truth. The second word in the original language is ***geneseoos.*** You should recognize this as the word for the title of the first book of the Bible, Genesis. The Book of Genesis is the record of creation. It is all about the beginning of things. It means the origin or the beginning of the existence of. The third word is ***Ieesou,*** which means ***of Jesus***, and the fourth word is ***Christou,*** which is ***of Christ.***

A translation of this verse in the original Greek would be: ***The Bible, record, or book of the beginning of the existence of Jesus Christ.*** Matthew's opening statement for the twenty-eight chapters of

The Book of Matthew in actuality reads, "the Bible of the genesis, which means origin, beginning of existence of Jesus Christ." Everything within me cried out against this statement. This is not the way to begin a presentation of Jesus Christ, the King. Matthew's purpose in writing was his attempt to present the Jews with an evangelistic message that would win them to Christ. They did not believe Jesus was the Messiah, and Matthew must convince them of His Divinity. He should have started with the great acclamation of Jesus being God. But he did not!

John knew how to begin a Gospel account. In his opening statement, he wrote, ***In the beginning was the Word, and the Word was with God, and the Word was God,*** (John 1:1). He confronts his readers with the sovereignty of Jesus. This information says Jesus is the omnipotent, omniscient, and omnipresent God. John wanted the Jews to be completely aware of the Christ they had nailed to the cross. He got the attention of the Jews as he began his evangelistic message.

Mark also knew how to present a convincing argument concerning Christ. He wrote, ***The beginning of the gospel of Jesus Christ, the Son of God,*** (Mark 1:1). He knew how to introduce Jesus to an unbelieving world. Jesus is God. He is the Divine One. He is the second member of the Trinity. Jesus is sovereign God, the creator of all things. He is the omnipotent One, the omniscient One, the immutable One, and the omnipresent One. This sort of statement describes Jesus in a proper way. These statements put His story in a proper setting.

But Matthew does not begin his Gospel account in such order! He starts by saying, ***Let me give you the record, the book of the beginning of the existence of Jesus Christ.*** Matthew begins with a total focus on the manhood of Jesus Christ. I know Jesus is God among us because I have read all of the Gospel accounts. Jesus' Divinity is very important. He could not have redeemed us if He were not God. The cross would have only been a tragic death of a nice guy if Jesus had not been God. Matthew should have made the Jews to understand this before he presented any other truth.

Matthew begins his account with a focus on the humanity of Jesus. Before he is finished with his account, Matthew uplifts Jesus as God. He highlights the prophecy of Isaiah, ***"Behold, the virgin shall conceive and bear a Son, and shall call His name Immanuel,"*** (Isaiah 7:14). He repeatedly reveals Jesus as the Son of God. Matthew states Jesus' claim to Messiahship in no uncertain terms. But it is not the first impression he gives. And aren't first impressions important? Doesn't the opening statement set the tone for the entire book? His beginning statement should thrust us into the basic theme, creating the undertow of everything he wants to say about Jesus.

The proposition of his entire book is this. **This is the record of the beginning of the existence of Jesus Christ.** What does he mean by this powerful emphasis?

## God is Doing an Old Thing

## Matthew 1:1

Is God doing an old thing? ***This is the beginning of the existence of Jesus Christ.*** Isn't it a new thing? God became flesh. That is the beginning of the existence of the second member of the Trinity, in the flesh. It is a new thing. There is no argument against this statement.

But we want to see all of this through the eyes of Matthew. He does not recognize it as a new thing. This is the first verse of the statement of genealogy. Matthew is going to tell us about forty-two generations of time (1:17), when God has been at work. He has a long range dream. God has a plan straight from His heart, and He wants to redeem the world. God has put this plan into place. He will pull the strings and manipulate the histories to accomplish this ancestry. This will require miracle after miracle. Here we are at the beginning of this old thing.

For the remainder of his book, Matthew will highlight how old it really is. He tells us of the prophecy of the olden days, and shows us that it is fulfilled in Christ. There are two kinds of prophecies given to us in the Old Testament. There is the symbolic predictive prophecy. Something or someone in the Old Testament is a type or symbol of something or someone in the New Testament. For example, the sacrificial lamb was a symbol of the coming Christ, who would die on a cross. Hundreds of these symbols in the Old Testament are fulfilled in the New Testament. God wove within the fibers of the Old Testament's ceremonies and traditions, these kinds of symbols. These prophecies reminded the Jews daily of the coming Messiah. God was doing an old thing. The symbolic predictive prophecies made it easier for the skeptics to say we just made up these prophecies after the fact.

But there is another type of prophecy. It is the verbal predictive prophecy. A man, called a prophet, stood before the people and spoke the words which described what was going to take place. He often did this hundreds of years before the event. We can look back, read what he spoke, and see exactly how it was fulfilled. There are three hundred and thirty-two verbal predictive prophecies given about the Messiah in the Old Testament. Jesus fulfills every one of these prophecies. The chances of one man fulfilling all three hundred and thirty-two of these prophecies are one chance out of eighty-four with one hundred zeros after it. Matthew fills his book with these prophecies as he tells us God is doing an old thing.

When writing of the birth of Christ, Matthew saturates the subject with the resounding phrase, ***it might be fulfilled which was spoken by the Lord through the prophet.*** Isaiah tells us that Jesus will be born of a virgin (Isaiah 1:23). Think of how long ago he said that. The wise men came from the East seeking a new King. Herod immediately called on the scribes, the students of the Old Testament, to see where this King would be born. They told him that Bethlehem was the place (2:5). They received this information through one of these prophecies. Think how long ago God made His plans. This is an old thing. The angel appeared to Joseph in a dream and warned him of the danger from King Herod. He took Mary and the baby Jesus into Egypt, but then it was already foretold by the prophet this would happen (2:15). These are really old plans. God didn't dream up a new idea, but He planned and determined the histories of the world around the old plan He already had. God is doing an old thing.

## God is Doing an Old Thing in Becoming One of Us

## Matthew 1:1

What is this old thing? It is God's redemption of the world. But redemption could not come from above. God could not spoon feed redemption from the heavenlies. He could not drop it from the seventh heaven. It was man who got us in this mess, so man would have to get us out. Redemption had to flow from below, not from above. But where is the man who is capable of accomplishing this? There is none! There was not a man with the qualities necessary to pay the penalty or the debt of sin. The Redeemer would have to be a man who needed never to offer sacrifice for his own sins. Every person we have known has been busy repenting of his own sins. Where is the man who could totally focus his attention on the sins of others because he has none of his own?

So it became obvious! One from above would have to come below and become one of us. God would have to become man. ***This is the record of the beginning of the existence of Jesus Christ.*** He could not be a superman. He could not be a fake man. He could not be a man without risk. This man could not have qualities other men did not have. If He had resources at His disposal, which others did not have, we could never be like Him. He would have to be tempted like we are, with the same possibility of sin and defeat. He would have to know our pressures, and have the need to wear deodorant, just as we do. His body would need to get tired, just like ours. This man needed to be without the knowledge to know what to do in each situation.

This is the scene of the first verse of Matthew. ***The book of genealogy of Jesus Christ, the Son of David, the Son of Abraham.*** To the Jew, there is an inclusiveness about the Son of Abraham. Not every Jew of Matthew's day could claim to be a descendant of King David, but every one of them could claim Abraham as His Father. Matthew says Jesus became one of us. He has on our skin; He wears our shoes. He smells like we do, and He eats our kind of food. He is tempted at every point as we are tempted. He has the same kind of emotions and feelings we have.

Jesus has a history. He has a grandfather and a lineage. He came through a process. He was not a vision, and He was certainly not an illusion. Jesus was not God making an appearance we could understand, but not really a total man. He had a birth certificate. He was one of us.

But I react to this picture of Jesus. I do not want Jesus to be like this. I want the emphasis to be upon the fact He is God. If He became like me, with only the resources I have, then all of my excuses are gone. I can no longer say, "I cannot be like Jesus. After all, He was God and I am only a human being." He became exactly what I am, therefore I can be called to be like He is. We all fight against this concept. But there it is. ***The record of the beginning of the existence of Jesus Christ, the Son of David, the Son of Abraham,*** (1:1).

## God is Doing an Old Thing for a Purpose

## Matthew 1:1

God must have had a great purpose in mind to become one of us. Matthew fills his twenty-eight chapters proclaiming this purpose. God's purpose was to redeem us by becoming the Messiah King. He became one of us to become a King over us. Isn't that the point of the genealogy? Didn't He need to prove His lineage, thus showing His right to claim the throne of David and rule as King over the Kingdom of God? Didn't He make this sacrifice to become man in order to get to rule over everyone and everything?

No! No! You have missed the purpose. The purpose was not just for Him to be King. In reality, He was already King? As the second member of the Trinity, He could rule over everything and everyone. He did not need to become man in order to rule. He was always sovereign God; He did not need to sacrifice in order to exert His authority. He is the creator of all things, and all things exist in Him (Colossians 1:16).

Now the purpose becomes clearer. Jesus became one of us in order to rule as one of us. It is one thing to rule from above as God, and it is another thing to come to earth to rule as a man. No! No! We still do not see the picture Matthew wants us to see. Jesus could have become a man and ruled as a king without being born in a stable. He should have been born in a palace. He did not need to have cows looking on at His birth, but He should have been in the luxury of a royal court. He should have had royalty bowing at his cradle, not shepherds. The Christ child should have been in with the leadership of Israel. He should have joined their ranks instead of constantly alienating them. What was He thinking when He washed the disciples feet? He did not need to do that in order to reign as King. That did not make Him one of us. The idea of the cross is ridiculous. If you want to be King and rule as one of us, there is no need for a cross.

The miracles of Jesus greatly impacted the crowds who witnessed them. Jesus fed five thousand men, besides women and children. After the feeding, and a short nap, these folks gathered up their doggy bags of leftovers and surrounded Jesus. It was their intent to take Him by force and make Him their King (John 6:15). Being the King was not difficult for a miracle worker to achieve.

But this is not the Kingship, or the kind of Kingdom Jesus wanted to establish. He was not becoming one of us to be a King to rule over us. He wanted to embrace us as His royal family. He became one of us in order to make us one of Him. He became what we were intended to be in the first place. When you see Jesus, you see exactly what you are supposed to be. You are to be like Him, not in theory, not in the ideal, but in the practical, reality of your life. The way Jesus lived is the way we are to live. The resource He had, we are to have.

So God did not do an old thing. He did not become one of us to rule over us. He became one of us to serve us. The Kingdom He established is different from any other kingdom. All other kings are interested in having people serve them, but Jesus became King to serve us. All other kings want to have their feet washed, but Jesus became King to wash our feet. All other kings require their subjects to die for them, but Jesus came to die for us. He is our King. All other kings live according to their self style, but our King lives out the cross style.

Jesus embraces us as royal family, brothers, in order that we might live the same style in our world. He took all the resource available to Him as a man, and He utilized it totally for others. We are to embrace Him and find the same total resource. That will make us like Him, having the same style. We are to be like Jesus. He wants you to have everything He has. All that He is He wants to give to you. The old thing was for Him to be the first one of a new group of people, who are just like Him. The resource He has, you have; the power He has, you have; the death He died, you must die; and the resurrection He experienced, you now experience.

Will you accept Him as King with the cross style?

# Matthew 1:1

# Jesus, The Son

A few summers ago, I met some people who were fascinated with the scope of my travels. They informed me they had never left the boundaries of their state. As our conversation proceeded, I discovered they had never even ventured beyond the outskirts of their county. Oh, they had watched television. They knew there was a world out there, but it had little effect on them. They had never tasted of it. They didn't know what it smelled like, and they certainly had never rubbed shoulders with its hurting people. These people were isolated in their comfortable surroundings, untouched by the vastness around them. This added to my growing concern about how small and narrow our lives can become. It is really sad when life is so compact the highlight of the week is going out for ice cream.

For the majority of us, however, this is not the case. We know what it is to travel outside our county, state, and maybe even our country, but we still seem to have narrow perimeters for our living. Our thoughts seldom go beyond our family, our business, our personal needs, or what we can see. Our motto seems to be, "Me, my wife, my son, John, my daughter, Sally, us four and no more!" We are immersed in our family, our town, our time, our church, our denomination, and our interests. We become very narrow in our vision. Oh, to see the big picture!

It was not easy, but Matthew had caught the vision. He had walked with Jesus for three years, and Jesus had forced him to a world view. The twelve men Jesus chose as His disciples were very narrow in their thinking. They had never been more than one hundred miles from their homes. All they knew was their little Jewish world. They were focused on their fishing businesses on the Sea of Galilee. This minority group had isolated themselves from the heathen population surrounding them. They had, on purpose, drawn in their borders and stayed within themselves. Jesus stretched their minds. When His death and resurrection took place, it was overwhelming to them. Can you imagine what it would have been like to talk with the resurrected Lord, who had been to hell and back? From His viewpoint, Jesus told them of the Kingdom which was beyond the borders of their world. When Pentecost happened, they began to see with the eyes of God. It shook their world. This group of narrow-minded Galileans suddenly became world evangelists, taking the Gospel to the utter most parts of the world. They began to build the Kingdom about which Jesus told them.

You can see this kind of vision in the parables of Jesus. In the Parable of the Great Judgment, the vision is visible. Jesus began the parable with these words. ***"When the Son of Man comes in His glory, and all the holy angels with Him, then He will sit on the throne of His glory. All the nations will be gathered before Him,"*** (Matthew 25:31-32). Do you get the feel of this? ***All the nations*** is the emphasis.

We are not speaking of our little group only. This is not about a minority sect called Christians, an opinionated group among many other religions. When all the nations are gathered together, there will be no other opinion. Christianity is a huge, all embracing, world influencing movement.

Jesus relates this feeling in the Parables of the Kingdom (Matthew 13). He says, ***"So it will be at the end of the age. The angels will come forth, separate the wicked from among the just,"*** (13:49). This is not a Christian thought process which the world has outgrown. Christianity is "a beyond comparison thrust." Our God holds the reins and will one day bring all things to an end.

Matthew writes an evangelistic message to his own people. He calls the Jewish nation to see the big picture. They must think beyond their own traditions, ceremonies and patterns. He paints the picture of their role in history according to God's movement in the world. They can no longer be a minority group, receiving an occasional pat on the head from Jehovah. The Messiah has come, and He has shaken the world. Matthew gives this view from the outset of his book. He says, ***The book of the genealogy of Jesus Christ, the Son of David, the Son of Abraham:*** (1:1).

## Jesus is the Focal Point of History
## Matthew 1:1-16

All the genealogies of the Old Testament were written in the same pattern. Matthew startles the Jews by reversing that pattern when he writes the genealogy of Jesus. He is making a bold declaration. From the outset of his writing, he plants a billboard as a resounding reminder to every Jew.

Every genealogy in the Old Testament begins with an opening statement, which names the forefather from whom each descendant received life. The purpose of the genealogy was to document the offspring of the forefather, the first entry in the genealogy. Every offspring derived his value and place from the forefather. If Matthew followed this pattern, he would have opened with these words. "The book of the genealogy of Abraham." In verse two he begins with Abraham, listing the descendants until he comes to the birth of Christ (1:16). Jesus derives His place in the history from Abraham. But this is not the genealogy of Abraham, this is ***The book of the genealogy of Jesus Christ, the Son of David, the Son of Abraham.***

Matthew does not follow the normal pattern of listing the descendants of Jesus. He gives a list of the ancestors of Jesus. This means Jesus is not dependant upon these ancestors for His life and meaning. They are dependent on Him. Jesus is the focal point of history. The descendants of Abraham do not point back to their forefathers; they all point to the One who is to be born.

Every one Matthew lists derives his meaning from Jesus. Each person is not listed because he is the descendant of Abraham or David, but because he is the ancestor of Jesus Christ. God, in His sovereignty, directed the history of Israel, and preserved David's line, because of His plan to send Jesus. By closing the genealogy with the birth of Jesus, ***who is called Christ*** (1:16), Matthew highlights Jesus' uniqueness and superiority in terms of fulfillment. Instead of Jesus' identity and character being discovered through His forefathers, the forefathers are subordinate to their last descendant, Jesus. Matthew shows Jesus as the One who gives meaning and significance to Israelite history.

## Jesus is the Focal Point of Your History
## Matthew 1:1-16

I will never be able to communicate this adequately. Jesus is the focal point of YOUR history! He is not the focal point of history in general, but He is the focal point of your individual history. In the genealogy, each ancestor derives his meaning from Jesus. Why are their names listed? What is the significance of the roles they play? It is all about Him! They are remembered in the histories of the world as to how they relate to Jesus Christ.

Most of us have been taught the circular view of history. It appears in statements like this. "What goes around, comes around," or "History repeats itself." These statements give the false impression that mankind is trapped in a huge circular motion. Year after year, man is going through the same experiences. Nothing seems to change. Therefore, this philosophy leaves one with the impression that you might get a second chance to make things right.

But this is completely contrary to the Word of God. The Biblical view of history is not circular, but linear. It is going somewhere. Matthew teaches that history is in a direct line. We are aiming at the target. We will not repeat this moment or regain this opportunity. We see this clearly in the story of Jacob and Esau. Jacob is the one listed in the genealogy. ***Abraham begot Isaac, Isaac begot Jacob, and Jacob begot Judah and his brothers,*** (1:2). Esau is nowhere to be found, even though he was the first born. It was his birth right. But the writer of Hebrews warns us concerning the ***root of bitterness,*** which might spring up and cause us trouble, ***and by this many become defiled: lest there be any fornicator or profane person like Esau, who for one morsel of food sold his birthright,*** (Hebrews 12:15-16). Esau had returned from hunting, but had caught nothing. Due to his hunger, Jacob connived him into giving his birthright for ***bread and stew of lentils,*** (Genesis 25:34). The end result of this foolish action was tragic. ***For you know that afterward, when he wanted to inherit the blessing, he was rejected, for he found no place for repentance, though he sought it diligently with tears,*** (Hebrews 12:17). Regardless of his sincere repentance, he could not undo what he had done in those life determining moments.

Why is this deed so important? It finds its meaning, as do all deeds, in how it relates to the person of Jesus Christ. Everything is going somewhere. We are headed for the bulls eye. Some men who were included in the genealogy should have been excluded, and some men who were excluded should have been included. Esau and Jacob are the examples. Their lives were going somewhere. The final bulls eye is Jesus. How do they fit into Him? You interpret their history through Christ.

Let me contrast this negative example with a positive one. You will notice there are four women who are included in this genealogy. Three of them are Gentiles. One of them is an adulteress. ***Salmon begot Boaz by Rahab, Boaz begot Obed by Ruth, Obed begot Jesse,*** (1:5). Ruth was not a Jew, but was a woman of Moab (Ruth 1:4). There were two Jewish brothers living in the land of Moab with their father and mother. Each reached the age of manhood, and married a

Moabite woman. First the father died, and then both boys died. This left the three women alone. One of the widows went back to her Moabite family. But Ruth refused to leave her mother-in-law, returning with Naomi to her people in Bethlehem. It was in Bethlehem, while gleaning in the fields of Boaz, a romance began. What is the significance of Ruth's decision? Why are we still talking about this romance of Boaz and Ruth? Ruth's decision to follow Naomi led to the birth of Obed, the grandfather of Jesus Christ. Ruth's value and worth, as well as all of history, is seen in relationship to her descendant, Jesus.

It is a reality! This same principal applies to us. A simple matter of life becomes a monumental turning point because of how it relates to Jesus. Your life is going somewhere. Your days count! You will ultimately be seen in light of Him. Your inclusion or your exclusion is determined by Him. Your meaning and your history will be determined by the perspective seen through Him

There is another valuable lesson we can learn from this verse. It will narrow the view.

## Jesus is the Focal Point of Redemptive History

### Matthew 1:1

The title, ***Son of David,*** is given to Jesus many times in the New Testament. It is used again and again, almost like a name. The phrase has become synonymous with the title "Messiah." This was true among the scholars and the common folks. It was a common teaching among the people. ***When Jesus departed from there, two blind men followed Him, crying out and saying, "Son of David, have mercy on us!"*** (Matthew 9:27). Upon their witness of a demonic deliverance, the multitudes were amazed. They began to ask the question, ***"Could this be the Son of David?"*** (Matthew 12:23). Even a Canaanite woman, a Gentile by birth, untrained in Jewish tradition, cried out to Jesus, ***"Have mercy on me, O Lord, Son of David!"*** (Matthew 15:22). On his way to Jerusalem for the last time, Jesus passed through Jericho. Two blind men ***cried out, saying, "Have mercy on us, O Lord, Son of David!"*** (Matthew 20:30). The crowds tried to get them to be quiet and not bother Jesus, ***but they cried out all the more, saying, "Have mercy on us, O Lord, Son of David!"*** (Matthew 20:31). At the great celebration called Palm Sunday, the people shouted in the streets, ***"Hosanna to the Son of David!"*** (Matthew 21:9). After Jesus cleansed the temple, the children were heard ***crying out in the temple and saying, "Hosanna to the Son of David!"*** (Matthew 21:15).

Jesus put the issue in its proper perspective during a day long debate with the leaders of Israel. After all of their questions, Jesus ends the discussion with a couple of questions of His own. ***Jesus asked them, saying, "What do you think about the Christ? Whose Son is He?"*** Jesus knew this would be a determining factor in their belief about the Messiah. ***They said to Him, "The Son of David,"*** (Matthew 22:42). Of course, they gave the right answer. Yet, there remained an issue with which they were not willing to deal. Jesus tackles this issue in his next question.

> ***"How then does David in the Spirit call Him 'Lord,' saying:***
> ***'The Lord said to My Lord,***
> ***"Sit at My right hand,***
> ***Till I make Your enemies Your footstool?"'***

> ***"If David then calls Him 'Lord,' how is He his Son?"*** (Matthew 22:43-45)

Jesus is superior to David. Do we not understand this? David is the greatest king Israel has ever known. He was the sweet Psalmist of Israel. But he was only significant because God made him a promise. It came to King David through the prophet, Nathan. ***"And your house and your kingdom shall be established forever before you. Your throne shall be established forever."*** (2 Samuel 7:16). David recognized and believed this promise. As he was dying, he recognized his children were not following God, and he cried out,

> ***"Although my house is not so with God,***
> ***Yet He has made with me an everlasting covenant,***
> ***Ordered in all things and secure,"*** (2 Samuel 23:5).

Matthew places this concept in the opening statement of his book. An amazing thing takes place with the phrases ***the Son of David, the Son of Abraham,*** (Matthew 1:1). The word ***Son*** is distinct, and carries a unique focus of its own. It is contrasted with another Greek word which is often translated "child." Throughout the Scriptures, these two words are used interchangeably. But it is significant to note the Greek word "child" is never applied to Christ. The focus of the Greek word for "child" is the passive, or dependent relation, of the children to the parents. But the focus of the word ***Son*** is on the person Himself, rather than on His dependency upon His parents. It suggests individuality rather than descent. The idea of descent is involved, as it is in this passage, but it is mentioned to state the son was worthy of his parents.

Matthew carefully chooses his words to relate the truth about Jesus Christ. He is the ***Son of David, the Son of Abraham,*** but He is not their child. Jesus does not depend upon them. He is absolutely worthy of all they are and more. In reality, they depend upon Him. They did not make Him; He made them. His position in the redemptive histories of the world is not because of them; their position in the redemptive histories of the world is determined by Him.

Now here is the thrilling thing! This same word is used in relation to us. Listen to these statements.

***For as many as are led by the Spirit of God, these are sons of God,*** (Romans 8:14).

***For you are all sons of God through faith in Christ Jesus,*** (Galatians 3:26).

***But when the fullness of the time had come, God sent forth His Son, born of a woman, born under the law, to redeem those who were under the law, that we might receive the adoption as sons. And because you are sons, God has sent forth the Spirit of His Son into your hearts, crying out, "Abba, Father!" Therefore you are no longer a slave but a son, and if a son, then an heir of God through Christ.*** (Galatians 4:4-7).

Matthew gives us insight into the glory of redemption and our thrilling position in Christ. We are not just children in a massive group. We are not just names, mixed in with all of the other names in the great list of the descendants of Christ. We are not children, but we are sons. We have distinction and individuality. Our forefathers do not determine who we are! We are not the product of our traditions, or what we have been taught by our parents, or of the circumstances of our childhood. We no longer live under the bondage of our past.

We are sons of God! There is a redemptive force moving with us. We are not born in a certain month, with a certain sign, and because of this we are a certain way, being unable to do anything about it. We are sons of God! We are unique individuals, designed by Him, filled with Him, and we have become the focal point of all redemptive history. We no longer derive our meaning from our forefathers.

If you want to draw your correct genealogical tree, you start with God, and then there is you! That is the entire tree. This brings a new sense to what Paul told the people of Corinth. ***Therefore, from now on, we regard no one according to the flesh. Even though we have known Christ according to the flesh, yet now we know Him thus no longer. Therefore, if anyone is in Christ he is a new creation; old things have passed away; behold, all things have become new,*** (2 Corinthians 5:16-17).

Live as sons of God. By the power of God, shake yourself loose from all the dependencies that bind you. You are no longer in bondage. You are free to be all God has dreamed for you. You are a son of God.

# Matthew 1:1-17

## God's Plan Still Accomplished

Genealogy was very important to the Jew. While Matthew had broken the normal pattern of the Old Testament genealogy, he did follow the normal format. Instead of listing the descendants of his subject, Matthew listed the ancestors of Jesus. But he did demonstrate a standard Jewish practice. It was the giving of a pattern promoting easy memorization. It was very important for the Jews to have in their hearts, and especially in their minds, a knowledge of their heritage. They had to be able to trace their genealogy back to their tribe, and memorization was the best method. Some information was often sacrificed for the sake of a concise pattern for easy memorization, allowing the Jew to maintain his genealogy's information in his mind.

Many scholars have gone to great lengths to highlight the numerical system of a genealogy. In this genealogy, there are three sections, each having fourteen ancestors. In counting the third section, there are some ancestors missing, unless you count David twice and include Mary. Ancestors, who could have been included, were left out to keep the number at fourteen. Some scholars have said Matthew did this because of the Hebrew spelling of David. The letters of his name number fourteen. There are three letters which represent the numbers four, six, and four. Why would anyone go to all of this trouble? What is the significance of the precise number of fourteen in each section, in light of the message Matthew wants to reveal?

Matthew has a distinct reason for including three periods in Israel's history. This message can be translated into our lives.

## Theocracy - God's Plan Established
## Matthew 1:1-6

Theocracy is a government ruled by or subject to religious authority. "Theo" is the word for God. Thus, a theocracy is a nation ruled by God. In the case of Israel, it was Jehovah. The very word "Israel" means people of God. They received their direction for living, their laws, their daily patterns of life, and their protection from God. Matthew states this first period of time in the first six verses of the genealogy. He gives us the theocracy in the first fourteen ancestors listed in the summary statement (1:17).

God has a plan. He has always had a plan. God is going somewhere. This is easy to forget when you are engrossed in the happenings of day to day events. Each of the ancestors mentioned by Matthew has a history of his own, with problems, relationships, and material needs just like us. Their daily lives contained crisis events. When we get involved in their stories, it is easy to forget God has a plan and is going somewhere. That is also true of our individual lives. When we are living out our personal events, the flat tire, the ringing telephone, and the squalling baby, it is hard to remember God has a plan. But when you step back and see the histories unfold, the perspective becomes clearer.

God never intended to separate Himself from His plan for us. He is heavily involved in His plan. It is as if He and the plan are the same. He is consistently relational in intent. The very name of "Israel" means people of God. God has a relationship with the people of Israel and the events of their lives. The Israelites were not the chosen people of God because He loved them more than others. They were not special because they had qualities no one else had. It had nothing to do with their talents or personal resources. God Jehovah wanted to do something through them. That was the plan. Sin captured mankind, and God needed to redeem the world from this sin. His plan was to do this redemption through Israel. Christ, the Redeemer, would come into the world through the Israelite lineage. God and man were related to fulfill the plan.

It is not any different for us. God has a plan for our lives. He is right in the middle of all that is taking place. God is intimately involved in every event of our lives. We are born from the dreams of God. He did not make us and then decide how He wanted to use us. He has a plan, a design, a dream, and we are essential to how God will fulfill the satisfaction of His heart.

A third factor in the plan is very simple. God never expects us to be anything other than who we are. This enables Him to be who He is. He wants man to be who man is, so God can be God. In this relationship, God will be God in our lives. This is God's plan. We can see it unfold in this first section of the genealogy. ***So all the***

***generations from Abraham to David are fourteen generations,*** (Matthew 1:17).

Throughout this time period, Israel has one characteristic which differs from the world around her. God is her King. All pagan nations had a man as king. But this was not so for Israel. Israel had God, and He was guiding and directing her life. God established Israel as a nation when He called Abram out of the Ur of Chaldees. God gave Abraham a covenant, and He sealed it with the sign of circumcision. He provided Israel's homeland. Abraham journeyed to the Promised Land under God's, direction, and He gave the law to this new kingdom. Israel went to God when they needed deliverance in battle, because God was in charge of the plans for war. He would be their God, and they would be His people. They needed no other King. The pagan nations feared the Israelites because of her God. Everyone knew that God Jehovah was Israel's King, and He protected her.

This has always been God's plan, and He has not changed it. The King will come from the heavens riding on a great white horse, and He will direct the final wrap up of the world.

***And He has on His robe and His thigh a name written:***

**KING OF KINGS**

**AND LORD OF LORDS.**

Revelations 19:16

God is establishing His Kingdom. It will be forever and ever. Matthew hounds this message in his book. Jesus is the Kingly Messiah. He has come to bring the Kingdom. He will reign as a King from a cross throne.

We need to translate this into our everyday living. God has never had any other plan for us. This has been, and this is His dream for us. He wants to be our King. God is driven by love, not some selfish thing. We were built for this. Nothing works properly without God being who He is in us. He is God, and He cannot be anything else. ***He cannot deny Himself,*** (2 Timothy 2:13). God cannot relate to us in any other manner. There is no relationship without his Kingship. Either God is Lord of all, or He is not Lord at all. We find our fulfillment in His accomplishment. God's dream must be our plan!

## Monarchy - God's Plan Exchanged
## Matthew 1:7-11

Matthew is summarizing Israel's history in the second part of the genealogy. ***From David until the captivity in Babylon are fourteen generations,*** (1:17). All the ancestors listed in this section were kings over Israel, in the monarchy period. A monarchy simply means a government ruled by a monarch, and a monarch is a sole and absolute ruler.

God's role in his relationship with man is to be King. It has always been His plan. The pagan nations which surrounded Israel had a man as their monarch, but not Israel. Man ruled by man is always an expression of self-centered carnality, but this was not the way of the Kingdom of God. The Israelite people longed for a king they could see with their physical eyes. God had brought them deliverance from war, but they wanted a physical man to lead them into battle. Samuel, the prophet, gathered all of the people in Mispah and said to them, ***"But you have today rejected your God, who Himself saved you from all your adversities and your tribulations; and you have said to Him, 'No, set a king over us!' Now therefore, present yourselves before the LORD by your tribes and by your clans,"*** (1 Samuel 10:19).

What a sad day it was! What worse thing could Israel have done? What would have resulted in stronger consequences? Israel's deeds were characterized by idolatry. This was beyond idolatry. This was the expression of an attitude. This attitude would set the tone for the next fourteen generations, and it would establish the platform for the tragedy of the third phase of her history. It would lead to her destruction.

A man king exercised authority to impose taxation. He demanded of his subjects personal services and labor, and he had the complete power to do so. Having this kind of power and authority naturally led to his distinction above the average person. He had special honors and luxuries. He gradually built a magnificent court. During this particular era, the king of Israel sat on a throne of ivory, covered with pure gold, and at the foot of the throne were two figures of lions. He dressed in royal robes, (1 Kings 22:10, 2 Chronicles 18:9). His insignia was a golden crown with gems (2 Samuel 1:10; 12:30; 2 Kings 11:12; Psalms 21:3), and a royal scepter. He was treated with the utmost honor and respect. Those who approached him bowed to the ground.

Israel exchanged the plan of God for her own foolish plan. She reaped the terrible consequences. Would she ever be the same? When would God again be her ruler? In this condition, how could Judah not be taken into captivity? Who can she blame but herself?

Can you apply this phase of Israel's history to your personal life? The negative plight of our lives is similar to Israel's. We substitute our God King for a man king. We dethrone God and enthrone ourselves. The awful condition of our lives is not pornography, drug addiction, alcoholism, adultery, nor any other deed we might mention. We substitute God's plan for our lives with our own cheap, destructive replacement. We overthrow His Kingship.

This results in the elimination of our relationship with God. We are no longer intimately involved in the fulfillment of His dream. His plan is to never be apart from us. Only in Him can we experience fulfillment. On our own we find the foolish fulfillment of our own nightmares, rather than the fulfillment of His dream for us. We become our own king. We are not satisfied to be who we are. We want to be who He is. We have substituted our role for His role. We try to make Him like us, instead of allowing His image to be seen through us.

It is inevitable that we end up in bondage just like Israel. We are in captivity. We fight fears and emotions we were never meant to fight. We create our own monsters, and they scare us to death. Will we ever be who we were destined to be? Will God's dream ever be fulfilled in us?

How can the story get worse? Oh, the end is not yet. We now enter into the dark ages of Israel's history.

## Hierarchy - God's Plan Eliminated

## Matthew 1:12-16

***And from the captivity in Babylon until the Christ are fourteen generations,*** (1:17). There are no kings in this section of the genealogy. Israel was without a king for fourteen generations. Year after long year, she was under the domination of a foreign power. A hierarchy is a body of persons having authority. Those who wanted to rule, swept through the promised land of Israel like vultures. Judah was in exile while in her own country. Finally, the Roman Empire was officially established on January 16, 27 BC, by Augustus. Being under such a great political power, how could Israel ever know her own king?

But this was only one of Israel's evidences of the dark ages. For four hundred years of this time period, Israel did not hear from God. During the four hundred year period between the Book of Malachi and the Book of Matthew, the heavens became brass. God no longer brought fresh revelation of Himself. There were no reports of burning bushes or dark clouds descending upon the mountains. It was as if God had abandoned them. But is it not proper? Had they not rejected His Kingship and gone their own way?

This does not mean they were without religion. Ceremonies, traditions, programs, and rules flourished in abundance. But God was not there. Those things which are present when God is King were absent. It was the Dark Age, indeed!

My heart breaks when I think of the parallel in our personal lives. It isn't that religion does not flourish. Churches are on every corner in our towns. Religious programs keep us busy to the point of dismay. Time demands and money requirements stretch us to keep buildings and material necessities intact for the programs. But where is the King? Have we entered into the dark ages? Has God left us alone? Has He abandoned us to our own rulership? Is there no one to turn to except each other? Are we alone with our thoughts?

Wait! There is a message! It all ends with Christ! ***So all the generations from Abraham to David are fourteen generations, from David until the captivity in Babylon are fourteen generations, and from the captivity in Babylon until the Christ are fourteen generations,*** (1:17).

Here He is - ***the Christ.*** He was the answer then, and He is the answer now. When we are at our lowest, without hope, there He is! When it appears we have been abandoned, He appears!

God's plan is still intact. What He started in the beginning, He has not abandoned. Here He is - ***the Christ.*** In the darkest hour of Israel's history, He is present. When the destructive process of our own choosing has done its worst, He appears. The King has arrived! Not an inferior king like you have chosen in the past, but the true King. God dreamed of being in your life. You and He are together again in partnership. The dream is fulfilled. God is accomplishing His plan.

# Matthew 1:1-17

## The King of the Cross Style

The doctrine of holiness has received criticism throughout the ages. Holiness, through the centuries, has received a "bum rap." You might disagree, or you might say it deserves exactly what it gets. But the doctrine is not the culprit here. The people who say they live by the doctrine of holiness are not always what they ought to be. There are many people who live only an imitation of holiness. Their actions are plastic and synthetic. But when something has an imitation form, you can be sure the real thing is around somewhere.

In order to clarify and identify true holiness, we will use other words to describe the doctrine. We call it CROSS STYLE. Though we have defined the cross style in different situations, and on many occasions, it bears repeating. The cross was an event in the life of Jesus Christ. But it was much more than an event. We do not want to undermine the significance of this historical happening, but in the heart of God, the cross was beyond the accomplishment of an event. It was not something Jesus had to endure, or get past. The cross was the demonstration of a life style. The cross event allows us to see the attitude, perspective, and internal flow from the heart of God.

Jesus lived the cross style. The first picture we see of Him is one where He leaped off His throne as God and became a man (Philippians 2:5-8). Jesus refused to live for Himself. He gave His life for others. It is the style of the cross. He demonstrated this style when He embraced the leper (Matthew 8:3), and when He washed the disciple's feet (John 13:5). He performed miracles, and then told the people who received His miracles not to tell anyone (Matthew 9:30). He was not trying to build a reputation by the miracles. He simply wanted to help those in need. The style of living for others had captured Jesus.

He taught this to His disciples! ***If anyone desires to come after Me, let him deny himself, and take up his cross, and follow me,*** (Matthew 16:24). This statement tells us Jesus is going somewhere, and His life has a style by which He will get there. He wants the disciples to think like He thinks, and see as He sees. It is the cross style! ***For whoever desires to save his life will lose it, but whoever loses his life for My sake will find it,*** (Matthew 16:25). Here lies the basic principle of the cross style. There is life in the midst of death. In the middle of losing your life, you will find it. The person who lives the style of the cross is always redemptive, pouring his life out for others. The cross style is true holiness.

The basic criticism of holiness, or the cross style, comes in one of several forms. First, there is the issue of **SUPERIORITY.** There has often been an attitude of "holier than thou" among those who claim the holiness life style. Though it may not have been their intention, many people have left the impression that they felt they were better than others. The Pharisees certainly expressed this kind of superiority. They asked the disciples, ***"Why does your Teacher eat with tax collectors and sinners?"*** (Matthew 9:11). They were shocked that Jesus would mingle with a group of sinners.

But the cross style knows nothing of this kind of attitude. Jesus embraced every individual as an equal in value. He reached out to the woman taken in the act of adultery (John 8:3-11), just as quickly as He went to the home of a Pharisee (Luke 11:37). James, the brother of Christ, caught this truth in his book. He wrote, ***My brethren, do not hold the faith of our Lord Jesus Christ, the Lord of glory, with partiality,*** (James 2:1). He then gave an illustration of how we treat the rich in comparison to our treatment of the poor. He thundered to the climax of it all by saying, ***But if you show partiality, you commit sin, and are convicted by the law as transgressors,*** (James 2:9).

But do not allow yourself to be captured by the illustration of doing! We must focus on the attitude of the heart. The cross style will not tolerate any feelings of superiority. There is no room at the cross for those who claim their own personal greatness. There is only room for those who beat their chests in repentance. Only those who understand their total failure, and emptiness without Him, have a place here. Christ is the distinguishing factor between the Christian and non-Christian. If there is any holiness found in us, it is because of Him.

The members of the holiness movement have been called **SEPARATIONISTS.** It is another one of the criticisms against us. A natural result of superiority is the removal of ourselves from those around us. The Pharisees exhibited this action during Jesus' day. They were constantly avoiding people who would defile them. They had a variety of laws designed to protect them from those who were not holy.

The monks are an example of those who isolate themselves from others. They live in monasteries, remaining apart from the world. We will not go to the length of physical separation, but we create the same separation in our minds and emotions. There are certain people with whom we will not associate. One of the biggest obstacles to evangelism in our churches is that of getting people to break out of their religious cliques to befriend someone who is not as holy as they are.

This expands into other areas of life. Race has always been a central issue. It was a part of the separation of the Jew from the rest of the world. The Jews referred to all non Jews as "Gentile dogs." But this attitude is not restricted to the Jewish element. We live in a day of the white supremacist. They are militant in their efforts of restriction. This depraved attitude has raised its ugly head throughout history. We would never admit to being a part of such a movement. However, streaks of this attitude seem to remain in our souls. Unexpressed feelings abide deep within our beings. Watch what happens when your daughter dates a person of another race. The only victory we find over this attitude is in the death of the cross! The cross style will not permit any residue of this to remain.

Small mindedness, narrowness, or **LEGALISM** has also been a base for criticism. It is a major struggle for holiness people to keep their focus. It is difficult for us to push aside the distractions of life and concentrate on Jesus. We must never forget that holiness is "not" our emphasis. Our emphasis is Jesus! We receive everything that is holy from Him. We are legalistic when we focus on the by-product rather than on the source.

A sense of ownership sometimes possesses us. When we own something, we have the need to protect and guard it. When we want to keep others out of our territory, we build walls and forts around us. Holiness was designed to get everybody in. It is the passionate heart of God. Legalism is the opposite of holiness. It makes loving others impossible. Holiness is perfect love, and it embraces the hurting people of the world. By nature, holiness is evangelistic. The people of cross style are always redemptive.

Another basis of criticism comes in the equation of holiness and **SAINTHOOD**. The world has given sainthood a twisted and negative definition. It is something impossible to attain, and if one could attain sainthood, it is not desirable. It has the reputation of a dusty museum piece. It is only good to view on certain occasions. No one who is interested in real living, or living on the edge, will consider the life of a saint.

The Bible's picture of sainthood is very different. There is attractiveness in the ultimate picture of sainthood as demonstrated by Jesus. Life is abundant, and it flows with meaning and destiny. Jesus has an intimate relationship with God. The very thought of this captivates us. The cross, which is repulsive in character, becomes our glory. ***That I may know Him, and the power of His resurrection, and the fellowship of His sufferings, being confirmed to His death,*** (Philippians 3:10).

This is the message Matthew presents in His book. Jesus spoke of His coming death and resurrection (Matthew 16). The disciples are fighting for the position of control in their group (Matthew 18). The Pharisees propose a question to Jesus. ***"Is it lawful for a man to divorce his wife for just any reason?"*** (Matthew 19:3). Jesus answers their question with the purest message of the cross style. Two disciples, accompanied by their mother, come to Jesus wanting the right and left-hand positions beside Him. Jesus says to them, ***"Whoever desires to become great among you, let him be your servant. And whoever desires to be first among you, let him be your slave - just as the Son of Man did not come to be served, but to serve, and to give His life a ransom for many,"*** (Matthew 20:26-28). He again expressed the style of the cross. It is the Kingdom style. He continues to express the cross style in the Garden of Gethsemane (Matthew 26), and in the entirety of the crucifixion (Matthew 27). It is the style of never living for yourself!

But Matthew does not reserve this message for the latter days of Jesus' ministry. He presents it in the genealogy. Matthew strongly declares the cross style as the very heart of God. It is the essence of all of God's dreams and plans from the beginning. The redemption of the world is displayed in the birth of Christ. God declared redemption in His very selection of the ancestors of Christ. The genealogy proclaims the style of the cross.

None of the criticisms of holiness are correct when they are seen in the framework of the genealogy. If you have only the knowledge of the ancestors of Jesus, you have what you need to understand the redemptive nature of the style of the cross. God removes every barrier which keeps us from His heart. He displays the style of the cross. It spills forth from His inner being.

If you study the genealogy of Jesus Christ (Matthew 1:1-7), you will find there are four women who are included (not counting Mary, the mother of Christ). The inclusion of these four particular women, in an otherwise male genealogy, is interesting in itself. Each of these ladies is a Gentile. Two of them are involved in adultery, and one of them is a harlot. Matthew gives a declaration of the theme of His book by their inclusions.

Cross style removes barriers.

## The Abuse of the Past

## Matthew 1:3

The story of Tamar and Judah is a most intriguing story. It would play well on the modern day soap opera. Er was the elder son of Judah. He was the age to marry. He needed a wife, so Judah made the proper arrangements, according to the custom of their culture. His firstborn would marry a young lady by the name of Tamar, a Gentile. Er was a very wicked man, and he soon died because of his wickedness. As was the custom, Judah's second-born son, Onan, took Tamar as his wife in order to raise an heir to his brother. Because of his selfishness, he refused to raise an heir to his brother. Due to his wickedness, he also died suddenly.

Judah had a third son, Shelah, but he was too young to be married at the time of the second son's death. Therefore, Judah told Tamar to return to her father's house and remain there until this third son came of age and could marry her. In his mind, Judah had no intention of giving this third son to Tamar as a husband. After all, two of his boys were already dead. Time passed, and Tamar was forgotten. Shelah was now of the age for marriage, but Judah did nothing.

One day Tamar decided to take matters into her own hands. Judah's wife had died. He decided to take some time to have his sheep sheared by a friend. This friend would also comfort him. Tamar heard about this plan, and she fixed herself up to look beautiful. She covered her face and sat in a public spot. Judah thought she was a harlot and secured her services. He promised to send her a goat from his flock, and in order to guarantee payment, he gave her his signet and cord, and also his staff. But later, when he sent one of his men with the goat, Tamar had disappeared.

Tamar returned to her fathers home. She was with child from the relations with Judah. In fact, she was carrying twins. In about three months, Judah received word concerning this situation. He was told that Tamar had played the role of a harlot, and she was with child. Judah was furious and demanded she be dragged out and burned. Tamar immediately produced the signet, the cord and the staff. When Judah saw these, he realized he was the father. Judah repented and said, ***"She has been more righteous than I, because I did not give her to Shelah my son,"*** (Genesis 38:26). The twins are both mentioned in the genealogy, but Perez became the actual ancestor of the coming Messiah.

There is no doubt in my mind that Matthew is giving the message of grace and mercy in the style of the cross. He could have eliminated any reference to this story, yet he highlights it. ***Judah begot Perez . . . , Perez begot Hezron,*** (Matthew 1:3). This would have been enough, but he includes the phrase, ***and Zerah by Tamar.*** He calls for the attention of every Jew who will read this genealogy and this dramatic story. At the heart of the genealogy of Jesus Christ, the Messiah, there are these kinds of people.

Christ was not born in a vacuum of righteousness. He was born in the midst of the cross style, which redeems and transforms the hurts and abuses of people into love and redemption. The cross style is not just the experience of death, but it is the very heart of Christ's birth. Can we implant Matthew's message into the middle of our family's circumstances? Can you see this truth in the midst of the abuse and hurts you have experienced in your past? Some of these hurts and abuses have come from our natural family, but many have come from our church family. Christ is bigger than all of the misdeeds and complications of your life. His plan stands in the middle of your hurts. Perez is destined to be an ancestor to the Redeemer of the world, who will in turn redeem him from his own personal pain.

## The Atrocities of the Past

### Matthew 1:5

The time had come for Israel to cross the Jordan River and invade the land of Canaan. Joshua sent two men into Canaan to spy out the land. They traveled as far as Jericho. In that city dwelt Rahab, "a harlot." She lived in her own home, even though she had family there. Strange men were always coming and going from her house. Two more men would not create suspicion, so the spies sought lodging from Rahab.

But the King of Jericho received word about the two spies. He sent word to Rahab, saying he wanted her to deliver the two men to him. Rahab knew of the progress of Israel. She had heard about the passage of the Israelites through the Red Sea and how they had repeatedly overthrown their enemies. She was convinced that Jehovah purposed to give Canaan to the Israelites. When the spies arrived at her home, Rahab took them to her roof top. She had some stalks of flax laid out there to dry. These stalks became the hiding place for the spies. Rahab reported to the King that the two men had come to her house, but she did not know who they were. She said they had run out of the city at dark when the gates were being shut. The King's men immediately pursued the spies on the road which led to the Jordan River at the location where they could cross.

Rahab told the spies of her faith in Jehovah. She made them promise when Israel returned to Canaan and her city of Jericho, that they would spare her family. Rahab's house sat on the city wall. When the spies gave her their word, she lowered them out of a window by means of a rope. That rope became the signal to Israel's army when they returned to Jericho. Her testimony to the spies was the encouragement in their report to Joshua. That encouragement prompted Joshua to take immediate action to conquer Jericho.

The author of Hebrews said, ***By faith the harlot Rahab did not perish with those who did not believe, when she had received the spies with peace,*** (Hebrews 11:31). The location of this verse is startling. It is located in the chapter of the "Heroes of Faith." This chapter contains the illustrations of the faith of great men such as Abraham, Isaac, Jacob, Joseph, and Moses. There in the midst of these great men is Rahab, "the harlot." The author makes no attempt to distinguish between these great men of faith and this harlot. That sounds just like Jesus. It is the cross style.

Matthew did not need to include the name of Rahab in this genealogy. He says, ***Salmon begot Boaz . . . , Boaz begot Obed,*** (Matthew 1:5). That was all of the information needed. Why did he add the phrase ***Salmon begot Boaz by Rahab?*** He wanted to deliver the message of the cross. It is not just an event at the close of the ministry of Jesus. The message of the cross is at the heart of Christ's birth as well as His death. This message flows eternally from the heart of God. God does not have a problem including a harlot in the genealogy of the Redeemer of the world. This is His passion and His heart! God does not have a problem including you either. Whoever you are, and whatever you have done, is not beyond His redemptive reach. His grace and mercy are abundant. He has a dream for you. You play a key role in His plan.

## The Ancestry of the Past
## Matthew 1:5

There was a great famine in the land of Israel. Elimelech and his wife, Naomi, had two sons. They were from Bethlehem of Judah, but because of the famine, they went to Moab to live. Elimelech soon died, leaving Naomi with her sons. After a period of time, the two sons married two women of Moab. Orpah and Ruth joined the family of Naomi. Approximately ten years later, both of the sons died, leaving the three women to care for themselves.

Naomi planned to return to her home in Bethlehem of Judah. She had received the news that the famine was over, and she wanted to be with her own people. She encouraged the two daughters-in-law to return to their own families as well. Orpah finally consented to do so, but

Ruth would not leave Naomi. She pledged herself to Naomi's people and to her God.

> ***"Entreat me not to leave you,***
> ***Or to turn back from following after you;***
> ***For wherever you go, I will go;***
> ***And wherever you lodge, I will lodge;***
> ***Your people shall be my people,***
> ***And your God, my God.***
> ***Where you die, I will die,***
> ***And there will I be buried.***
> ***The Lord do so to me, and more also,***
> ***If anything but death parts you and me,"***
> (Ruth 1:16-17).

Naomi and Ruth arrived in Bethlehem at the very beginning of the barley harvest. Ruth needed to support herself and her mother-in-law, so she went out to glean in the harvest. In the gleaning she met a relative of Naomi's named Boaz. When Boaz learned that Ruth had come with Naomi from Moab, he not only gave her permission to glean in the field among the sheaves, but he told her to appease her hunger and thirst with the food and drink of his reapers, (Ruth 2:1-16). When Naomi heard of the kindness of Boaz, she counseled Ruth to seek an opportunity to tell Boaz the claim she had upon him as the nearest kinsman of her deceased husband. Ruth followed her advice, and Boaz promised to fulfill her request, provided the nearer redeemer, who was still living, did not perform his duty (Ruth 3:1-13). The relative was unwilling to marry Ruth. Therefore, Boaz obtained a release from him, redeemed for himself the patrimony of Elimelech, and took Ruth to be his wife (Ruth 4:1-13). Eventually she became the great-grandmother of King David.

Why did Matthew include her name in the genealogy? ***Boaz begot Obed . . . , Obed begot Jesse,*** (Matthew 1:5). That would have given all of the necessary information for the genealogy. But Matthew included ***Boaz begot Obed by Ruth.*** Matthew once again attempts to tell us of the width of the arms of the cross style. The arms of God did not stretch wide only at the point of the crucifixion, but they have been open all of the time. Included in the genealogy of Jesus is a Gentile woman. Race has never made a difference to Jesus. Who your father is, or who he is not, is not an issue with Him. God dreamed, and you were born out of the dreams of God. God has been using famines and the tragedies of your life to bring you to where He has dreamed you could be. It is the cross style in the genealogies.

## The Adultery of the Past
## Matthew 1:6

Matthew refers to the story of David and Bathsheba in the genealogy of Jesus. ***And Jesse begot David the king, David the king begot Solomon by her who had been the wife of Uriah,*** (Matthew 1:6). He does not mention the name of Bathsheba, but everyone knows the story of David's great sin.

It was in the Spring of the year. It was the time when kings go out to war. The battle plans were established. David wanted to take things a bit easier than in the years gone by. He had led his men into battle time after time. He was not getting any younger and the travel was hard. He ordered Joab to lead the army to destroy the people of Ammon and besiege Rabbah. In his boredom, David was walking on the rooftop as he waited to hear how the battle was going. He looked across the way to another rooftop and saw a beautiful woman bathing. He made inquiries about her, and discovered her name was Bathsheba. He was married to Uriah, the Hittite, one of his soldiers, who was now out to war.

David laid, and carried out, the plans of adultery. This resulted in the birth of a child who would die. In order to cover up his sin, David sent for Uriah to come home. When Uriah returned home, he told David he could not go to live in comfort with his wife while the army of the Lord was encamped in the open fields. Therefore, Uriah slept with the servants of the King.

David then sent Uriah back to the battle with a letter for Joab. Joab was instructed by David to ***"Set Uriah in the forefront of the hottest battle, and retreat from him, that he may be struck down and die,"*** ( 2 Samuel 11:15). David moved from the sin of adultery to the sin of murder. Following a period of mourning for her husband, Bathsheba was legally married to King David. She became the mother of four sons, one of them being Solomon.

Why did Matthew call such strong attention to this in the genealogy? He could have written, ***And Jesse begot David, the king, David the king begot Solomon. . . .*** (Matthew 1:6). But Matthew went on to point out, not only who Solomon's mother was, but also that she was the wife of Uriah. Perhaps it is just as remarkable King David is included in the genealogy as is Bathsheba. It is all about the reality of the cross style. The cross is not an event at the end of Jesus' ministry, but it is a reality in the birth of Christ. It is seen in the fulfillment of the dreams of God. Murder and adultery cannot stop the great arm of the forgiving God, who has a dream to redeem all of mankind.

Do you have any other questions concerning Matthew's intent? The story of Christ is a story of the cross style. Grace and mercy flow from the heart of God to the world. There is no barrier He cannot penetrate; there is no gap He cannot bridge. He has made provision to include you in the fulfillment of His dreams. What is the wall between you and all God has dreamed for you? What has happened to you, which has left you feeling like you can never be what God intended you to be. What have you done which has so scarred you, you believe you can never receive the best from God? Take a fresh look at the cross! Do not see it only at the close of Jesus' earthly life, but at the beginning, with His birth. See the redemptive work of Christ in the very selection of His ancestors. The dreams of God for your life can still be fulfilled. Trust Him in the style of the cross!

# Matthew 1:16

## Jesus, The Son of Mary

Matthew was just an ordinary man. But under the inspiration of the Holy Spirit, his writing skills are amazing. When you think you have discovered what he is saying, he does an abrupt turn and expands the truth beyond comprehension. This is what he does with the genealogy. What startling revelation could come from the monotonous facts of a genealogy? It is fairly basic and routine, but there it is. It explodes before you in a life changing manner.

Matthew gives three phases of Jewish history. He divides the genealogy into three distinct sections, each having fourteen generations. God had a dream for mankind. He wanted to be their King. But Matthew reveals the digression of Israel through the generations of the genealogy. They wanted their own king. Their digression led them into captivity, which resulted in their having no king at all. They finally returned to their own land, but they were constantly under the domination of the stronger countries around them. They had no chance of freedom. All hope was gone. But wait! There is Christ Jesus. The

King of Kings and Lord of Lords is born among them. Matthew explodes with the message of hope in the Messiah, the Deliverer.

Matthew reveals the heart of God when he includes four women in the genealogy of Christ. God did not wait until the end of Jesus' earthly life to acknowledge the style of the cross as the heart of His Kingdom. The cross style is present in the birth of Christ as well as in His death. The cross style is present in the genealogy. There is no obstacle which can block the redemptive heart of God. It is the style of the cross, and it has been in the heart of God all along.

In the process of studying Matthew's writings, when you think you have the truths understood and can relax in what God is doing, He releases a greater than ever revelation. Instead of ending the genealogy with a conclusion, Matthew ends it with a question mark. He raises a question, which is somewhat confusing, and demands an answer. It appears Matthew undermines everything he has accomplished. You think you understand, only to realize there are other factors which change the equation of the birth of the King.

What you think is a climax to the genealogy is, in reality, the introduction to the next section. Matthew opens the door for you to walk through, if you have the courage.

## The Physical to the Spiritual

Matthew 1:16

Look closely at this verse. ***And Jacob begot Joseph the husband of Mary, of whom was born Jesus who is called Christ,*** (1:16). One might not be able to see the question which Matthew raises in the English translation of this verse. All appears to be very routine.

Joseph and Mary are husband and wife. Jesus was born from their relationship. This pretty well follows the story of the genealogy. Matthew names the forefathers as he lists the ancestors of Christ. You can trace the genealogy of Jesus through the seed of the forefathers. Even when Matthew mentions the four women in the genealogy, he always lists their husbands and points to them as the forefathers of the Messiah (1:3,5,6). Matthew then comes to the climax of the genealogy and states, ***Joseph the husband of Mary, of whom was born Jesus who is called Christ.***

But when you read this scripture in the original language of the Bible, you see that Matthew does something unmistakable. He does not quietly do this, as if by accident. He is blaring and bold. His revelation explodes on the scene. It is contained in the words ***of whom.*** This is not a problem if it relates to Joseph as the forefather of Jesus. That is the pattern of the genealogy. And there is no problem if it relates to both Joseph and Mary. But Matthew raises a tremendous issue if this relates to Mary alone.

But how can we know for sure what Matthew's intention was in his writing? There are masculine and feminine pronouns in the English language. Everyone understands when you write about a man, you do not use the pronoun "she," which is feminine, but you use the pronoun "he," which is masculine. In the English language, when you use the pronoun "who" or "whom," these can be either feminine or masculine. The noun to which you refer determines the feminine or masculine. The Greek word which translates ***of whom*** in this verse is feminine!

This means ***of whom Jesus was born*** does not refer to Joseph, but to Mary. Matthew does not even include Joseph in this statement.

Matthew lists an entire genealogy of male forefathers. He comes to the end, and where Joseph should be the father of Jesus, Matthew bypasses him and leaps to Mary. He boldly states that Joseph is not the natural father of Jesus. There is no linkage between Joseph and Jesus.

But you are far ahead of the process of Matthew, because you have read the end of the story. You know Jesus has Divine origin. You know about the truth of His virgin birth. But what if this was all new to you? What if you had never read of the virgin birth? You would read what Matthew writes in the genealogy and find yourself in utter confusion. Who is the father of Jesus? Who is the subject of, ***was born?*** How can Jesus be the son of David if Joseph is not the natural father?

Matthew boldly says Jesus cannot be understood in the terms of physical descent. ***And Jacob begot Joseph the husband of Mary, of whom was born Jesus who is called Christ,*** (1:6). The focus is on the legal descent, rather than the physical descent. In the Jewish teaching, if a man acknowledged a son as his own, then he was considered that son's father, without further question. Matthew can thus show that Jesus was a legal descendant of David through Joseph, and at the same time he emphasized the unique aspect of Jesus' birth through the virgin Mary. Up to this time, the emphasis was on the physical ancestors and the roles they played. Now Matthew makes a shift to the spiritual reality of the Holy Spirit's involvement with Mary. Joseph is left out of the birth process, except for the legal aspect.

But it has been the heartbeat of God forever, to take us from the physical to the spiritual. Every created thing in the physical realm was made to glorify and display God. ***For by Him were all things created that are in heaven, and that are on earth, visible and invisible,***

***whether thrones or dominions or principalities or powers. All things were created through Him and FOR HIM,*** (Colossians 1:16). Paul captured the essence of this truth when he discovered man is without excuse. There is no man who can plead ignorance in knowledge, or in seeing God. ***Because what may be known of God is manifest in them, for God has shown it to them. For since the creation of the world His invisible attributes are clearly seen, being understood by the things that are made, even His eternal power and Godhead; so that they are without excuse,*** (Romans 1:19-20).

In the midst of God's creative action is His crowning creation, man. God built man to be the stage upon which the spiritual would act and could be seen clearly by other men. God created man to be His home. ***Do you not know that you are the temple of God and that the Spirit of God dwells in you?*** (1 Corinthians 3:16).

Matthew moves us from the physical ancestry of Jesus to the spiritual thrust of God acting in the life of man. But this radical and abrupt shift does not complete the emphasis. Matthew moves us from the physical to the spiritual. Now he has another move to make.

## The Spiritual to God's Heart

## Matthew 1:16

***And Jacob begot Joseph the husband of Mary, of whom was born Jesus who is called Christ,*** (1:16). Throughout the genealogy, Matthew uses the word ***begot.*** Now we come to verse sixteen. Matthew refers to Mary's involvement in the birth of Jesus, and he translates the begot into ***was born.*** In the original language of the Bible, it is the same word. However, while the basic root word is the same, the ending has been changed slightly. Matthew changes the word in verse sixteen from an active verb to a passive verb.

In other words, the verb ***begot,*** used thirty-eight times in the first fifteen verses of the genealogy, is always active. Now in reference to the birth of Jesus Christ, as it relates to Mary, Matthew uses the same word, but changes it to a passive verb. The difference between an active and a passive verb is very simple. An active verb is illustrated by the sentence, "The boy hit the ball." In this statement, the verb "hit" is an active verb. It means the subject of the verb is responsible for the action of the verb. This is how Matthew uses the active verb ***begot*** the first thirty-eight times. He lists the forefathers who were responsible for each of the offspring. Now he comes to the birth of Christ. He uses the feminine form of ***whom,*** which means there is no linkage between Joseph and Jesus, except in the legal sense. He uses the passive form of the verb ***begot,*** which means the subject is not responsible for the action of the verb. This form of the verb can be seen clearly in the following sentence, "The boy was hit by the ball." In other words, Matthew clearly states the shift from the active form of the verb to the passive form. Mary was not the source of the birth of Christ. She was acted upon by the Holy Spirit.

This may not confuse you, but it was confusing to those who read it first. You already understand the vital teaching of the virgin birth. You know the birth of the Christ was not the result of good family planning, and it was not an immoral act. It was the result of the action of God upon Mary. Matthew introduces this great truth with verse sixteen. It is the threshold into the reality of truth. Jesus was born of God.

Throughout the Gospel accounts, the originator of the word ***begot,*** in the spiritual realm, is most often God. He is constantly acting to bring about birth. John is strong about this in his Gospel account. He always seems to give the point of origin of the word ***begot*** to God. ***But as many as received Him, to them He gave the right to become children of God, to those who believe in His name: who were born, not of blood, nor of the will of the flesh, nor of the will of man, but of God,*** (John 1:12-13). Jesus was very clear in His discussion with Nicodemus, a ruler of the Jews. ***Jesus answered, "Most assuredly, I say to you, unless one is born of water and the Spirit, he cannot enter the kingdom of God,"*** (John 3:5). Kingdom life can only come from the Spirit. There is a life style change which takes place in the birth process of God in our lives. John speaks of it when he writes, ***Whoever has been born of God does not sin, for His seed remains in him, and he cannot sin, because he has been born of God,*** (1 John 3:9). He previously wrote, ***If you know that He is righteous, you know that everyone who practices righteousness is born of Him,*** (1 John 2:29). The chief characteristic of this righteousness is love. ***Beloved, let us love one another, for love is of God; and everyone who loves is born of God and knows God,*** (1 John 4:7). John tells us, ***For whatever is born of God overcomes the world,*** (1 John 5:4).

The author of the Hebrews writes of the dream of God. He wanted ***many sons of glory,*** (Hebrews 2:10). His passion was not one Son, but many. Sharing His life with us is the heart of God. If you have been able to move with us from the physical to the spiritual, then you can move from the spiritual to the heart of God. You can now realize what God did in Jesus, He wants to do in you. As the life of God was placed in the womb of Mary, so God wants to impart into you the Divine life. You are to be born of God!

Now we are ready to move on in the story.

### God's Heart to the Fulfilled Dream

### Matthew 1:16

***And Jacob begot Joseph the husband of Mary, of whom was born Jesus who is called Christ,*** (1:16). Matthew gives a brilliant finish to the progression of the genealogy. He is ***Christ,*** and He is the fulfillment of the dreams of God. The Greek word for ***Christ*** is equal to the Hebrew word for "Messiah." It means to anoint or to smear. He is the anointed One, the Deliverer. The Israelites have dreamed of the arrival of this great One for years. The arrival of the Divine One has been the dream of God. He has manipulated three groups of fourteen generations (1:17), in order to bring this to pass. His manipulation is for the redemption of the world. Christ is the fulfillment of all God wants and dreams!

***Who is called Christ*** is a very important statement. The verb ***is called*** is in the present tense. The original Greek word is a passive participle. Present tense means it is now. Since it is passive, it means Jesus is being acted upon by the speaking. He is not the cause of it, but it is the action of the people. The participle acts like an adverb, giving content to the noun ***Jesus.*** This indicates what the people continue to call Him. ***Called*** does not mean He is named ***Christ,*** but it means people have applied the title to Him. In other words, "The people will call Him the Christ," or "People say, 'He is the Christ.'"

Even the common man recognizes what God is doing. God has moved us from the physical to the spiritual. Tremendous spiritual activity is taking place through the life of Jesus. God acted to bring about the birthing process of a Son. It is a direct reflection of His heart. This Son was born of God, not man. Joseph was not responsible; Mary was acted upon! God brought it to pass! Jesus is the fulfillment of the dream of God, and He made redemption possible in the world. The result is deliverance, and it was the goal of the birthing process.

It was the dream of the Father to ***bring many sons to glory*** (Hebrews 2:10). Jesus is the prototype of a new breed of people. As the nature of God was born in the womb of Mary, so He wants to be born in you. As God lived in and through the flesh of Christ, so He wants to live in and through you. ***By which have been given to us exceedingly great and precious promises, that through these you may be partakers of the Divine nature, having escaped the corruption that is in the world through lust.*** (2 Peter 1:4).

God continues the redemptive flow of His life in and through you. Sons of God appear in every arena of life. Each Son of God flows the redemptive force of God into the world. God acts upon the stage of each life to bring about the fulfillment of His dream. If you are born of God, and you flow with His life, you touch your world, and you are the fulfillment of God's dream.

# PART TWO

# Matthew 1:18-25

## The Cross – The Birth of a King

The Cross Style in the Incarnation

# Matthew 1:18

# The Incarnation

Matthews opens his Gospel account with the genealogy of Jesus Christ, then immediately inserts the announcement of His momentous birth. Verse eighteen is essential to understanding the rest of the book. Jesus is the climax of the Old Testament. Every individual in the Old Testament finds his or her purpose in the person of Jesus. Therefore, this verse gives proper interpretation to the Old Testament as a whole. And more than that, it gives us the proper lens through which we can view the life and ministry of Christ. If you do not understand His birth, you will not understand His life. If you do not understand His origin, you will certainly miss the significance of His death.

Matthew uses one verse to plainly state the birth of Jesus. This gives credence to the Divine inspiration of the Scriptures. It is not natural for a human author to do such a thing. Such important information would need many chapters of explanation, often confusing the issue. But through the inspiration of the Holy Spirit, Matthew states it simply.

***Now the birth of Jesus Christ was as follows:*** (Matthew 1:18). Matthew opens the verse with the word, ***Now.*** It is a conjunction. It is coordinating and continuing in its impact. He wants you to take a new look at the genealogy as he has just listed it. The primary way to translate the conjunction is "but." Matthew writes with great detail about the physical heritage of Jesus, as traceable through the lineage of King David. This is important for the fulfillment of prophecy, and, in the mind of the Jew, it was the primary test of anyone claiming to be the Messiah. ***But*** it is not all there is to consider. He indicates this by eliminating Joseph as the earthly father of Jesus, (Matthew 1:16). With the elimination of Joseph, Matthew raises the issue of who Jesus' Father really is, and he gives the answer in the contrast of the genealogy.

***The birth*** is an important pronouncement. Matthew uses the word, ***begot,*** to highlight the birthing process thirty-eight times through the Old Testament genealogy. Now he changes the word for birth. It is not a new word, for he used it in his opening statement of the account. ***The book of the genealogy of Jesus Christ, the son of David, the son of Abraham:*** (Matthew 1:1). The Greek word translated ***genealogy*** (Matthew 1:1), is the same word translated ***birth*** (Matthew 1:18). A literal translation means "origin" or "beginning." Thus, Matthew gives us parallel genealogies. The first genealogy was of Jesus Christ, through His legal father, Joseph. Now he states the genealogy of His natural Father, without much detail. The line of ancestry is not long. Jesus is simply born of God.

Here is how he says it: ***After His mother Mary was betrothed to Joseph, before they came together, she was found with child of the Holy Spirit,*** (Matthew 1:18). Again we see Matthew eliminate the earthly father. In the doctrine of the church, we call this the "incarnation." It means "the act of assuming flesh." In our doctrine it means "the gracious, voluntary act of the Son of God, assuming a human body and a human nature." The Lord Jesus Christ is one person with two natures. These natures are indissolubly united, the one nature being that of the eternal Son of God, and the other being that of man, in all respects human, "yet without sin." Who can know the depth of such statements?

We must understand the long range aspect of this concept. When God finished the activity of creation, He walked with man in the cool of the day. Intimacy was established between God and the human race. Then the most tragic event in human history took place. This event has affected more people, and produced more ramifications, than any other. We call it the Fall. God dealt with the situation by giving a promise. It is the first Messianic promise. He said to the serpent,

> ***"And I will put enmity***
> ***Between you and the woman.***
> ***And between your seed and her Seed;***
> ***He shall bruise your head,***
> ***And you shall bruise His heel."*** Genesis 3:15

Did you notice the use of the word, ***seed***? In a technical sense, seed belongs to the man. Mary was with child by the seed of God. It is the only instance in human history where a woman had a seed within her that did not come from a human male. The idea of ***your seed,*** and ***her Seed*** speaks of both a corporate and an individual usage. Those experiencing the life of the serpent, and those born of God, are in major conflict. Neither side will be without suffering. The war will rage for all time. But those of ***her Seed*** will triumph. In the singular sense, ***her Seed,*** refers to the one great, final, glorious product of a woman. This ***Seed*** will be the Lord Himself. He will be born without male seed. Paul wrote about it in one of his epistles. ***But when the fullness of time had come, God sent forth His Son, born of a woman, born under the law,*** (Galatians 4:4). There is no human father presented in this verse. Jesus had to have one human parent, or He would not have been human, but He also had to have a Divine Father, or He would not have been the adequate sacrifice for our sin. This is the story of the incarnation. Who can understand it, even in its simplicity?

The teaching of the Trinity is strong, both in the Scriptures and in church history. We believe the Trinity is three distinct personalities, making one Godhead. This is not one person fulfilling three roles or manifestations. A man has many roles. He is a husband, a father, and a grandfather. He is a trinity in function, but not in person. This is not the Trinity in which we believe. H2O can manifest itself in gas (steam), solid (ice), and liquid (water). It is a trinity only in manifestation. This is not our God, the Trinity. There are three distinct personalities, yet, we do not believe in three Gods. Our Trinity is only One. They are one because of the cross style. Each One has died to self and lives totally for the other Two. In losing Their lives to each other, They have become One. Marriage is the best describes the earthly illustration of this. A husband and wife lose their lives to each other, becoming one flesh. The church is another example of this oneness. The believers lose their lives to each other to become one body.

God perceived redemption in His eternal plan. The first member of the Trinity volunteered to become the Law Giver. He acts as the supervisor over the plan. We call Him, Father. This is not a name, but it is the function which He performs for us. The third member willingly becomes the individual who will permeate the heart of man. He serves as the agent for the resource of redemption. In order to affect man from within, He will need to be a Spirit. Since He is holy, we call Him, Holy Spirit. This is not a name, but it is the function, He performs for us.

The second member of the Trinity graciously accepts the challenge to leap off His throne and become man. He becomes the redemption resource for man's salvation. He will experience the incarnation. We can never comprehend the depth of the sacrifice the Trinity made for us. The risk involved to Their relationship is immeasurable.

Matthew 1:18 focuses upon what takes place with the second member of the Trinity. What did it mean for Him to become a man? Was He a superman? Could He go into a telephone booth and change from His man costume to His God reality? Did He really feel like we feel? Did He need to sleep? Did He get hungry? Was He attracted to girls? Did He need deodorant? These are all valid questions which need answers. Your understanding of the rest of the Book of Matthew will be determined by your answers. The quality of your holy lifestyle will be determined by how you see Jesus.

We do not doubt that Jesus is God. He is absolutely, unmistakably God. We will not attempt to discredit this fact in our discussion. We all understand if Jesus is not God, there is no redemption for us. God alone is able to sufficiently make the sacrifice for us all.

However, when He left His throne and became total man, this raised some important questions. As God, Jesus has all the attributes of God. He is omnipresent, omniscient, omnipotent, and immutable. But when He became man, did He have these same qualities present and available for living?

As God, Jesus is omnipresent. But as man, was He everywhere at one time? This seems to be the easiest quality to understand. The obvious answer is, no! Jesus, as a man, was limited to one space at one time. When He wanted to go the fifteen miles from Jericho to Jerusalem. He had to walk just like everyone else. As God, He possessed the quality of omnipresence, but He decided to limit Himself to be a man. He took His omnipresence, which is rightfully His, and set it aside to become man. This does not lower our view of Jesus, but highlights it. He voluntarily surrendered His right to be everywhere at one time.

As God, Jesus is omniscient. He knows everything. But now He has become man. Does He know everything as a man? This quality is a bit harder to decipher clearly. There seems to be times when Jesus knew things a normal man would not know. Yet, if there is one fact that Jesus as a Man does not know, then He is not omniscient. When He spoke of His second coming, Jesus told His disciples, ***"But of that day and hour no one knows, not even the angels of heaven, nor the Son, but only the Father,"*** (Mark 13:32). Luke gives us the only insight we have into the childhood of Jesus. He wrote, ***And Jesus increased in wisdom and stature, and in favor with God and men,*** (Luke 2:52). In the Book of Hebrews we read, ***though He was a Son, yet He learned obedience by the things which He suffered,*** (Hebrews 5:8). All of these verses leave us with the awareness that as Jesus set aside His omnipresence, so also He set aside His omniscience. He chose to limit Himself to the knowledge and learning processes of a human being.

It is more difficult to comprehend Jesus as a man when we look at the quality of omnipotence. As a man, did Jesus have God power? His miracles seem to indicate He had an ability other men do not possess. Did Jesus surrender all of the other attributes, but decide to hold tightly to His power as God? If we believe He limited Himself in this area, we must explain how He was able to do the things He did. The answer becomes clear when you recognize Jesus did not do any miracles until He was baptized by John the Baptist. Matthew records, ***When He had been baptized, Jesus came up immediately from the water; and behold, the heavens were open to Him, and He saw the Spirit of God descending like a dove and alighting upon Him,*** (Matthew 3:16). Here is the secret! Jesus was filled with the Holy Spirit. What He did, He did not do. It was the Father, through the Spirit, doing it through Jesus. He did not do what He did because He was God. He did what He did because He was a man filled with God.

Paul states it clearly in the Kenosis passage. ***Let this mind be in you which was also in Christ Jesus, who, being in the form of God, did not consider it robbery to be equal with God, but made Himself of no reputation, taking the form of a bondservant, and coming in the likeness of men. And being found in appearance as a man, He humbled Himself and became obedient to the point of death, even the death of the cross,*** (Philippians 2:5-8). This is the incarnation in plain words. The second member of the Trinity became man, and set aside all He knew as God, to be a total man.

The style Jesus lived is the style God intended for all humanity. Jesus lived the cross style. He did not live out of Himself. His life was not self-initiated. He constantly relied on the Father, through the Holy Spirit, to act through Him. Christ likeness is the call of Christianity. It is not a call to act like Him, or to attempt to do what He did. It is a call to surrender to Him as He surrendered to the Father. Christ will be like He is through us, as the Father was who He is through Jesus.

Think of the sacrifice Christ made for us. It is impossible to comprehend! Stretch your imagination with me. In an attempt to understand the sacrifice, imagine an entire warehouse filled with millions of spiders. There are spiders of all sizes, shapes and species. Imagine that you have a special love for these spiders. Every day you fellowship with, and care for them. One day you notice something is wrong. Sin has entered your spider world. It is evident by their actions. Groups of spiders have formed gangs. They are destroying other spiders. Something must be done to stop this.

You attempt to communicate with them. You speak to them directly. They do not understand English, and they simply pass your words off as thunder. You write them a love letter, but they do not read English, and they do not bother opening the pages of your book. You create a lovely environment for them, but they destroy it without concern. Finally, it becomes evident to you that there is only one way to save them. You have to become a spider. You set aside all you know and enjoy as a human. You do not become a spider man, but you think, speak, walk, eat, and live like a spider. You are a real spider.

You show the spiders love. By your life style, you reveal to them the way spiders should live. They see how different you are and despise you. They plot to kill you, and they finally pull it off. They nail you to an eight legged cross. But you are raised from the dead, and you return to the spider world.

I know this is a silly illustration, and it does not parallel the depth of what took place in the Trinity. But think of what it would mean for you to become a spider, and of all you would set aside. Even though becoming a spider would be a tremendous sacrifice, may I suggest that sacrifice is only a small percentage of the sacrifice Jesus made, to leave all He knew as God and become man. Our story of the spiders does not portray the involvement of the Trinity in Their sacrifice.

But there is another major consideration in the story. If you became a spider for three months, and you lived to be eighty years old, your life as a spider would only be a minute portion of your overall life. Let us suppose after three months as a spider, you regained your manhood and all you enjoy as a man. The three month sacrifice would be great, but it would not begin to compare with the eternal sacrifice of never returning to your human form. Eternal means forever, and your sacrifice for the spider means you will forever be a spider.

Is this the real story of the incarnation? Did the second member of the Trinity leap off His throne and become a real man? Did He set aside everything He knew as God? Was this emptying of Himself more than just thirty-three years? Did He become one of us forever? Did He become the first one of a whole new breed of mankind called Sons of God? He made an eternal sacrifice, and the answer to all of these questions is, YES!

Now we must question the issue of motive. In our world, there is always an angle. What was God's angle in making this great sacrifice?

Was it a matter of money? Is my tithe what He really wants? This is a preposterous thought. The Trinity can turn streets into gold with the mere thought of Their creative mind. God does not need my money. Perhaps He is after my service. Think of the millions of man hours which are given to God. This, too, is a ridiculous consideration. God made angels with nothing but service in mind. They can serve Him better, faster, and more efficiently than any of us.

What is God's motive? It is love. ***For God so loved the world that He gave His only begotten Son,*** (John 3:16). It is the style of the cross. His love demands He be redemptive. He loves us. This kind of love demands my total life. Think of the sacrifice He made! How can you possibly live for yourself? We cannot go on living our self-initiated lives? His love demands the unreserved availability of our lives for His activity. Anyone who loves us this much can be trusted with our total lives. We must surrender to Him! It must be a complete surrender. Anything less would be mockery. Lukewarmness makes all He did cheap and insignificant. You can understand what the author of Hebrews meant when he said, ***they crucify again for themselves the Son of God, and put Him to an open shame,*** (Hebrews 6:6). We cannot compromise. We cannot give only a part of our lives. We must be totally His!

# Matthew 1:18-2:23

## The Protected Plan

Matthew writes to the Jews in an attempt to convince them Jesus is the Kingly Messiah. He is bold and direct in his communication of the truth. He lists the genealogy of Jesus through King David. This is essential, because it is the first test of anyone claiming to be the Deliverer of Israel. Jesus has no right claim to the throne of Judah without being a descendant of King David. Matthew begins his book by giving the legal genealogy of Jesus Christ (Matthew 1:1-17).

Once Matthew establishes this claim for Jesus, he immediately eliminates Joseph as the natural father of Jesus. He does so by using the feminine pronoun, ***of whom,*** which relates only to Mary (Matthew 1:16). Joseph, the legal father of Jesus, had absolutely nothing to do with the birth of Jesus. This raises questions in the mind of the Jew, which Matthew must answer. He begins an entirely new genealogy (Matthew 1:18). Though this genealogy is very short, it is no less powerful in its truth. Jesus is born of God! It is the genealogy of the natural Father of Jesus.

***Now the birth of Jesus Christ was as follows:*** (Matthew 1:18). The Greek word, translated ***birth,*** is the same word, translated ***genealogy*** (Matthew 1:1). Though Matthew previously used the words, ***begot*** (Matthew 1:2-15), and ***was born*** (Matthew 1:16), he does not use either of those words now. He uses the same word to introduce the second genealogy (Matthew 1:18) as he does to introduce the first genealogy (Matthew 1:1). He boldly declares the birth of Jesus is a direct result of the action of God. The birth of Jesus cannot be explained without the action of God. God is the natural Father of Jesus!

God starts a new adventure in Christ. It has been His dream from the beginning. It was His purpose in creating Adam as the first man. God did not stop when His plan was thwarted by sin. Throughout the unfolding of His plan in the Old Testament, God kept His dream alive. ***But when the fullness of time had come, God sent forth His Son, born of a woman, born under the law,*** (Galatians 4:4). He was beginning a new breed of humanity. He instituted a new category of existence. He called them sons of God. These sons would know the very life of God. They would participate in the very nature of God, and they would be born of God. The dream the Father had for Jesus is the same dream He has for you and me. What took place in Jesus is what God wants to take place in us. As Jesus was filled with the Spirit of God, so we are to be filled with the Spirit of God. As Jesus lived in the power of God, so we are to live in the same power. As Jesus lived a God initiated life, so we are to live in response to God. The new beginning takes place in Christ. He is born of God.

As Matthew tells of the birth and early years of Christ, he expresses how God feels. Matthew relates this period in five narratives, all from the perspective of Joseph, thus highlighting his role in the life of Jesus.

First, Matthew writes of the **EMERGING OF JESUS** (Matthew 1:18-25). In this section, Matthew gives the new genealogy of Jesus. He clarifies the questions which he raised at the close of the first genealogy. Jesus is born of God. But how does Joseph feel about all of this? Evidently Mary did not tell Joseph what the angel told her. Can you imagine his shock when he discovers Mary is with child? He has great turmoil in his heart. What is he to do? The answer comes to him in a night time dream when an angel of the Lord appears to him. He immediately marries Mary.

The second narrative is the **ENTRANCE OF THE WISE MEN** (Matthew 2:1-12). The wise men have come from the East to Jerusalem. It was their custom to travel with an army. This entourage was in search of this new King. Herod, then the king of Judea, became involved in the investigation of the wise men. With the help of the chief priests and scribes, Herod discovered Christ was to be born in Bethlehem. He informed the wise men, fully expecting them to return with the information of the exact location of this new baby king. But God intervened through a dream, and He instructed the wise men to go home another way.

Joseph was again visited in a dream by the angel of the Lord. This time his instructions were to take Mary and the baby Jesus, and **ESCAPE TO EGYPT** (Matthew 2:13-15). Joseph did not hesitate, but immediately responded. They departed for Egypt in the night hours. They were to remain in Egypt until the death of Herod.

None of this was hidden from Herod. He realized he had been deceived by the wise men. He could not tolerate the idea of a new king being born, and his temper got the best of him. His twisted mind had an easy solution. He would simply have all the male children, two years and under, killed. Surely this would eliminate the new king. So the **ELIMINATION OF ALL THE BOYS** took place (Matthew 2:16-18). The cruelty of such an event is hard to imagine. An earth shattering wail came from nearly every home in Bethlehem and all of its districts.

In the final narrative, we find the **EXCURSION FROM EGYPT** (Matthew 2:19-23). Herod is now dead. An angel of the Lord appears a third time to Joseph in a dream. He instructs Joseph to return to Israel with Mary and the baby Jesus, because those who sought to kill the new King are all dead. However, there is still some conflict in Judea. Archelaus, the son of Herod, is now ruling over Judea. He has inherited the same kind of insanity and thirst for cruelty that his father had. Again God warns Joseph in a dream, and the family settles in Nazareth, which is in Galilee.

My heart rejoices greatly when I note certain observations from these narratives. They reveal something about the person of God. He is faithful, and He protects His children.

## Prophecy

We have dealt with the subject of prophecy before, but Matthew highlights it repeatedly in the opening stories of his account. The Jews knew and understood prophecy, and Matthew uses it as a key argument in his writing. It is a simple reminder of the plan of God. Each of these five narratives makes a reference to prophecy.

In the **EMERGING OF JESUS** (Matthew 1:18-25), we clearly see prophecy. An angel appears to Joseph in a dream. This angel plainly speaks the message. Joseph is to marry Mary, because that which is conceived in her is of the Holy Spirit. Then the angel makes an incredible statement. ***"And she will bring forth a Son, and you shall call His name Jesus, for He will save His people from their sins,"*** (Matthew 1:21). Then Matthew reminds us of the reason for this, ***that it might be fulfilled which was spoken by the Lord through the prophet, saying: "Behold, the virgin shall be with child, and bear a Son, and they shall call His name Immanuel," which is translated, "God with us,"*** (Matthew 1:22-23).

In the **ENTRANCE OF THE WISE MEN** (Matthew 2:1-12), they come to Herod in Jerusalem. Herod calls for the chief priests and the scribes. He instructs them to look into the Scriptures to see where the Christ child was to be born. ***So they said to him, "In Bethlehem of Judea, for thus it is written by the prophet:***

> ***'But you, Bethlehem, in the land of Judah,***
> ***Are not the least among the rulers of Judah;***
> ***For out of you shall come a Ruler***
> ***Who will shepherd My people Israel,'"***

(Matthew 2:5-6).

This new family follows the instructions of the angel of the Lord to **ESCAPE TO EGYPT** (Matthew 2:13-15). The angel appears in a dream, and Joseph, Mary and the baby get up in the middle of the night to begin the journey to Egypt. Matthew footnotes this scene when he writes, ***and was there until the death of Herod, that it might be***

***fulfilled which was spoken by the Lord through the prophet, saying, "Out of Egypt I called My Son,"*** (Matthew 2:15).

Matthew highlights prophecy again in the narrative of the **ELIMINATION OF THE BOYS** (Matthew 2:16-18). Herod decrees that all male children, two years and younger, in Bethlehem and its districts, be put to death. ***Then was fulfilled what was spoken by Jeremiah the prophet, saying:***

> ***"A voice was heard in Ramah,***
> ***Lamentation, weeping, and great mourning,***
> ***Rachel weeping for her children,***
> ***Refusing to be comforted,***
> ***Because they are no more,"*** (Matthew 2:17).

In the final narrative, **EXCURSION FROM EGYPT** (Matthew 2:19-23), Herod is dead. The angel of the Lord appears again to Joseph in a dream. He is to return to Palestine and live in Nazareth. Matthew writes, ***And he came and dwelt in a city called Nazareth, that it might be fulfilled which was spoken by prophets, "He shall be called a Nazarene,"*** (Matthew 2:23).

It is a tremendous plan! Things are not left to accident or happen chance. God is fulfilling His dream! He is working things out in a systematic order. Step by step, He is carrying out the plan. He does not invent things as He goes along. The events do not determine His actions. God is not reacting to each event. Each event fits into His plan. He has had this plan throughout the eternities. God allowed the prophets of old to see parts of the plan as He was on the move, fulfilling His dream.

How can I convince you that you are a vital part of this plan? The plan is never for the multitudes. It is for the individual. God has specifically ordained you for these moments! Your significance does not lie in the bagging of groceries at the local supermarket. The histories are being fulfilled in your day. This is about more than preparing another meal for your children. You are fulfilling the plan of God. Live beyond the meager, the small, and the mundane. Live in the vision of God! He has a plan!

### Prompting

You must see the complete picture. God did not create a plan and put you in charge of carrying out the details. It is not your plan. The truth of the matter is, we only know small parts of the plan. But what we do know is so startling, we can hardly imagine what the full plan might be. We are not in charge of the plan; He is! He is fulfilling His plan through us.

God guides and intervenes in the midst of His plan. In four out of five of the narratives, there is direct Divine guidance given. In the opening narrative, **EMERGING OF JESUS** (Matthew 1:18-25), Joseph is in extreme turmoil because he is a just man. He is stunned by the news of Mary's condition. From his position, it is obvious that she has had an affair with someone else, while she is betrothed to him. He does not want to stone her to death, but at the same time he does not want to continue with a marriage when she has been unfaithful. He decides to handle it in a private manner. ***BUT while he thought about these things, behold, an angel of the Lord appeared to him in a dream,*** (Matthew 1:20). God has a plan, and in that plan He includes a way to protect the reputation and purity of both Mary and Joseph. He sends an angel of the Lord to intervene in the thought process of Joseph. He will not allow the plan to go astray. God is guiding and directing His plan.

In the second narrative, the **ENTRANCE OF THE WISE MEN** (Matthew 2:1-12), the plan is again threatened. Herod the king aids the wise men in their search for the Christ child. He appears to be supportive in their mission to find the child to worship Him. He tells the wise men, ***"Go and search carefully for the young Child, and when you have found Him, bring back word to me, that I may come and worship Him also,"*** (Matthew 2:8). But he is deceptive. His true plan is to destroy this new King. God does not allow this to happen. The wise men were ***divinely warned in a dream that they should not return to Herod,*** (Matthew 2:12).

This was no small matter. Herod was a powerful man, high in the political arena of his day. God was not threatened by the supposed power of Herod, and He does not let His plan be thwarted. God is aware of Herod's scheme, and He takes action before Herod can. In the next narrative, the **ESCAPE TO EGYPT** (Matthew 2:13-16), ***an angel of the Lord appeared to Joseph in a dream, saying, "Arise, take the young child and His mother, flee to Egypt, and stay there until I bring you word; for Herod will seek the young Child to destroy Him,"*** (Matthew 2:13). Even as the angry Herod orders that all male children, two years and younger in Bethlehem and its districts, be put to death, the new King is protected by the guidance of God. God is intimately involved in the unfolding of His plan. He guides the action step by step. Everything, and everyone, are under His watchful care and concern.

Finally, in the last narrative, the **EXCURSION FROM EGYPT** (Matthew 2:19-23), God again guides this new family. The angel of the Lord appears to Joseph in a dream and makes him aware that ***those who sought the young Child's life are dead,*** (Matthew 2:20). God not only makes the plan, but He also carries it out. He is in the middle of the plan, directing the drama. God is the plan! He is reconciling the world to Himself.

The truth is about more than five narratives, which took place two thousand years ago. It is about you and your life. God has a plan, and you were born out of the dreams of His plan. God is involved in your life and its details. Do you see the opportunity you have for being involved in the action of God for your day? He knows where to go and what to do. You can totally rest in that knowledge. His guidance is forth coming. He has not deserted you. Will you totally surrender to His plan and His guidance?

## Protection

The truth we have observed to this point is enough to make us rejoice forever. But we must not miss the final declaration from the narratives. There is no political power, or man-made institution which can stop what God desires to do! No evil is equal to the active involvement of God's protective arm as He protects His plan.

The narratives declare it! The **EMERGING OF JESUS** (Matthew 1:19-25), reveals how dedicated and detailed the protection of God is for His plan. The customs and practices of the day would demand that Mary be stoned as an unfaithful young lady, who has betrayed her betrothal. At the very least, the scandal connected with the birth of the Messiah will undermine its good. Nothing else can present a greater evil than this situation. But God protects His plan. He arranges for Joseph, by marriage, to keep the birth of Jesus in the place of integrity.

In the second narrative, the **ENTRANCE OF THE WISE MEN** (Matthew 2:1-12), the most insane rulership Judea has ever seen, is on the throne. Herod's evil is visible by the list of unthinkable acts his history reveals. Herod will add another to his list, if he can. He will murder the new King. But God protects His plan. He will not allow the wise men to report back to the King. In the **ESCAPE TO EGYPT** (Matthew 2:13-15), God removes the Christ child from the reach of King Herod. Even with his long reaching authority, Herod is still no match for the protective arm of a sovereign Jehovah. The plan will not be stopped.

In the last narrative, the **EXCURSION FROM EGYPT** (Matthew 2:19-23), even as the holy family returns from Egypt, the protection of God is covering Christ. God warned Joseph in a dream to make his way into Galilee, where the family was to settle in Nazareth. Archelaus was now the ruler of Judea. He was the son of Herod, and he was not free from the insidious insanity of his father. God still protects His plan. Nothing will stop Him from redeeming His world.

What a message this is to our hearts! God has a plan. He is prompting and guiding the details of this plan. He brings all the sovereign power of His being to bear on the protection of His plan. I want to yield myself to the plan of God. It is the only safe place to be. I want every moment of my life to be under the direction and guidance of God's protection. I am willing to surrender any dream or plan I might have, for His perfect plan to flow through my life. No ego or pride will stop me from a humble submission to the guided plan of my Father. What possible reason could I find to risk going my own way? What gain could be achieved by striking out in my own wisdom? I resist all such foolishness to know the perfect plan of my God's guidance and protection.

I recognize this truth in the most intimate areas of my life. I also see it in the simple and complex functions of my being. From my career, to my daily routine, I submit to His leadership. Moment by moment I will flow with His presence, and let Him shape my responses. No relationship will be outside the plan. I will allow no financial decision to waver from His design. Materialism will not rule, for there is no protection found in that. I want the total plan of God to flow in my life. His guidance will be my only focus. Only there will I know safety.

## Matthew 1:18

## After and Before

***Now the birth of Jesus Christ was as follows: After His mother Mary was betrothed to Joseph, before they came together, she was found with child of the Holy Spirit,*** (Matthew 1:18). In the original Greek, planted in the middle of the verse, is a small word. The word only has one letter. We have many translations of this verse, but none translates this word. It seems to have been ignored. It is a primary particle, and it makes a distinction between two connected terms. This particle is used to mark a difference. Sometimes it is translated "or," other times "either," or it can be translated "than."

There are two verses in the New Testament which I can give you to illustrate the use of this particle. ***No one can serve two masters; for either he will hate the one and love the other, or else he will be loyal to one and despise the other. You can not serve God and mammon,*** (Matthew 6:24). The primary particle in this verse is translated ***either,*** and ***or else***. The second illustration is in the verse, ***Either make the tree good and its fruit good, or else make the tree***

***bad and its fruit bad; for a tree is known by its fruit,*** (Matthew 12:33). Again the particle is translated ***either*** and ***or else?*** One is used to distinguish things which exclude each other, and one is used to take the place of another.

In the verse we are now studying (Matthew 1:18), the primary particle is in-between the Greek word, translated ***before,*** and the Greek word, translated ***they came together.*** If this particle carries with it the comparison of two situations, then the meaning is clear. Matthew contrasts the plans of Mary and Joseph for marriage with what is really taking place. Mary is with child outside of the marriage relationship.

There is little information available about Mary. We learn from the Scriptures she had a sister named Salome, who was the mother of James and John (Matthew 27:56). According to the genealogy given by Luke, we understand she was of the lineage of David (Luke 3). She was a native of Nazareth, and she came from a fairly poor family. We know she was related to Elizabeth, who was the mother of John the Baptist.

There was something significant about Mary's spiritual condition. It played a major role in her being chosen by God to be the mother of Jesus. After the Angel Gabriel's announcement that she would be the mother of ***the Son of God,*** Mary said, ***"Behold, the maidservant*** (bond slave) ***of the Lord! Let it be to me according to your word,"*** (Luke 1:38). She never questioned the angel. She assumed what he said was true. She did wonder, ***"How can this be, since I do not know a man?"*** (Luke 1:34). The Holy Spirit testified to Mary's belief and response. ***"Blessed is she who believed, for there will be a fulfillment of those things which were told her from the Lord,"*** (Luke 1:45). Mary expressed her deep commitment in what the scholars call her magnificent Magnificat. ***"My soul exalts the Lord, and my spirit has rejoiced in God my Savior. . . . For He who is mighty has done great things for me, and holy is His name,"*** (Luke 1:47-49).

We know even less about Joseph than we do about Mary. His father's name was Jacob (Matthew 1:16). He was a craftsman, a construction worker, probably a carpenter (Matthew 13:55). He was a ***righteous man*** (Matthew 1:19). And after the childhood of Jesus, Joseph disappears from the narrative.

It is important to understand the difference between the betrothal and the actual marriage. It is probable, both Joseph and Mary were quite young when they were ***betrothed,*** (Matthew 1:18). Girls were often betrothed as young as twelve or thirteen, and boys when they were several years older. The Hebrew marriage involved two stages, the betrothal and the marriage ceremony. The marriage was arranged by the families of the bride and groom. The young people were almost never consulted. A contract was made between the bride's parents and the groom's parents, and it was sealed by the payment of a dowry, or bride price. This was paid by the groom, or his family, to the bride's father. It served to compensate the father for the wedding expenses, and it provided a type of insurance for the bride, in the event the groom became dissatisfied and divorced her. The contract was considered binding as soon as it was made, and the man and the woman were considered legally married. Often the marriage ceremony and consummation of the marriage did not take place until a year later. This betrothal period was a time of probation and testing of fidelity. During this period, the bride and the groom usually had little, if any, social contact with each other.

Joseph is shocked to find out what has taken place in his betrothal period to Mary. It is a moral disaster! When the angel made the pronouncement to Mary, she went to visit her cousin Elizabeth for a period of three months (Luke 1:56). When she returns home, she is physically demonstrating the announcement. As far as we know, she had no contact with Joseph during this time. She does not explain to him what has happened. Would he believe her explanation? Evidently she relies on God to handle Joseph. It is an act of trust.

Joseph struggles with what to do (Matthew 1:19). Should he report her to the magistrate at the city gates and allow the death penalty provided by the Old Testament to take place? He is deeply shamed by her obvious unfaithfulness to him. His love for Mary and his love for God tell him to simply divorce her privately and let the rumors spread as they will. But either way, Mary's reputation and future life are in jeopardy. Think of what this will do to the plan of God. Not only is the moral character of Mary at stake, but the legitimacy of Jesus' birth is at stake as well. Joseph finds himself in the middle of a tremendous dilemma. What shall he do?

Matthew presents two contrasting pictures. A righteous young man has definite plans for marriage, a home and a future. He is betrothed to a pure and blessed young lady, who is pledged to be his wife. All their plans are in place. Their parents have agreed, and the dowry has been paid. Everything is just as it ought to be. Then there is a sudden upheaval. A factor is injected into the equation, which upsets all the plans. The entire picture changes. Mary is with child! This turns a good picture bad. A pure, wholesome, virgin appears to be unrighteous and unfaithful. The future home, marriage, and children are twisted into scandal, possible death and no marriage. The situation has changed from glory into shame.

Who is responsible for this awful change? It is not an adulteress affair. It is not another man. It is God! The Holy Spirit has overshadowed Mary, and the child to be born will be the Son of God. God has interfered in this beautiful scene. God is responsible! What gives God the right to impose His will upon this young couple and ruin all their plans? If another man had done this, we would call him evil. Yet, God has done this thing, and we call Him holy.

The answer resides in the well-established background of the Old Testament, and in the message to the church in the New Testament. Mary and Joseph lived in the hour of the Old Testament. Matthew paints the picture for us of the relationship between God and His people. It is the picture of the bridegroom and his bride.

If you take an exhaustive concordance and view the word, harlot, it appears repeatedly throughout the Old Testament. Most often it refers to the spiritual life of Israel. In their state of idolatry, God refers to Israel as a harlot. You can read it in the following words concerning Jerusalem. ***"How degenerate is your heart!" says the Lord God, "seeing you do all these things, the deeds of a brazen harlot. You erected your shrine at the head of every road, and built your high place in every street. Yet you were not like a harlot, because you scorned payment. You are an adulterous wife, who takes strangers instead of her husband. Men make payment to all harlots, but you made your payments to all your lovers, and hired them to come to you from all around for your harlotry. You are the opposite of other women in your harlotry, because no one solicited you to be a***

***harlot. In that you gave payment but no payment was given you, therefore you are the opposite. Now then, O harlot, hear the word of the Lord!"*** (Ezekiel 16:30-35). God considers His people to be His wife. He is a broken hearted husband who has discovered His unfaithful wife. He, like Joseph, sees the one He loves as unfaithful. What shall He do?

The Book of Hosea in the Old Testament is written from this view point. Hosea is told by God to marry a harlot so he will understand how God feels about His people. After Hosea's wife has been unfaithful to him, God speaks again to Hosea. ***"God again, love a woman who is loved by a lover and is committing adultery, just like the love of the Lord for the children of Israel, who look to other gods and love the raisin cakes of the pagans,*** (Hosea 3:1). Through the prophet Hosea, God cries out to Israel like a husband longing for the return of his wayward wife. God sees His people as Hosea sees His bride.

The Old Testament picture is somewhat negative, but in the New Testament, we are able to see the positive view. ***Husbands, love your wives, just as Christ loved the church and gave Himself for her, that He might sanctify and cleanse her with the washing of water by the word, that He might present her to Himself a glorious church, not having spot or wrinkle or any such thing, but that she should be holy and without blemish,*** (Ephesians 5:25-27). Paul cries out, ***Oh, that you would bear with me in a little folly - and indeed you do bear with me. For I am jealous for you with godly jealously. For I have betrothed you to one husband, that I may present you as a chaste virgin to Christ,*** (2 Corinthians 11:1-2). Listen to the final moment of time, ***And I heard, as it were, the voice of a great***

***multitude, as the sound of many waters and as the sound of mighty thunderings, saying, "Alleluia! For the Lord God Omnipotent reigns! Let us be glad and rejoice and give Him glory, for the marriage of the Lamb has come, and His wife has made herself ready." And to her it was granted to be arrayed in fine linen, clean and bright for the fine linen is the righteous acts of the saints. Then he said to me, "Write: Blessed are those who are called to the marriage supper of the Lamb!"*** (Revelation 19:6-9). ***Then one of the seven angels who had the seven bowls filled with the seven last plagues came to me and talked with me saying, "Come, I will show you the bride, the Lamb's wife,"*** (Revelation 21:9).

We could go on with many kinds of declarations. We are His bride, and He is the Bridegroom. The relationship He wants to have with us must be viewed from this perspective. He wants to impregnate us with His life! The kind of relationship taking place between Joseph and Mary is a type of the relationship God wants to have with us.

## Commitment

Perhaps the culture of Mary and Joseph's day is a better symbol of God's relationship with us than is our own culture. Even the betrothal (engagement) was so binding that breaking it was punishable by death. Sexual impurity simply was not tolerated by Jewish law. A contract was in place, and a price had been paid. This was not a romantically inspired promise which would change when someone else more appealing came along. This was not a light, superficial, emotional agreement, which would change when the emotion was gone. This was a legal, binding contract involving commitment.

This same strength of commitment is experienced in the covenant relationship of the Old Testament. God is interested in having a covenant with us. The prophecy of Jeremiah 31:31 says that God views us in the New Testament as a new covenant. Every covenant is sealed with the shedding of blood. The strength of this new covenant is the cross. It shows us how far God has gone in His commitment to this marriage with us, His bride.

This contract results from the commitment of our will, not the emotion of a high moment. God forgives us! We have been far too fickle in our relationship with Him. We have acted like Israel of old and played the role of the spiritual harlot. We have committed spiritual adultery and turned to other husbands. We are betrothed to Christ alone!

## Completeness

The marriage relationship between Joseph and Mary was to be twofold. There was the betrothal, followed by the marriage ceremony. The two individuals were to be in complete unity. Mary was going to belong exclusively to Joseph, and Joseph to Mary. No one else was to be in the picture!

Mary's life would become focused on Joseph. She was not planning how she could make room for another man besides Joseph. Her entire planning revolved around him. How she decorated the house and arranged the living room furniture would depend upon what Joseph liked. Her days were going to be spent in light of Joseph's schedule. She would not fix dinner without thinking about him. Herod, the king, required that every person of the lineage of David would go to

Bethlehem for the census. Mary would not go alone, but she would go with Joseph. All of her life would revolve around Joseph.

Joseph would focus his entire life upon Mary. Mary was not to be one of Joseph's wife. She was to be his only wife. She was going to be the pervasive influence in His life. How he spent his money, what kind of home he built, where he would go, and how he would act, all revolved around Mary. Even in the most tragic moment (Matthew 1:19), Joseph was thinking how he could do what needed to be done and still protect Mary.

Is this not what God wanted from Israel in the Old Testament? Is this not what He wants from us in the New Testament? There is no other focus. He cannot be in one section of life. We are His bride, and He only has one thought on His mind. It should be the same with us. All of our plans, our view of the future, how we act, and where we go, all have to do with our total focus on the Bridegroom.

### Companion

Joseph has just received the heart breaking news about the one to whom He is betrothed (Matthew 1:19). He does not care about Mary having other friends. Certainly he is not upset about her visit to Elizabeth, and the family relationship represented there. But she is to be his companion. She is to have a special depth of intimacy with him alone.

But Mary is with child. This bespeaks an intimacy beyond friendship. This has to do with the "one flesh." It is the kind of relationship between two people, where there are no secrets and everything is shared. Is this what our Bridegroom desperately wants from us, His bride? Will He be satisfied with anything less than this? Will He tolerate any other attitude within us? Certainly not, for we are His bride!

# Matthew 1:19-21

# Focus on Jesus

Fear is a fundamental emotion in everyone's life. Though there are many other emotions present in the human personality, fear seems to be the basis of them all. We all battle fear in some form or other in our lives. It is not surprising that the Bible has much to say about overcoming fear.

When we discuss fear, we face a language problem. The English language is very thin. It lumps many ideas together under the term, fear. But this is not so in the original language of the Scriptures. There is a Greek word which expresses the idea of fearing God. It is reverence and awesomeness in relation to the person of God. It is encouraged throughout the Scriptures. This is not a negative, but a positive. But this is not the word in this passage. The word here for fear is the total opposite.

The Greek word here means "to frighten or to terrorize." A good example of its usage is found when Jesus walks on the water (Matthew 14:26). The disciples have battled the storm all night. It is probably about three o'clock in the morning. They are extremely tired. They cannot go forward or backward. The storm waves are crashing over the sides of the boat. They are bailing water with all the strength they have, trying to keep the boat afloat. Suddenly these men look up to see a ghostly figure skipping from one wave to another, and they are very afraid. What English word would properly describe what the disciples are feeling? Terrorized, frightened, or the slang phrase "scared out of their wits" come to mind.

Another example of the use of this Greek word is the experience of the two ladies and the soldiers at the tomb on Easter Sunday morning (Matthew 28:1-5). They are all in the area of the tomb where Jesus' body was laid to rest following the crucifixion. An angel appears and removes the stone. The earth quakes, and even the supposedly fearless soldiers ***shook for fear.*** By the end of this event, the Scripture says they ***became as dead men.*** Their fear built and progressed, and as their minds began to comprehend what was taking place, their bodies could not tolerate their emotions, and they fainted. The two ladies experienced the same overwhelming fear.

In the passage we are studying, Joseph finds himself in a crisis moment. The news about Mary has delivered a crushing blow. How can this possibly be? Mary, returning from a three-month visit to her cousin, Elizabeth (Luke 1:56), is showing physical evidence of her pregnancy. The rumors, which have been spread all over town, are true. Mary makes no attempt to explain or defend her situation to Joseph. She trusts the Holy Spirit, who is accomplishing the plan of God within her, to make it known to Joseph. He, no doubt, hears the rumors and asks others to verify their reality. His heart is struck with terror! What will this mean? What should he do?

***An angel of the Lord appeared to him in a dream, saying, "Joseph, son of David, do not be afraid . . ."*** (Matthew 1:20). There are several intriguing things about this situation. Every human being in the Christmas scene deals with the issue of fear. The wise men have come to Jerusalem, traveling with their army, which was their normal custom. ***When Herod the king heard this, he was troubled, and all Jerusalem with him,*** (Matthew 2:3). The troubling Herod feels is based on his fear. The wise men have been warned about Herod, and they certainly have a fear of him. After they see and worship the Christ child, they return home by another route, because they have been warned about this insane king (Matthew 2:12). Mary and Joseph have fear in their hearts as they flee for their lives into Egypt (Matthew 2:14). When Herod issues his decree to have all male children, two years of age and below slaughtered, think of the terror which arises in the hearts of the families with little boys. Every such family in Bethlehem and its surrounding districts are visited by soldiers who kill their baby boys (Matthew 2:16). Fear is a major emotion in the Christmas story. This brings us to the conclusion that fear is the common element in all of us. None of us are exempt from this emotion.

Secondly, we are told not to fear seventy-five times in the Scriptures. This exhortation seems to be needed often in regard to the human personality. Man is always getting himself into situations where he needs to hear the words, ***do not be afraid.***

Another important element in the exhortation not to fear, is the challenge to go beyond the absence of fear. The grammar structure of the Scripture's exhortations tells us we should stop having fear and begin to do the opposite of that emotion. This challenge is not just a negative. It is a positive. The Gospel pursues much more than just the absence of fear. Fear is to be replaced with the great elements of joy, rejoicing, and worship. So the exhortation, ***do not be afraid,*** is not just the removal of fear. We are to pursue all that is the opposite of fear.

In the fourth element of real importance, the angel gives Joseph definite, step by step instructions to follow, which will replace his fear with joy. The angel uses the word, ***for,*** immediately after his exhortation, ***do not be afraid.*** This word assigns a cause. So the angel is saying, "Don't be afraid, and here is the reason why."

We need to look at this from Joseph's perspective. Matthew writes this unfolding drama of the birth of Christ through Joseph's eyes. His fear is in a specific area, not a general sense. The fear is in the area of his marriage. They have been planning this for some time. How will he carry out those plans? It will be difficult because of the new element of Mary's pregnancy. Suddenly fear takes a strong hold in Joseph's life. There are so many unknown factors in the equation now. How will this affect their future relationship? Their culture will make things difficult, because peer pressure and peer acceptance affects everything. There are both spiritual and moral implications in this new development. Joseph is afraid. What is the answer?

## Remembrance

## Matthew 1:20

Did you notice how the angel addresses Joseph? ***An angel of the Lord appeared to him in a dream, saying, "Joseph, son of***

***David . . .*"** (Matthew 1:20). God calls Joseph to remember who he is, and how intimately God has been involved in his life. Joseph is a son of David, and that is no insignificant matter. Matthew's genealogy is proof that the lineage of Jesus can be traced through King David. Jesus has a right to be on the throne of David. Joseph is in this same lineage.

Joseph resides in a lineage of people who have experienced the mighty **PROTECTION** of God in their lives repeatedly. Abraham knew the covenant promise of God being fulfilled through him. King David was delivered from the threat of Goliath. Joseph can stand tall, knowing that his lineage begins with Abraham and leads up to King David. It spills through a multitude of stories of men who were constantly evil, and yet, God would not abandon His plan. God saved a people, even in the midst of captivity. His long-suffering is proven again and again. Joseph is a part of this story. The same God who would not allow any nation, king, or people to thwart His plan will not be overcome by Joseph's situation!

Joseph resides in the lineage of people who have experienced the mighty **PROVISION** of God in their lives from beginning to end. He provided quail in the bush and manna from the sky. He gave them water from the rock, and He controlled the Red Sea. He gave them a government organization and laws for conduct. God's provision and forgiveness to them was present and forthcoming. Everything the Israelites could need was provided by their sovereign God. Will Joseph's need go unheeded in his moment of great fear?

Joseph resides in the lineage of people who have experience the mighty unfolding **PLAN** of God in their lives again and again. This was why they were formed. Who could look at this list from beginning to end and not admit the One in charge has a significant plan? The plan does not come from an introverted mind, who wants to please Himself. It is the plan of a gracious, unselfish God, who wants to redeem a world. His design is to redeem the physical and spiritual world from the clutches of damnation. Joseph finds himself in the middle of this plan! Will he allow his fear over the moral crisis in his life to stop this unfolding of God's plan? Joseph must remember he is a ***son of David.***

We are not exempt from the message of the angel. There is no need for you to fear. Remember who you are! You are in the list of God's people, who have experienced the deliverance of God in their lives. Jesus has delivered you repeatedly. He always intervenes in the lives of the sons of God. He delivered Joseph, and He will deliver you. He has provided every detail of your life's needs. He showers you with blessing after blessing. Remember! There is no need to allow the fog of fear to cloud your vision.

## Reigning God
## Matthew 1:20

The angel immediately focuses on the specific problem which is at the heart of Joseph's fear. He does not give general advice for overcoming the fear. He says, ***"Do not be afraid to take to you Mary your wife,"*** (Matthew 1:20). Then the angel assigns a cause by using the word, ***for.*** He addresses the fact of Mary's pregnancy, which has caused Joseph's fear. The angel says, ***"Do not be afraid to take to you Mary your wife, for that which is conceived in her is of the Holy Spirit,"*** (Matthew 1:20).

The basis of Joseph's fear is the conception of Jesus within Mary. He has only one explanation for such an event. Joseph's response to the angel's declaration is significant. He accepts it, and he does not argue about the fact that what seems to be immoral and devastating, is really of God. How can something this awful be of God? How can something which disrupts the most intimate relationship known in human life be of God? Have you ever asked these kinds of questions?

Could it be that what is taking place is beyond Joseph's knowledge? Could it be that things are not as they appear? Can Joseph trust God in what he does not understand? Can fear be replaced with trust? You do not have to understand something to over come fear, but it does demand faith. Will Joseph trust a reigning God who has a plan?

The Greek word for ***that which is conceived*** is the same word, translated ***begot,*** in the genealogy. The focus of the word is not upon the method or act which causes the conception, but it is upon the reality of the fact. The angel states the reality of the conception, and then he assigns the cause of this fact to the Holy Spirit. Matthew gives us no insight into the method of the conception. However, he does make it very plain, Mary is a virgin before the moment of conception, and Mary remains a virgin until after the birth of Jesus Christ. Matthew says Joseph did exactly what the angel commanded him to do. He ***took to him his wife, and did not know her till she had brought forth her firstborn Son,*** (Matthew 1:24-25). It is very plain that the method of conception is not a sexual relationship.

Luke, in his Gospel account, gives additional information. The angel of the Lord announced to Mary that the conception will happen in her. She does not question the reality of it, but only requests additional information about the method of conception. She asks, ***"How can this be, since I do not know a man?"*** (Luke 1:34). The angel proceeds to give the additional information when saying, ***"The Holy Spirit will come upon you, and the power of the Highest will overshadow you;"*** (Luke 1:35). There are two different and important Greek words, which are translated ***will come*** and ***will overshadow.***

The Greek word, which is translated ***will come,*** means "to over take." It is used in the Scriptures to refer to sleep, disease, calamities, enemies, and the Holy Spirit overtaking a person. There is something all encompassing about the idea. It affects the entire being.

The Greek word, which is translated ***will overshadow,*** means something of the same sense. It is used in only three scenes in the New Testament. It is dominate at the Mount of Transfiguration. The scene is recorded in three of the Gospel accounts (Matthew 17:5; Mark 9:7 and Luke 9:34). In each case, this Greek word describes the movement of the cloud, which contained the Father's presence and encompassed the disciples. This Greek word is used in relation to Peter, whose shadow would ***overshadow*** those who were sick, and they would be healed (Acts 15:5). The third place this word is used is in the conception of Jesus within Mary.

This is a powerful word! The idea of the word means to "invest with preternatural influence." The dictionary defines the word, preternatural, "to transcend the natural or material order, something that is not physical." This points us back to the spiritual activity of God. This conception within Mary was not the result of the physical, but of the spiritual. It has the same sense of what took place in the re-creation of the world. ***The earth was without form, and void; and darkness***

***was on the face of the deep. And the Spirit of God was hovering over the face of the waters,*** (Genesis 1:2).

Perhaps what happened to Mary was not isolated. We must understand the fact of conception happened only once in the history of man, but God used the same method repeatedly. It is the wonder of His presence overshadowing, encompassing, permeating the totality of our beings. There need be no fear in the results of this hovering of the Spirit. It is creative! It brings about the will of the Father and fulfills the plan of God in our lives. In the Old Testament, it is a foretaste of how God wants to envelope you and me.

But there is a risk involved. It is the same risk Mary took as she submitted to God's will and the overshadowing. What will the end result be? How will it develop in my daily life? What changes will this bring to me? When you are overtaken by the Holy Spirit like this, you lose all control of what happens. The creative flow of the Spirit of God will manifest Himself as He desires. There is no need to fear!

## Resolution

## Matthew 1:21

Here is the angel's final statement to Joseph. ***"And she will bring forth a Son, and you shall call His name Jesus, for He will save His people from their sins,"*** (Matthew 1:21). Where does this movement of God, the overshadowing, finally bring us? It seems God only has one focus in His actions! It is Jesus! There is no need to fear, if it is of Jesus.

I know there is a section of church history which got off focus and looked to Mary. Mary became the recipient of the prayers of many people. It is easy to move from a wrong focus to the upgrading of saints. These saints then became the focus of many people's prayers. But this mistake in focus only teaches us there must be a proper focus. It is never about Mary or the saints. It is always been about Jesus.

Maybe we are not among those who focused on Mary, but we seem to get focused on many other things just as wrong. Sometimes we focus on the church instead of on Christ. We become man centered instead of Jesus centered. We give our energy to programs instead of Jesus. Any time our focus is not on Jesus, we are going to live in fear. It is in being captured by Christ all fear is pushed aside by the faith which He alone stimulates in us.

I can hear the thoughts of Joseph as he struggles with Mary's pregnancy. What should he do? Everywhere he turns, there is fear. Whatever he decides to do will be the wrong thing. It is not going to turn out as he dreamed. There is no proper solution. Fear blocks him from doing the right thing. What is the purpose of the angel? The angel is to bring Joseph back to focus on the plan of God, which is Christ. In this focus, Joseph will find himself able to do what He could not conceive doing. The thing he could not consider as the answer, is now clearly the only solution. He must completely focus on Christ.

When we live in fear there are no adequate answers. Our view is clouded. At best we can only select the better of the wrong answers confronting us. We cannot see what we are to do because of the fear. We have only one solution. We must focus on Christ.

# Matthew 1:21

# The Name

Matthew presents the ***angel of the Lord*** at least four times in the first two chapters of his book. He does so to make a strong statement. After the wise men consult with Herod, they find the Christ child, but they return home another way because of a Divine warning. The ***angel of the Lord*** appears to Joseph and instructs him to go with his family to Egypt to avoid the slaughter of the baby boys (Matthew 2:13). This same ***angel of the Lord*** appears to him in another dream to let him know when it is safe to return to Judea (Matthew 2:19). In the first chapter of Matthew, it was the ***angel of the Lord*** who gave Joseph the instructions concerning Mary (Matthew 1:20-21).

A valuable part of the message Matthew wants to communicate to his readers is that Joseph and the wise men responded to the ***angel of the Lord,*** (Matthew 1:24). This angel intervened for the purpose of fulfilling God's plan. There are definite levels to the angelic host. There are ordinary angels, but there is an angel of Jehovah, who is mentioned in the Old and New Testaments. This is the ***angel of the Lord.***

We cannot be dogmatic in how the ***angel of the Lord*** differs from the ordinary angels. It appears the ***angel of the Lord*** has an attachment with the person of God Himself. This angel is not an actual appearance of God. But at times there seems to be a merging of the angel and the presence of God, until what takes place in the angel is a foretaste of what we experience in the fullness of the Holy Spirit. The ***angel of the Lord*** is an angel who can merge with the Spirit of God, and he is being used to speak the words of God Himself.

This is important in regard to the Christmas story. Because this event is so significant, God has come to supervise. God intervenes in the life of Joseph to direct him in his decision. It is God who delivers the message. The message is especially meaningful to Joseph, but as the message continues, we see its importance to the entire Book of Matthew. It becomes important to us. It becomes a slogan or a banner in the truth presented by Matthew. The message of the ***angel of the Lord*** stands on its own and becomes a summary of the message which Matthew will deliver in the rest of his book.

The whole of Jesus' life is manifested in one bold statement. Everything He is going to do has one focus. His life has one purpose. He will not accomplish many things, but He will be remembered for one very important thing. ***"And she will bring forth a Son, and you shall call His name Jesus, for He will save His people from their sins,"*** (Matthew 1:21).

## The Purpose of the Name

Part of the angel's message was the Son would have a special name. ***"And you shall call His name Jesus."*** In the day of Christ, this was a **COMMON NAME.** It is the translation of the Hebrew name, Joshua. It is a sentence name in the Hebrew language. It means, "Yahweh saves." The name holds great significance. The name of God is very sacred. In Jewish history, the sacred name, Yahweh, was not pronounced when reading the Scriptures. Instead, the words, "my Lord," were substituted for the name, Yahweh. The name was too sacred to speak aloud. If a man used the name in cursing, by law he could be stoned to death.

But when Jesus comes on the scene, an amazing shift takes place. He is ***Immanuel, which is translated, "God with us,"*** (Matthew 1:23). His name is upon the lips of every man. His name is used in conjunction with miracles, and it cures lepers and calms the seas. Demons tremble at the name. The name, Jesus, will be known by all far and wide. This One will be God seeable and knowable. We will embrace and cherish His name.

Jesus was a common man with a common name. Jesus was a common name up to the early second century. The same Greek word for ***Jesus*** (Matthew 1:21) is used in a variety of places in the New Testament. This word is used in Stephen's address to the Council, but it is translated, Joshua (Acts 7:45). The author of the Book of Hebrews speaks about ***a rest for the people of God,*** (Hebrews 4:9). In this context, he speaks of Joshua, who was not the one who gave them the rest (Hebrews 4:8). Again the Greek word is the same as used in Matthew, and there are many other usages in the New Testament (Luke 3:29; Matthew 27:16; Acts 3:16; Colossians 4:11).

The name of Jesus is a **COSTLY NAME.** The Book of Matthew begins, ***The Book of the genealogy of Jesus Christ,*** (Matthew 1:1). The name, ***Christ,*** is Jesus' official name. It is the Greek translation of the Hebrew word for Messiah. It means "the anointed One." But His personal name is ***Jesus.*** This bespeaks His identification with humanity. He became one of us. It means He has come to our level, so He might bring us to His level.

We see this highlighted in the verse at hand. ***"And she will bring forth a Son, and you shall call His name Jesus, for He will save His people from their sins,"*** (Matthew 1:21). The Greek word, translated ***for,*** means to assign a cause. The statement, ***He will save His people from their sins,*** has something to do with calling Him ***Jesus***. In order to save His people, He will have to become one of them. Therefore, contained within the name is His connection with humanity. Do not miss the strong reference to ***His people.*** He has become one of us, and we have become one with Him.

The separation, which was experienced between God and man in the Old Testament, is gone forever. God will no longer dwell in the Holy of Holies, to be visited once a year by a human representative. He has ripped the veil from the top to the bottom (Matthew 27:51). He will no longer be a cloud on top of the mountain. God has made a permanent connection. In great sacrifice, He has surrendered all that cannot be contained within that union. He has eliminated every barrier which makes Him different from us. He set aside everything necessary to join us forever. His name is ***Jesus,*** and His sacrifice is great.

There is another purpose for this name. It is a **CRUSHING NAME.** There is an undercurrent in the language the angel uses in his statement. We find it in the opening segment concerning Mary. ***And she will bring forth a Son.*** Matthew uses an astounding Greek word to describe how Jesus will be ushered into the world. The verb is translated as an active verb, which makes the subject responsible for the action. This means Mary will be directly involved in the process of the birth. It is in the indicative mood, which indicates a simple statement of faith. This is not a description or explanation. It is a fact.

All of this gives insight, but the startling fact comes from the word itself. This Greek word has not been used in any other part of this chapter up to this time. In all the births mentioned in the genealogy, this word is not used by Matthew. Matthew paints a picture for us to see. He uses the word four times, and Luke uses the word five times. But it is only used in relation to the birth of Christ. The focus of this word is on the process of birth. It describes the entrance of the babe into the world. John said it this way, ***"A woman, when she is in labor, has sorrow because her hour has come; but as soon as she has given birth to the child, she no longer remembers the anguish, for joy that a human being has been born into the world,"*** (John 16:21).

Matthew says Jesus will not be born without pain. Travail is the style of the birth. This style will apply again and again, throughout the redemption of the world. It is ingrained into the very first Messianic promise:

> ***"And I will put enmity***
> ***Between you and the woman,***
> ***And between your seed and her Seed;***
> ***He shall bruise your head,***
> ***And you shall bruise His heel."*** (Genesis 3:15)

Redeeming mankind is a major war, and it will not be without suffering.

We consistently see suffering throughout the Christmas story. ***When Herod the king heard this, he was troubled, and all Jerusalem with him,*** (Matthew 2:3). The presence of a new King is a crushing blow to Herod's control. The people of Bethlehem and its surrounding districts give additional testimony to suffering. The Old Testament prophecy says they will weep for their children and will refuse to be comforted (Matthew 2:18). Their baby boys are all killed due to the birth of the Son. Mary and Joseph certainly knew the crushing blow of His presence from the announcement of His conception to their flight into Egypt. Great travail comes with the presence of Christ.

Is it safe to conclude that to invite Jesus into your life is to embrace trouble and upheaval? When Jesus comes, He inevitably brings a cross. The suffering does not come only in His ministry and at His death, but it also comes at His birth. The style of the cross is who He is! To embrace His name is to embrace His style, the style of the cross.

## Person of the Name

I will tread lightly now, because I do not want to offend your traditional view of the name of Jesus. I am concerned we have attached magical qualities to this name. We pray His name. We cast out demons and ward off trouble in His name. We control circumstances in His name, and constantly call on His name. It is as if the name, Jesus, has a magical power. But that was not true in the day Matthew is writing. We have developed this mysticism for the name of Jesus through years of religious practices. Have we become more attached to the name of Jesus than we have to the person of Jesus? It is something we need to consider.

In this verse, the Greek word translated, ***name,*** points to the character and work of the person. The significance in the Biblical context is that one cannot call upon the name of Jesus without calling on the person of Jesus. His name is not a magical charm! It is the living Person, who has the power to save.

The early apostles were very careful about this issue. Peter and John were used by God to heal a crippled man at the gate called Beautiful (Acts 3:6). The leaders of Israel became quite concerned when the people of Jerusalem began to talk about what was taking place in their city. They asked the disciples, ***"By what power or by what name have you done this?"*** (Acts 4:7). Peter was filled with the Holy Spirit and addressed them (Acts 4:8). He was blunt and clear. ***"Let it be known to you all, and to all the people of Israel, that by the name of Jesus Christ of Nazareth, whom you crucified, whom God raised from the dead, by Him this man stands here before you whole,"*** (Acts 4:10). Did you notice how he linked ***the name of Jesus Christ, . . . by Him?*** Peter said the man was healed by the name of Jesus Christ, and the man was made whole by the Person of Jesus Christ. There is no difference between the name and the person. Peter went on to make a broader statement. ***"Nor is there salvation in any other, for there is no other name under heaven given among men by which we must be saved,"*** (Acts 4:12). He clearly links the person and the name. They are the same. He says salvation cannot be found in any other person, and then He continues to uplift the name by which we can be saved.

Paul gives us insight into the sacrifice Christ made as He left heaven, humbled Himself, and became one of us. ***Therefore God also has highly exalted Him and given Him the name which is above every name, that at the name of Jesus every knee should bow, of those in heaven, and of those on earth, and of those under the earth, and that every tongue should confess that Jesus Christ is Lord, to the glory of God the Father,*** (Philippians 2:9-11). Again the name of Jesus is linked with the person of Jesus. ***Therefore God also has highly exalted <u>Him</u> and given <u>Him</u> the <u>name</u> . . . .*** Some Bible scholars make a distinction between "the name of Jesus" and "the name, Jesus." The indication of the Philippians passage may be that the name of significance is not Jesus, but ***Lord.*** This may mean the focus is still on the person as the One we are to confess.

In the New Testament, we find several references to the person of Jesus as simply "the Name." ***"So they departed from the presence of the council, rejoicing that they were counted worthy to suffer shame for His name,*** (Acts 5:41). ***Is anyone among you sick? Let him call for the elders of the church, and let them pray over him, anointing him with ail in the name of the Lord,*** (James 5:14). ***Because they went forth for His name's sake, taking nothing from the Gentiles,*** (3 John 7).

I fear we are more comfortable using simply the name. When it is a magic charm, we are in control. We can scare the demons away, heal physical ills, and bring about the miracles we desire. We can use the name for our benefit. But when we involve the person of Jesus, He is in control. Every time we personally involve Him, His will becomes the priority. Suddenly it is His plan, not ours. The only way to get Jesus involved in any situation is to come into total submission.

Even His name calls us back to total surrender. It is the style of the cross. In recognizing Him for who He is, we totally abandon what we want, and we embrace all He wants to be and do through us. His name, which is His person, becomes our life.

# Matthew 1:21

## The Purpose of His Name

Matthew closes The Book of Matthew with the great crucifixion/resurrection declaration (Matthew 27-28). All Christianity knows this declaration is foundational to the existence of our faith. To remove these events would be to reduce Christianity to mere religion. The absolute focus of these events is on the person of Jesus Christ. This declaration is not about the events. It is about the person. The pronouns are everywhere in Matthew's story. ***But the angel answered and said to the women, "Do not be afraid, for I know that you seek <u>Jesus</u> who was crucified. <u>He</u> is not here; for <u>He</u> is risen, as <u>He</u> said. Come, see the place where the <u>Lord</u> lay,"*** (Matthew 28:5-6).

The resurrection is focused on the person of Jesus Christ. Every eye is upon Him. Those who are worshiping, worship Him. There is only one hope, and it is in Him. No one speaks about a new theology of eternal life. This is not about philosophy, theology, or doctrine. It is about the person of Jesus. He stands before them, raised as conqueror of hell and death. The ***infallible proofs*** (Acts 1:3) experienced by the eleven disciples, during the forty days after His resurrection and prior to His ascension, were completely centered in the experience of His resurrected person. They touched, saw, and smelled Him. They tasted of His goodness again. It was an experience of His person.

While this is true of the closing days of Jesus' appearance on earth, it is just as true of the beginning moments of His birth. Everyone in the Christmas story is focused on the arrival of a person. Mary is focused on the new life in her womb. This new life within Mary is troublesome to Joseph (Matthew 1:19). Wise men from the East come to Jerusalem in search of the new king. ***"Where is <u>He</u> who has been born King of the Jews? For we have seen <u>His</u> star in the East and have come to worship <u>Him</u>,"*** (Matthew 2:2). The angels announce the birth to the shepherds. ***"For there is born to you this day in the city of David a Savior, who is Christ the Lord,"*** (Luke 2:11). The shepherds seek the person, whose birth the angels announced. Their praise and worship were for the person of Jesus (Luke 2:16-17). Simeon is in the temple awaiting the fulfillment of the promise of the Holy Spirit (Luke 2:25-26). The answer to his dreams is the person of ***the Child Jesus.*** Everywhere one searches in the Christmas story, Jesus is the focus of attention.

This is true in the opening narrative (Matthew 1:18-25). ***Behold, an angel of the Lord appeared to*** Joseph ***in a dream.*** This makes the message to follow very important. The angel represents the merging of the presence of God with the angelic person. When this angel speaks, God is speaking. The first part of His message is focused on the special decision Joseph needs to make. But as the message develops, we are all confronted with the central truth of the Gospel.

The angel says, ***"And she will bring forth a Son, and you shall call His name Jesus, for He will save His people from their sins,"*** (Matthew 1:21). What a magnificent statement! It is the great mission statement of the Messiah. It is the key slogan of the Kingdom of God. This statement is the title page for the Book of Matthew. The angel presents a summary of all Jesus will accomplish. The purpose of the incarnation is made clear as the angel says, ***". . . for He will save His people from their sins."***

In light of this, we need to consider three key parts to the concept contained within the **PURPOSE OF HIS NAME.**

**The Savior**

**Matthew 1:21**

The purpose of Christ is contained within the name of ***Jesus***. The angel of the Lord is very specific about what this Son is to be named. This is the personal name of the Savior of the world. It bespeaks His identification with us. He takes on a common name, and He empties Himself of every thing which makes Him different from us. The purpose of this becomes clear as the angel says, ***". . . for . . ."*** It assigns a cause. Here is why the Messiah will be called ***Jesus.*** The purpose of His name is discovered in the phrase, ***". . . He will save His people from their sins."***

No additional resource is needed for salvation. The total focus is on the person of Jesus. He does not need a group of angels to help Him save His people. He does not need additional personnel to help Him invent or manufacture redemption. He will not start something which will need additional saviors to save His people from their sins. The complete salvation of His people will be in Him.

The angel is emphatic about this issue. The Greek verb, translated ***will save***, indicates the personal pronoun, ***He,*** by its ending. ***He will save*** is a proper translation of the verb. However, the angel is not satisfied with this. He adds an additional Greek word, which is the pronoun, ***He.*** The angel says the pronoun twice for double emphasis. It literally says, ***"He, for He, will save His people from their sins."*** Or it could be translated, ***"for He Himself will save His people from their sins."*** The American Standard Version translates this verse, ***"for it is He that will save His people from their sins."***

Do you remember Peter's declaration to the family of the high priest? In a tense moment, the elite controllers of Israel wanted to know the source by which the crippled man was made whole. Peter, without hesitation, declared the source was Jesus. But he quickly went on to say, ***"Nor is there salvation in any other, for there is no other name under heaven given among men by which we must be saved,"*** (Acts 4:12).

Paul, addressing the Israelites in a public meeting, built a case for Christianity from their own history. He reminds them how God gave them the land of Canaan. God gave them judges for a period of four hundred and fifty years, but then allowed them to have their own king, Saul first, and then David. Then Paul boldly says, ***"From this man's seed, according to the promise, God raised up for Israel a Savior - Jesus,"*** (Acts 13:23).

Let me be sure we have stated this correctly. It is the person of Christ who is the Savior. It is not Jesus, plus anything else, which ***will***

***save His people from their sins.*** Salvation comes in Jesus alone! You must understand that salvation is contained within His person. It is not something He gives us, apart from Himself. It is what He is. In embracing Jesus, we experience salvation. Jesus is our only hope.

John Calvin makes a bold statement in his **Institutes.** This statement is found in book two, chapter sixteen, under the title, "The Knowledge of God the Redeemer in Christ."

> The moment we turn aside from him in the minutest degree, salvation, which resides entirely in him, gradually disappears; so that all who do not rest in him voluntarily deprive themselves of all grace. The observation of Bernard well deserves to be remembered: The name of Jesus is not only light but food also, yea, oil, without which all the food of the soul is dry, salt, without which as a condiment whatever is set before us is insipid; in fine, honey in the mouth, melody in the ear, joy in the heart, and, at the same time, medicine, every discourse in which this name is not heard is absurd (Bernard in Cantica., Serm. 15).

## Salvation

### Matthew 1:21

Salvation in this verse is clearly stated as ***". . . for He will save His people from their sins."*** "Sin" is addressed before the birth of Christ. We find it in the announcement and purpose of His mission. Sin must be seen in the context of the war, declared by God in the first Messianic promise (Genesis 3:15). The ***enmity . . . between your seed***

***and her Seed*** displays itself in sin. The very attitude, which creates the ***enmity,*** is sin. He is not addressing the issue of the deeds of sin only, but the entire flow of sin in its nature, results and rulership.

When we consider the announcement of the Lord in the context of its pronouncement, it reveals the content of salvation contained in Jesus. Matthew writes distinctly to the Jews. He gives the genealogy to impress them (Matthew 1:1-17). Jesus will be born a Jew. This salvation effort will come through the Jewish nation. The salvation proposed is to save from the evils which block and obstruct the reception of the Messianic deliverance. Salvation is completely contained within Jesus. Therefore, every thing which hinders the total acceptance of His person is considered sin.

Matthew boldly proclaims it from the beginning. Jesus is King! The genealogy removes any doubt. Jesus has the perfect right to claim this position. He is ***the Son of David*** (Matthew 1:1). Every force, deed, attitude, structure, action, and plan which attempts to hinder the establishment of the Kingship of Jesus is sin. Salvation has to do with entering the Kingdom which embraces Him as King. Salvation is regarded as deliverance from the power and dominion of all contained outside the rulership of King Jesus.

The unfolding of the Book of Matthew reveals the conquest of this great Deliverer. Every miracle of Jesus was a work, which reversed the results of sin. The miracles of Jesus were always restorations of the unnatural to the natural positions. When Jesus cured disease, it was the restoration of man to the normal physical condition. He was taking away the results of sin. The resistance of the leadership of Israel had to do with control. They were using the legal religion of their day to establish a kingdom which opposed His rule. Their religious system had to die to the permeating life of the Kingdom of God.

The Greek word translated, ***sins,*** in this proclamation gives us the content of salvation in Christ. It is the most frequently used word for sin in the New Testament. It has to do with missing the mark, as a warrior who throws his spear and fails to strike his adversary, or as a traveler who misses his way. Contained within this word is the failing, or missing, of the true end and scope of our lives, which is Jesus. Sin is not seen within the content of the deed being done, but it is seen in how the deed relates to the person of Jesus. Anything which opposes His Messianic deliverance is considered sin, and is conquered by Jesus.

## The Severity
## Matthew 1:21

There is something severe about this statement. ***"And she will bring forth a Son, and you shall call His name Jesus, for He will save His people from their sins,"*** (Matthew 1:21). Matthew does not qualify this statement. He makes no attempt to present a disclaimer. It is simply a bold statement of fact. If you had nothing but this statement, you would conclude everything contained within ***sins,*** is destroyed in Christ.

Did you notice the word, ***from***, in the text? In the Greek language, it is a word which means "off, away or from." It denotes separation, departure, cessation, completion, or reversal. The intent of the statement is not to inform us Jesus will save us "in" our sins, but ***from*** our sins.

Adam Clarke in his commentary on this passage says:

> This shall be his great business in the world; the great errand of which he is come, namely to make an atonement for, and to destroy, sin: deliverance from all the power, guilt, and pollution of sin, is the privilege of every believer in Christ Jesus. Less than this is not spoken of in the Gospel; and less than this would be unbecoming the Gospel. The perfection of the Gospel system is not that it makes allowances for sin; but that it makes an atonement for it: not that it tolerates sin, but that it destroys it.

Everywhere we turn in the Scriptures, the message is forgiveness. John writes to a group of people he dearly loves. He calls them, ***My little children,*** (1 John 2:1). Early in his epistle he establishes the fundamental of forgiveness. ***And if anyone sins, we have an Advocate with the Father, Jesus Christ the righteous,*** (1 John 2:1). His purpose was not to discourage anyone, but to encourage them. This was not a message to create guilt over defeat, but to uplift Christ, the Savior, who is completely adequate to give victory over sin. John's message then becomes very strong. ***And you know that He was manifested to take away our sins, and in Him there is no sin. Whoever abides in Him does not sin. Whoever sins has neither seen Him nor known Him. Little children, let no one deceive you. He who practices righteousness is righteous, just as He is righteous. He who sins is of the devil, for the devil has sinned from the beginning. For this purpose the Son of God was manifested, that He might destroy the***

***works of the devil. Whoever has been born of God does not sin, for His seed remains in him; and he cannot sin, because he has been born of God,*** (1 John 3:5-9).

The author of the Book of Hebrews spends one entire chapter highlighting the sufficiency of the blood of Christ (Hebrews 9). Based upon this fact he approaches the subject of obedience (Hebrews 10). Evidently there was a group of people who wanted a Christianity that would only require partial obedience.

In the opening verses of chapter ten of Hebrews, the author describes the Old Testament sacrifice for sin. It was weak in that it must be done ***continually year by year*** (Hebrews 10:1). It does not make the worshiper perfect. ***For it is not possible that the blood of bulls and goats could take away sins,*** (Hebrews 10:4). While the Old Testament sacrifices failed to accomplish the task, their purpose was to deliver us from sin. The intent of the sacrifice was to give victory to the worshiper, so he would go forth and sin no more. He was expected to live in victory.

Then the author highlights the New Testament sacrifice of Christ. He writes, ***For by one offering He has perfected forever those who are being sanctified,*** (Hebrews 10:14). This was the very promise given by the prophets of old as they foretold the new covenant (Hebrews 10:15-17).

In conclusion of this matter, if you want a Christian experience which allows you to continue in sin, you must discover a new sacrifice other than those in the Old or New Testament (Hebrews 10:26). Both the Old and the New Testament sacrifices expected man to live in victory over sin. While the Old Testament sacrifice failed, the New Testament sacrifice exceeded abundantly. If you propose a sinning Christianity, where is your sacrifice? What sacrifice for sin has been offered which allows this?

Is there any doubt the Gospel is a message of total victory over all that stands in the way of the Messianic deliverance? Every thing which blockades you from having intimacy with God is destroyed in Jesus. There is no reason not to have victory in your life. Any claim to be a Christian without victory over sin is fake and fraudulent. Anything less than holiness is an embarrassment to Christ. It makes Him a joke. ***For He will save His people from their sins,*** (Matthew 1:21).

# Matthew 1:22-23

# The Scriptures and Jesus

When we come to these verses, it seems as though Matthew makes a bold shift in his first narrative. He has given the story of Joseph's obedience in taking Mary as his wife, knowing the child within her is not his. He gives an explanation of the consequences of this in the next two verses (Matthew 1:24-25), then changes his focus and returns to the long range plan of God in the Scriptures.

Matthew has a purpose in his writing. He wants the Jews to recognize that Jesus was, and is, the Kingly Messiah. He writes from his purpose, repeating a major principle which is paramount to his communication of this truth. Matthew builds nearly every paragraph, from the genealogy to the Sermon on the Mount, around one text of Scripture. He invites his readers to see Jesus in light of the Scripture, and the Scripture in light of Jesus. Matthew wants everyone to recognize the person, and the work of Jesus, as central to the Scripture's character. Do not take this lightly! Read it again and give it careful thought! **The**

**person and the work of Jesus are central to the Scripture's character.**

In this first narrative (Matthew 1:18-25), Matthew tells of the conflict which arises in the heart of Joseph when he learns of the conception of Jesus in Mary, his betrothed wife. ***An angel of the Lord*** appears to Joseph in a dream and gives him a message. This message will personally guide Joseph in the days ahead, but it is also a mission statement for the Messiah (Matthew 1:20-21). Matthew does not hesitate to remind his Jewish audience of the great Messianic prophecy found in Isaiah (Isaiah 7:14). We must see this narrative of the conception of Christ through the Scriptures.

The second narrative tells of the wise men (Matthew 2:1-12). They come to Jerusalem in search of the new King. Desiring to visit Him, they need to know the location of His birth. This information is in the Jewish Scriptures. Herod, the King of Judea, knows the scribes can discover this location through the prophets (Matthew 2:5). This narrative unfolds from the Scriptures the Jews have had in their possession all this time.

The third narrative comes from the prophets, Hosea and Jeremiah (Matthew 2:13-18). ***And angel of the Lord*** warns Joseph to take his family and flee to Egypt to escape Herod's slaughter of baby boys in Bethlehem and its surrounding districts. This was foretold in the Jewish Scriptures.

The closing event of the first Christmas is told in the fourth narrative (Matthew 2:19-23). Joseph brings his family to Nazareth after the angel tells him Herod is dead, and it is safe to return to Judea. This should not have been news to the Jews, because it flows from their Old

Testament Scriptures. Matthew declares the Jews must see Jesus in light of their Scriptures. From their Scriptures, the ones they hold dear, they can glean the understanding of who Jesus is!

But Matthew does not stop there. The Jews must see the story of John the Baptist (Matthew 3:1-12), in the light of the prophet Isaiah (Matthew 3:3). The temptation of Jesus in the wilderness is saturated with the view of the Old Testament (Matthew 4:1-11). Jesus consistently brings Satan back to the prophecies of the Messiah as seen through the Jewish Scriptures.

The Messiah's first acts of ministry, as recorded by Matthew, must be seen in view of the Scriptures.

> ***The people who sat in darkness***
> ***have seen a great light.***
> ***And upon those who sat in the***
> ***region and shadow of death***
> ***Light has dawned,*** (Matthew 4:16).

The Old Testament contains the mission of the Messiah, and how He will carry that mission out. Matthew carefully points the Jews to the truth that Jesus, their Messiah, is in direct linkage to their Scriptures. He paints a picture of Jesus for them to see, and this picture is in the shape and structure of their Scriptures. Matthew strikes a blow at the heart of the Jewish concept. They had developed their own cultural and personal view of the coming Messiah. This view had become twisted by their self-centered carnality. They believed it completely, but it was not the Messiah seen in light of the Scriptures.

This is what caused the disciples trouble when they were faced with Jesus. He did not match their preconceived concept of what a Messiah was to be. He was always breaking their Messiah rules. They struggled with Who He really was. The Pharisees were worse than the disciples. When you know what they expected, and what Jesus was, you can understand why the leaders of Israel had to get rid of Him. They could not tolerate such a powerful man going around deceiving people. He did not match their view of the Messiah.

One of their misconceptions of the Messiah, was that He was to be a military leader. That was the world in which they lived. They saw Jesus in light of their world, rather than through the eyes of the Scriptures. They had formulated a political and military structure for their Messiah. Their success, both personal and national, was measured in terms of political power. How many people do you have under your control? Finances also played an important part in this political control. The leaders of Israel had become the Sadducees and the Pharisees. The Sadducees were the wealthy businessmen and politicians of their day. They were comfortable in their present structure, and they did not want to be disturbed. Rome had given them freedom to continue their own religious government, as long as they complied with the Roman requirements. But Jesus, the Messiah, did not adapt well with either the Roman or the Jewish systems. He was a threat to all power and worldly authority. He was a threat, not because He was a great power, but because He proposed a Kingdom where you find life in death, exaltation in humiliation, and greatness in serving others. Jesus simply was not what they expected.

Can you imagine how the Jews felt when Jesus came to Jerusalem and presented Himself as the Lamb of God (Matthew 21)? During Passover Week, two hundred and fifty thousand lambs will be slaughtered as sacrifices in the temple. This was very important financially to the business system of the temple. The priests were in complete control of what lambs could be sacrificed. Each lamb had to be without a blemish, and the priests decided whether a lamb was blemished or not. The only lambs they were going to accept were the ones they sold in the Court of the Gentiles. The approved lambs were priced slightly above the market price, of course. The temple had its own money, because secular money could not be spent in the temple. Therefore, money changers were present to make the necessary change from secular to temple money, and there was a small fee for this exchange. Everything they did in the Court of the Gentiles had a fee, which brought financial gain to the temple. Every sacrifice was a money making proposition. Then Jesus comes and proposes they do away with their system, for He, the Messiah, had come. Their political and financial power will not allow this. They want a Messiah who will promote, or at the least endorse, things as they are.

The leaders of Israel did not see Jesus in the Scriptures. At one point Jesus turned to them and said, ***"You search the Scriptures, for in them you think you have eternal life; and these are they which testify of Me. But you are not willing to come to Me that you may have life,"*** (John 5:39-40). They studied the Scriptures. They said they lived and died by them. By their own words, their life was contained in the Law of God. But in all of their study, they never recognized the purpose of their Scriptures was a testimony of Jesus. He was the life coming from their Scriptures. They missed Life itself!

That was not all they missed in their Scriptures. Another key element is in the concept of sin. Their Scriptures plainly revealed man's self-centered carnality and sinful nature, but they ignored that in their studies. It was omitted from their present Jewish teaching. Consequently, their highest thought of the Messiah was that of a King and Deliverer, a military leader. This stemmed from their national life under the domination of Rome. The great hope of Israel was to be restored to their national glory. Because of this focus, they missed the important truth of the Messiah.

Matthew is bold in his declaration of Jesus as King. The genealogy establishes Jesus' right to the throne of David. But Jesus is not the military, or national King, they have conceived. The ***angel of the Lord*** proposes the purpose of the Messiah as found in His name. ***Jesus, for He will save His people from their sins,*** (Matthew 1:21). He forgives sin early in His ministry (Matthew 9:2). Demons are the promoters of sin, and many of Jesus' miracles involved the deliverance of those possessed by demons. Jesus began His ministry with a Manifesto (The Sermon on the Mount, Matthew 5, 6 &7). In this, He delivered the message of the Kingdom of God. He declared that righteousness in everyday life was the law, and the Jews never grasped that in their interpretation. The people ***were astonished at His teaching,*** (Matthew 7:28). The scribes missed the emphasis of their Scriptures about the priestly office of the Messiah. They saw Him as King, but not as a Kingly Priest. Matthew painted a new picture of the Messiah from their Old Testament Scriptures. The Messiah was One with a great purpose.

Jesus came to present Himself as the Lamb. He offered Himself, because He was His own priest. He did it on the cross. How could they miss the crucifixion in the Scriptures? They were blinded by their own selfish desires, and they shaped a Messiah who was not like the one found in their Scriptures. They must constantly adjust the interpretation of the Scriptures to fit the Messiah they wanted.

The Scriptures are very powerful. Though I am describing the Jewish cultural situation which Matthew addressed, I am also describing the structure I find in myself. The same passionate self-centeredness in the leaders of Israel abides within me. I have shaped my own Jesus to be comfortable with my life as it is. I have used and abused the Word of God, and I have not seen Jesus through the eyes of the Scriptures.

How else can I possibly explain the comfort of my living and the complete lack of impact I have on my world? How do I explain that I am a part of a large multitude of Christians who have not won any one to Jesus in the last year? Obviously, I have a Jesus who approves of this behavior, or at least tolerates it. Where did this Jesus come from? He came from my imagination. The Jesus of the Scriptures spends all His energy, and gives His entire life, for one mission. His accomplishments are demonstrated by the disciples in the Book of Acts. The Words of Jesus express Who He is. ***"But you shall receive power when the Holy Spirit has come upon you; and you shall be witnesses to Me in Jerusalem, and in Judea and Samaria, and to the end of the earth,"*** (Acts 1:8).

My life is filled with worry and concern over my style of living. It is my ambition to better myself, for the sake of my wife and children, of course. I spend thousands of dollars to see my children have straight teeth and college educations. Our schedule revolves around the educational system, not the church and its spiritual endeavors. My attention is consumed with my retirement. I need a strong financial stability to receive the benefits of life I have earned. The Jesus I have imagined approves of all of this. He wants the best for me. I still do not understand the story of the Rich Young Ruler. What did Jesus mean when He said, ***"If you want to be perfect, go, sell what you have and give to the poor, and you will have treasure in heaven; and come and follow Me,"*** (Matthew 19:21)? Surely what He said needs some adjustment or interpretation. Jesus could not have wanted the young man to waste his finances on the poor when we need a nice church building to gather in. You know how expensive church steeples are, don't you?

The Sermon on the Mount also disturbs me. ***"Therefore I say to you, do not worry about your life, what you will eat or what you will drink; nor about your body, what you will put on. Is not life more than food and the body more than clothing?"*** (Matthew 6:25). Jesus must not live in my culture. He could not understand how important such things are. Most of my thoughts are about what I am going to wear, how I look, and what I will eat. Doesn't my weight prove this? The Jesus I picture is very modern. He is a bit overweight and carries a notebook computer under His arm. I can embrace a Jesus like this.

It will be a major step for me to see Jesus through the Scriptures. What if He is not like I have pictured Him through the lenses of my culture and wants? Will I be able to make the kind of changes necessary in my life to adjust to a new Jesus? What kind of demands will the Jesus of the Bible make on my life? Will He be as radical as He was in His day?

## Matthew 1:22-23

## God With Us

**GOD WITH US** is a bold declaration (Matthew 1:23). It was a distinct change from what the Jews had known. The intertestimental period was four hundred years long. God had been silent during this time. This period stretched from the end of Malachi, the last book in the Old Testament, and the Book of Matthew, the first book in the New Testament. There were no burning bushes, and there were no Mt. Sinai events. There were no prophets declaring, "Thus saith the Lord!" It looked like God had abandoned His people. No one dared to say, "God with us." Though God seemed to be missing during this time, religion was strong.

Suddenly everything changed. ***But when the fullness of the time had come, God sent forth His Son, born of a woman, born under the law,*** (Galatians 4:4). Something that had never happened before was taking place now. There was a new revelation. ***God, who at various times and in various ways spoke in time past to the fathers by the prophets, has in these days spoken to us by His Son, whom***

***He has appointed heir of all things, through whom also He made the worlds;*** (Hebrews 1:1-2). ***God with us*** is the new and proper thing to say.

This declaration was the fulfillment of prophecy. ***So all this was done that it might be fulfilled which was spoken by the Lord through the prophet,*** (Matthew 1:22). God has dreamed a long range plan, and now He is fulfilling it. He has been moving to this point. It has been His heart's desire from the beginning. ***God with us*** was His intent from the start. Sin interrupted this plan, but now things are back on track. ***God with us*** is the new reality, and it can be experienced by all of us.

Matthew presents this fact with great strength. He opens and closes his book with this fact, ***God with us.*** He begins quoting a prophet, ***"Behold, the virgin shall be with child, and bear a Son, and they shall call His name Immanuel," which is translated, "God with us,"*** (Matthew 1:23). He describes this in detail throughout the rest of the book. He thunders to a climax, and ends his book with the words of Jesus, ***"And lo, I am with you always, even to the end of the age,"*** (Matthew 28:20).

The scope and depth of this statement are impressive. It is almost too much to grasp. ***God with us*** is beyond what we can imagine. Jesus wants to walk and talk with us. He wants to be involved in all of our affairs and needs. He wants to give us a new direction and purpose for living. We are no longer alone in the plight of our own making. God has come, and He is with us. It is a new day. It is a new start. God has drawn a line, and we can begin again. ***God with us*** is our salvation. It is our only hope!

If you are like me, your heart cries to know more. You want someone to give you a detailed description of what is involved in God being with you. You want the step by step instructions you need to follow to enter into such an experience. You do not want your hopes of knowing God raised, only to be dropped to the point of despair. How well can I know Him? Will it be the kind of relationship those in the Old Testament experienced? How will He be with us?

**The Mystery**

**Matthew 1:23**

The reality of ***God with us*** is shrouded with mystery. We know something about this, but we do not know everything. It is a mystery.

***God with us*** begins with the mystery of the virgin birth. The message, from the prophet of God, proposes this mystery. ***"Behold, the virgin shall be with child, and bear a Son, and they shall call His name Immanuel,"*** (Matthew 1:23). In the original language, the article, ***the,*** is included before the word, ***virgin.*** This makes the word distinct and refers to a definite virgin. Matthew quotes Isaiah, the prophet, from the Old Testament (Isaiah 7:14). The Old Testament was written in the Hebrew language. There are several words Isaiah could have used which refer to a young woman. However, he uses a specific word that refers to an unmarried woman. This Hebrew word is used a total of seven times in the Old Testament (Genesis 24:43; Exodus 2:8; Psalms 68:25; Proverbs 30:19; Song of Solomon 1:3; 6:8, and Isaiah 7:14). Each of these Scriptures contains the idea of a virgin.

Matthew now writes this message to his Jewish audience in the Greek language. He does not give the Hebrew term a Christian "twist," but he uses it with the same meaning all Jews used at that time. Even if there was a dispute over the precise definition of this Greek word, Christ being born of a virgin is a strong teaching from both Matthew and Luke. ***Now the birth of Jesus Christ was as follows: After His mother Mary was betrothed to Joseph, before they came together, she was found with child of the Holy Spirit,*** (Matthew 1:18). ***But while he thought about these things, behold, and angel of the Lord appeared to him in a dream, saying, "Joseph, son of David, do not be afraid to take to you Mary your wife, for that which is conceived in her is of the Holy Spirit,"*** (Matthew 1:20). ***And the angel answered and said to her, "The Holy Spirit will come upon you, and the power of the Highest will overshadow you; therefore, also, that Holy One who is to be born will be called the Son of God,"*** (Luke 1:35).

In Luke's Gospel, this statement is in reply to a question asked by Mary. She is responding to the angel's first declaration of this birth. Mary asks, ***"How can this be, since I do not know a man?"*** (Luke 1:34). While the angel gives the answer, it is still clouded with mystery. Who can know the depth of the movement of God to bring about this incarnation? In the pagan religions, even in our day, they say their deities had sexual relations with women. There is nothing in the Gospel accounts even close to this. The birth of Christ, and the entrance of God into the state of ***God with us,*** is completely beyond a sexually physical act.

The mystery of Christ's conception is parallel to the mystery presented by Nicodemus (John 3). Jesus challenged him with the mystery of being ***born again.*** The response of Nicodemus reflects the mystery involved. ***"How can a man be born when he is old? Can he enter a second time into his mother's womb and be born?"*** (John 3:4). Jesus gives some explanation to Nicodemus, only to receive this question. ***"How can these things be?"*** (John 3:9).

This is a mystery, but it is also reality. While ***God with us*** in the flesh of Christ, or ***God with us*** in the experience of the new birth may not be fully understood in worldly wisdom, it can be experienced in practical living. The mystery signifies it is God initiated. None of this can come from our own invention. This is the beating heart's desire of God for us. ***God with us*** is the summary of the dream of God in our behalf. It is a mystery, but it is a reality!

## The Mystical
## Matthew 1:23

Mystical is a word we do not want to use in the wrong way. There are two primary meanings of the word found in the dictionary. One definition means "having a spiritual reality or import not apparent to the intelligence or senses." A second definition means "relating to, or stemming from direct communion with ultimate reality or God." In other words, something is taking place which has to do with spiritual realities. It is not that it cannot be understood, but it is not necessarily apparent to the intelligence or senses of man. It is mystical!

It is the atmosphere of the name, ***Immanuel.*** If one trusts the steady orthodox interpretation of the church throughout the ages, this name denotes the same as God-man (theanthropos) and has reference to the personal union of the human nature and the divine in Christ. What was taking place in Jesus in the incarnation was so practical and earthy, yet, it was mystical and heavenly. It was two words coming together. Jesus was God made visible in our midst. The mystical world of God was suddenly made visible. This manifestation upset all our worldly patterns, because the tremendous plus factor of the mystical was added. Judgments, which had been made by the leaders of Israel based on what they knew of this world, suddenly became incorrect. There was a new addition to the equation. Everything needed to be re-evaluated.

***God with us*** would not look like anything we have ever seen. There would be no comparisons with any other experience. It would not be the normal. But clearly understand, ***God with us,*** as seen in Jesus, was simply the firstborn of a new breed of humanity, fulfilling the dream of God. What was taking place in Jesus is to be true in us! Jesus was ***God with us*** for thirty-three years. His example has become the standard for us. The same Divine nature within Him has now come to be shared with us! Within us there is the union of the Divine nature and our human nature (not carnal). As Jesus is ***God with us*** to our lives, so we are to become ***God with us*** to our neighbor. We have become the display of the mystical world. What could not be known has now become seen through us.

## The Medium
## Matthew 1:23

Now we come to the third part of the concept. According to the dictionary, one of the strong definitions of the word, medium, is "an intervening substance through which something else is transmitted or carried on, or an agency by which something is accomplished, conveyed or transferred." It is absolutely essential to understand ***God with us*** is the fulfillment of the purpose God had for the physical realm in the first place. God intended the physical to become the stage, or platform, upon which the mystical world of His presence could be manifested.

***God with us*** is the desperate need of our lives. It is our completion. This is fundamental and basic, and we have no other need. This single factor brings everything else into proper perspective. Regardless of the circumstances or pressures active in life, the single need is ***God with us.*** All apparent answers to our immediate crises are only temporary solutions. This is the answer God has given us.

Matthew brings a prophecy to our attention, which gives us the reality of this truth (Matthew 1:23). He quotes from Isaiah (Isaiah 7:14). In the context of the prophecy, the prophet delivers his message about seven hundred and forty years before Christ, in the reign of Ahaz, the king of Judah. Though he was the son of the great Uzziah, he was a wicked king. He filled Jerusalem with idols, reinstated the worship of Molech, and burned his own son as a sacrifice to that god. Rezin, king of Syria (Aram), and Pekah, king of Israel (also called Samaria at that time), in confederation decided to remove Ahaz and replace him with a king who would do their bidding.

During this time the kingdom of Judah, under the government of Ahaz, was reduced very low. Pekah, king of Israel, had slain in Judea, one hundred and twenty thousand persons in one day. His army carried away two hundred thousand captives, including women and children, together with much spoils. To add to their distress, Rezin, king of Syria, being confederated with Pekah, had taken Elath, a fortified city of Judah, and captured the inhabitants and carried them away to Damascus. In this critical conjuncture, is it any wonder that Ahaz was afraid that the enemies who were now united against him would prevail, destroy Jerusalem and the kingdom of Judah, and annihilate the family of David?

In the face of such a threat to the people of Israel, and to the royal line of David, Ahaz, instead of turning to God for help, sought the help of Tiglath-pileser, the evil king of the Assyrians. He even plundered, and sent to Tiglath-pileser, the gold and silver from the temple. Ahaz was looking to other things for the solution to his problems, instead of looking to God.

Isaiah came to Ahaz and reported God would deliver the people from the two enemy kings. But Ahaz refused to listen. Isaiah encouraged him to ask God for a sign, but Ahaz still refused. God gave him a sign anyway. ***Moreover the Lord spoke again to Ahaz, saying, ". . . Therefore the Lord Himself will give you a sign: Behold, the virgin shall conceive and bear a Son, and shall call His name Immanuel,"*** (Isaiah 7:10-14). The sign from God means not only Rezin and Pekah should be unsuccessful against Jerusalem, which was the fact; but Jerusalem, Judea, and the house of David, should be both preserved, notwithstanding their depressed state, and the multitude of their adversaries, until the time should come when the virgin should bear a son.

This is a most remarkable circumstance. The house of David could and would never fail, until the virgin should conceive and bear a son. But when that incredible and miraculous fact did take place, the kingdom and house of David became extinct! Their safety and security were contained within the plan of God through Christ. Everything focused on ***God with us.*** There is no other way for us to survive. It is as if we were made for this, and without it we are not functioning properly, and we will gradually end in destruction.

We were designed as the agent through which a sovereign God can manifest Himself. Think of the staggering privilege we have of being the life of God to our world! ***God with us*** has become God in us, and God through us. It is the focus of the way we are designed. It is the fulfillment of our destiny. Anything else creates only chaos and emptiness.

# Matthew 1:24-25

# The Obedience of Joseph

The first narrative of the Christmas story immediately follows the genealogy of Jesus Christ (Matthew 1:18-25). It introduces several significant concepts upon which the Gospel account of Matthew rests. These issues are fundamental. Matthew begins the narrative with a bold title page. It is a second genealogy, and in it Matthew declares who is the natural Father of Jesus. ***Now the birth of Jesus Christ was as follows: After His mother Mary was betrothed to Joseph, before they came together, she was found with child of the Holy Spirit,*** (Matthew 1:18). He presents the doctrine of the incarnation. Matthew introduces us to the virgin birth of Christ.

This is the story of Joseph. This narrative is told from his perspective. He struggles with the moral dilemma presented by the news of Mary's pregnancy. If he continues with his marriage to Mary, he will be admitting he is the father of the child, and that he had not been faithful to the betrothal commitment. Yet, he cannot conceive in his just heart of taking her to the magistrates and having her stoned to death.

His only other option is to ***put her away secretly,*** (Matthew 1:19). While he slept that night, an angel of the Lord came to him in a dream and gave him information and direction. The angel says, ***"Joseph, son of David, do not be afraid to take to you Mary your wife, for that which is conceived in her is of the Holy Spirit. And she will bring forth a Son, and you shall call His name Jesus, for He will save His people from their sins,"*** (Matthew 1:20-21). There is no question now as to what he should do, and why he should do it.

Then Matthew leaves the story and reminds us of the prophetic basis of all that is taking place. He quotes the prophet Isaiah, saying, ***"Behold, the virgin shall be with child, and bear a Son, and they shall call His name Immanuel," which is translated, "God with us,"*** (Matthew 1:23). This is strong verification to the truth of this birth. Seven hundred and forty years prior to this happening, a prophet foretold its reality. The reality of a ***virgin*** birth is proposed, which underscores the great truth, God has indeed come to be with us. This is especially important in the context of the four hundred years before the Book of Matthew, when it appeared God was not present. There was no evidence of His speaking to Judah, but now He has come to be with us.

After establishing this prophetic basis for the first narrative, Matthew returns to telling the story. He covers a six-month time period. Mary has visited Elizabeth for three months (Luke 1:39-40, 56). She returns to Nazareth. Matthew begins the narrative at this point (Matthew 1:19). Due to the instructions of the angel of the Lord, Joseph enters into the marriage ceremony with Mary, and they are now living together as husband and wife. The next narrative will begin with the wise men coming to Jerusalem at the actual time of the birth of Christ in Bethlehem (Matthew 2:1).

The focus of the six-month period is on Joseph's obedience. Naturally Mary is included in this obedience, but Matthew writes the narrative from Joseph's viewpoint. He was very glad for Divine intervention. He proves this by his immediate and consistent obedience to the voice of the Lord. ***Then Joseph, being aroused from sleep, did as the angel of the Lord commanded him and took to him his wife, and did not know her till she had brought forth her firstborn Son. And he called His name Jesus,*** (Matthew 1:24-25)

Matthew's introduction of these two verses is significant. ***Then*** is a distinctive conjunction, and its primary translation is "but." This conjunction establishes contrast and opposites. It highlights a certain picture, but immediately flashes the opposite picture into the equation. The narrative begins with this conjunction. ***Now*** (BUT) ***the birth of Jesus Christ was as follows . . .*** (Matthew 1:18). This contrast is between the opening genealogy (Matthew 1:1-17), giving the legal father of Jesus, and a second genealogy where Matthew proclaims the natural Father of Jesus (Matthew 1:18). Jesus is conceived by the Holy Spirit.

Matthew uses this distinctive conjunction five other times in the first narrative. He relates the moral dilemma which grips Joseph (Matthew 1:19). He uses this conjunction to contrast this dilemma with the knowledge that Jesus is born of God. Having presented this moral dilemma, Matthew goes on to use this distinctive conjunction four more times. He continually contrasts everything in this narrative with the moral dilemma of Mary's circumstance.

Matthew begins with the appearance of the ***angel of the Lord.*** Joseph cannot seem to resolve this moral dilemma in his mind. ***But while he thought about these things, behold, an angel of the Lord appeared to him in a dream,*** (Matthew 1:20). Matthew records the "mission statement" of Jesus, and it begins with this same conjunction. ***And*** (BUT) ***she will bring forth a Son, and you shall call His name Jesus, for He will save His people from their sins,"*** (Matthew 1:21). Matthew then contrasts the moral dilemma with the intent of prophecy. ***So*** (BUT) ***all this was done that it might be fulfilled which was spoken by the Lord through the prophet, saying: . . .*** (Matthew 1:22). Finally, Matthew contrasts the moral dilemma of Mary's pregnancy with Joseph's obedience. ***Then*** (BUT) ***Joseph, being aroused from sleep, did as the angel of the Lord commanded him and took to him his wife,*** (Matthew 1:24).

When you understand how severe the moral dilemma is, then you begin to comprehend how great is Joseph's obedience. The significance of obedience, in the midst of temptation, is always measured by the severity of the temptation. Joseph had undoubtedly never experienced anything as devastating as this. He is already officially married to Mary, and they are probably three or four months into the betrothal period. The legitimization of the birth of Jesus is hanging in the balance. The temptation for Joseph was to run away, to remove himself from the circumstance. What other answer could there be? But the angel of the Lord calls him to obedience. It is a call we have heard many times. What are the elements of this call and this obedience?

## Total Faculties
## Involving the Waking from Sleep
## Matthew 1:24

I have been struggling with the normal concept of "obedience," the same with which I was raised. Growing up in the parsonage, I have vivid memories of cottage prayer meetings. I remember sitting in a circle of adults, mostly white haired, singing the hymn, "Trust and Obey." The lyrics of this hymn are etched in my memory. My concept of obedience was like a son who has a father who wants him to do certain things. It is my responsibility to discipline myself to accomplish all of the things on the list. The problem comes when I discover my discipline is not adequate, and that produces tremendous guilt. As I grew older, I became more familiar with the things I should do, but I seemed less adequate to do them. I did not have trouble trusting Jesus to save me. The obstacle was in the discipline of obedience.

Matthew presents a very different picture of obedience. This obedience finds its strength in God. It is the discipline of the Holy Spirit in our lives. We simply respond to what God does in us. God is adequate for our obedience, not our ability to obey. That is a major shift. Christian living must not be explained in the terms of self-discipline, but in Christ alone.

Matthew begins his narrative with these words, ***Then Joseph, being aroused from sleep, . . .*** (Matthew 1:24). The Greek word, translated ***being aroused,*** is egeiro. It is used in the New Testament in connection with waking from sleep, rising from sitting or lying, and healing from disease. It is the word used for the resurrection of Jesus Christ from the dead.

The word probably comes from the root word which has the idea of collecting one's faculties. Joseph was to collect, or gather together, all of his faculties, to focus on the activity at hand, which in this case is obedience. What else could we expect from this arousing call from the angel of the Lord? The call of God brings us from sitting to standing, from sleeping to wide awake, from scattered to collected, from unfocused to concentration, from death to life, and from partial to total. The call of God never allows us to awaken by opening one eye and dozing off again. The call of God is so strong it demands the response of our total being.

***Being aroused*** is in the passive voice. This is significant. It tells us Joseph was not responsible for the action of this verb. He is being acted upon. He did not arouse himself. As one reads the narrative, the flow of the story suggests to us the angel of the Lord is the one acting. Joseph is not the one initiating the obedience. The angel issues the call, arouses Joseph from sleep, and enables him to gather his total faculties to respond.

This gives us tremendous insight into the action of obedience to which God calls us! It is not self initiated. It is God initiated. We are being acted upon by the Divine person. Not only has the call come from God, but He arouses us from sleep. He enables us to bring our total faculties to focus in response to Him. He captures us with His presence. He draws us to Himself in aggressive ways.

This is true from the beginning to the end of Christian experience. God calls us to repentance. It is not a call from the skies, and it is not in a language we do not understand. He comes personally to our hearts, and whispers the call in the inner ear of our being. We are aroused from sleep, and guilt grips our hearts. John Wesley called this "an awakening." It is the result of the action of God. One does not know guilt unless it is revealed by the Divine presence. One does not repent, and then God responds by coming to the heart. God comes to the heart and enables us to respond to the call of repentance.

This is the underlying concept in Paul's writings. ***He who calls you is faithful, who also will do it,*** (1 Thessalonians 5:24). ***Being confident of this very thing, that He who has begun a good work in you will complete it until the day of Jesus Christ,*** (Philippians 1:6). ***For it is God who works in you both to will and to do for His good pleasure,*** (Philippians 2:13). No one fails in Christianity because he or she lacks discipline, training, or the personal ability to respond. God comes to each of us and reveals His will. He arouses us from sleep and enables us to respond with our total faculties.

## Total Focus
## Involving the Response of the Heart
## Matthew 1:24

Matthew is not satisfied with highlighting Joseph's obedience in this manner. He now takes the concept and expands it dramatically for us. He says, ***Then Joseph, . . . , did as the angel of the Lord commanded him . . .*** (Matthew 1:24). There is a message contained within the word, ***did.*** It is translated from the Greek word, poieo. We have highlighted this word in other of our studies, but it is very significant here in its description. In the English, the verb, "to do," or "did," serves the purpose of many Greek verbs which have a large variety of meanings. Each Greek word has a slightly different flavor about it.

While it is not always true, the verb, poieo, most often refers to "doing good." It has a creative flavor. It can be contrasted with the idea of a habit or routine. It focuses on the method of "doing," and it has the primary meaning of "making." The thoughts and feelings of the individual are expressed by this "doing" action. It is an expression of what is within the person himself.

***Did*** is in the active voice, which means it is Joseph, and what is within him, that is responding to the call of the angel of the Lord. Something happens within Joseph which arouses him from sleep to respond. He is not acting out of himself. Certainly it is not a routine, duty or habit. God has come, through the angel of the Lord, in the midst of Joseph's sleep. God stimulates within him a new direction, with a new call. God arouses Joseph from sleep, and God enables him to collect and gather together all of his faculties. This creative force moves him into the action of ***did.***

This is not a self-initiated doing. Joseph did not think it over and come up with a plan. At this point in time, he knows little about the plan. We do not applaud Joseph for the rescue of the moral dilemma and the legitimizing of the birth of Christ. Was Joseph involved? The answer is yes! But he was not involved in doing. His involvement was in responding. The creative flow of God works upon, and within, this man.

Could it be this is the kind of obedience to which God calls us? We do not memorize a list of rules, keep them, and then become acceptable in our religious circle. We do not discipline our lives, limit our activities to the acceptable things, and thus, we are called "good." The obedience to which God calls us is not an act. We are not separated from His person or void of His resource. He is the one who calls us.

His resource enables and directs us. He arouses us, and He gives us the creative resources from within. He enables us to respond in obedience. It is not of us. It is of Him.

This does not take away our free will. We do not have to respond to the creative resource of God from within. However, a shift has taken place in the idea of obedience. Instead of struggling to obey, we must struggle not to obey. The only way to keep from responding to the flow of God's enabling resource is to resist the obedience which naturally comes. God wants to act upon and flow through our lives. Will we respond?

## Total Formation
## Involving the Enlisting of the Will
## Matthew 1:24-25

Then Matthew injects another idea in this concept of obedience. ***Then Joseph, being aroused from sleep, did as the angel of the Lord commanded him . . .*** (Matthew 1:24). The Greek word Matthew uses for ***commanded,*** is a larger concept than simply an order. There are specific instructions given to Joseph by the angel of the Lord. He was told, ***"Do not be afraid,"*** (Matthew 1:20). The instructions also included, ***"Take to you Mary your wife, for that which is conceived in her is of the Holy Spirit,"*** (Matthew 1:20). Specific guidance was given in the words, ***"You shall call His name Jesus, for He will save His people from their sins,"*** (Matthew 1:21). However, after all of these special instructions, Matthew reminds us that the impact of the angel's words are more a focus, or emphasis, than a specific order of things to do.

The Greek word for ***command*** actually means "to order," "to command," or "to impart an ethical direction or norm." It carries with it the idea of arranging, or setting things in order, towards an end. The word can be divided into a basic word and a prefix. The prefix means "towards." The basic word means "to arrange." This conveys the idea of a focus or direction. The angel of the Lord was not giving Joseph a list of things to do, but the angel was setting him in a direction, focusing him on an emphasis. The angel of the Lord called Joseph to something bigger than the accomplishment of a task which would soon be over, and once the order was completed, Joseph was free to do as he pleased. Joseph was to be involved in something which would compel him for the rest of his days. In one way or the other, this was going to become the focus of his entire life. God called Joseph into His great plan, and He called him into the direction He was going. The focus of Joseph's life was to become this great plan, and the great plan was Jesus. Is there any other focus?

This is verified by the insight Matthew gives in the very next verse. He writes, ***and did not know her till she had brought forth her firstborn Son. And he called His name Jesus,*** (Matthew 1:25). Jesus was conceived in the womb of a virgin, and He was born of a virgin. God called Joseph, and brought about His creative action within him, causing Joseph to set aside the normal intimacy of marriage relationship until after the birth of Jesus. The verb, ***did not know,*** is in the imperfect tense and has the definite sense of continual action. Thus, the emphasis is that Joseph continued not to know her. Was this a direct rule from God? We are not aware of any such command. Joseph responded from his heart. He was living in the focus and emphasis of the plan of God.

This is the obedience to which God calls us all. It is not a matter of doing the acceptable things to please God. God is calling us, and He is acting in us to answer that call. His Spirit moves us from within. We respond completely to God's call. The call is a focus, and it has to do with where He is going, and what He wants to accomplish. We are captivated by Christ. Our lives respond in ways which are beyond the natural function of human living. God lives His life through us. We live in His obedience.

# PART THREE

# Matthew 2:1-12

## Seeking the King

# Matthew 2:1-12

## Wise Men Still Seek

Matthew begins his Gospel account by presenting the genealogical proof of the Kingship of Jesus. Then he launches into the details of the story of Christ's birth as seen through the eyes of Joseph. It is an intriguing story of apparent betrayal, sexual scandal, senseless murder, and Divine interventions. He uses four main narratives to describe the events. The second one is the story of the wise men who came seeking the new born King (Matthew 2:1-12).

The thrilling and encouraging element of each narrative is the Divine intervention. Each time the situation looks hopeless, God marvelously saves the day. In the first narrative, Joseph decides to give Mary a private divorce and distance himself as far as possible from what is taking place within her. But in the night hour ***an angel of the Lord appeared to him in a dream, saying, "Joseph, son of David, do not be afraid to take to you Mary your wife, for that which is conceived in her is of the Holy Spirit,"*** (Matthew 1:20).

God's protection is seen again in the third narrative (Matthew 2:13-18). Just before Herod orders the death of all the baby boys in Bethlehem and its districts, ***an angel of the Lord appeared to Joseph in a dream, saying, "Arise, take the young Child and His mother, flee to Egypt, and stay there until I bring you word; for Herod will seek the young Child to destroy Him,"*** (Matthew 2:13).

The direction of God is actually given twice in the fourth narrative. After Herod's death ***an angel of the Lord appeared in a dream to Joseph in Egypt,*** (Matthew 2:19). The angel instructed Joseph to move his family back to the land of Israel. And ***being warned by God in a dream*** (Matthew 2:22), Joseph took them into the region of Galilee.

You may have noticed we skipped over the second narrative of the Christmas story (Matthew 2:1-12). This narrative also includes Divine intervention. However, this Divine warning is distinctive to this narrative. It produces an important truth which we must understand.

At first I thought God's action in behalf of the wise men was strictly an act of benefit to Himself and His own plan. He warned the wise men in order to keep them away from Herod. Herod must not receive the location of the Christ child! There would be no way to protect Him from certain death. So God was acting out of Himself to fulfill His overall plan of redemption.

The fullness of time had come and Christ was to be born. The forces of evil began to exert their influence in an attempt to stop the plan, but God would not permit it. He intervened as much and as often as necessary to bring about His plan. This Divine warning was a part of God's fulfillment of His plan. Herod's deception was not going to bring about the destruction of the Christ child. God would not allow it, and He entered the lives of the wise men with a Divine warning.

I found my interest peaked by this Divine warning. I was enthralled by the action of the wise men which brought about this intervention. Matthew tells us the Divine warning in this passage was more than God protecting His plan. He responded to the heart's cry of the seeking wise men. God clearly answered the deep longing of these men.

God in His sovereignty could have protected the Christ child in dozens of ways without warning the wise men. An army of angels could have encamped around the house in which the Christ child was staying. God could have stricken Herod with a disease, causing his death before he ordered the destruction of Christ. But the wise men allowed God to use them in His plan of protection because they were seeking and responding to Him.

We see this clearly in the message of Matthew. ***Then, being divinely warned in a dream that they should not return to Herod, they departed for their own country another way,*** (Matthew 2:12). The words, ***being . . . warned,*** are translated from one Greek word. One definition of this verb is in the participle mood, "to give a response to one who asks or consults." This participle gives content, or describes the main verb, ***departed.*** The subject, ***they,*** refers to the wise men. However, the participle, ***being . . . warned,*** is in the passive voice, which indicates the wise men are being acted upon or are receiving the action of this warning. They are "receiving an answer."

The word implies the wise men sought counsel of God and received the answer. Wycliffe, in his translation of the New Testament, refers to this Divine warning as ***an answer taken in sleep.*** The Amplified New Testament states this truth by paraphrasing the verse as, ***and receiving an answer to their asking, they were divinely instructed and warned in a dream not to go back to Herod; so they departed to their own country by a different way.***

God desperately wants to warn His people. He wants to guide us through the pitfalls of life and fulfill His plan through us. We do not need to fall victim to the demonic plotting of those around us. God wants to pour out His Divine warning upon us. What is the key to receiving the interactive warnings of God? It is "SEEKING" or "RESPONDING." It is vividly portrayed in the narrative of the wise men.

## The Seeking Focus

We know very little about these wise men. But there are some facts we can piece together. The Kingdom of Judah had fallen into the hands of the Babylonians six hundred years prior to the birth of Christ. The great stories about Daniel in the lion's den and the three Hebrew children in the fiery furnace took place during Babylonian captivity. In the Book of Daniel the wise men were among the highest-ranking officials in Babylon. With Divine intervention Daniel was able to interpret Nebuchadnezzar's dream. None of the other court wise men were able to do this. Because Daniel could, he was appointed as ***ruler over the whole province of Babylon, and chief administrator over all of the wise men of Babylon,*** (Daniel 2:48).

Because of Daniel's great wisdom, and because he had successfully pleaded for the lives of the wise men who had failed to interpret the king's dream, Daniel was highly regarded among them. This resulted in the wise men learning from this prophet about the one true God, the God of Israel, and about His will and plans for His people, which included the coming of the Messiah King. Many Jews remained in Babylon after the Exile and intermarried with the people of the East. It is most likely the Jewish messianic influence remained strong in the region even until the New Testament times.

Now God calls these wise men from the east to come to Jerusalem. They announce the arrival of the Kingly Messiah. They travel a great distance to recognize and honor a King in whose coronation they have no part. Historians tell us no Persian had ever become king without mastering the scientific and religious disciplines of the wise men (magi). In addition to this, they must approve and crown the king. They were powerful oriental kingmakers, but they saw this King Messiah as far greater than any they had ever, or would ever, set on a throne. They came to pay homage to One greater than they had ever known.

The situation Matthew describes in this paragraph takes place several months ***after Jesus was born.*** Herod was specific in his questioning of the wise men (Matthew 2:7). He wants to know the definite time when the star appeared to the wise men the first time. This indicates there had been a lapse of one to two years from the first appearance of the star until the events of this passage. Herod orders the murder of all the boys two years of age and younger. This indicates Jesus could have been as old as two years of age. The family of Jesus now resides in a house rather than the stable where He was born (Matthew 2:11).

In this passage the wise men have a single focus. They are seekers of the new King. There is no cost too great and no issue will sidetrack them from their search. Deception and evil leadership will not stop them. They respond to the original message of the star and the passion strongly motivates them. Though the journey is hard and the travel is long, their desire is not dampened. They are driven to find the new King.

In spite of their limited spiritual insight, the wise men immediately recognize God's light when it comes to them. Despite their paganism, quasi-science, and superstition, they recognize God's voice when He speaks to them. They set aside all of their other ideas and religious concepts to seek this one superior truth. They are willing to ***worship Him*** at great expense.

There was no way they could miss Him. They did not see a star and start seeking, but they had been looking for the reality of truth for a long time. The reason they saw the star was because they were seeking. It was not as clear in their minds as it was for the Jewish population in Jerusalem, but the influence of Daniel and the Jews of the ancient East had planted a seed which was still growing. Their concern was not religion, country, status or law, but where is the new King? Jesus is the focus of their seeking.

## The Seeking Facilitated

The measure of how focused they were on seeking Christ is seen in the sacrifices they made to find Him. It was TOTAL in its element. They use every means at their disposal to facilitate their search for the new King. They leave no stone unturned. They use their knowledge of the stars in their search. Is it not remarkable that the very paganism which should have kept them from Christ is used to drive them to Him?

In my early days of Christian searching, one of the books which impacted my life was **Crowded to Christ** by L. E. Maxwell. He proposed the basic concept that God uses everything in our lives to draw us to Himself. My confusion is not a barrier to finding the Truth. It is part of the instrument God uses to bring me to Himself. He brings my circumstances, traditions, positions, and peer pressure under the domination of the search for Him. Everything is facilitated to reveal His presence.

There was TROUBLE involved in the seeking of the wise men. Certainly you can visualize the difficulty involved. They left their families and the comfort of their homes to make the journey. This search may have lasted as long as a year or more. Think of the upset to their schedules and activities. They set aside all for the search. The action of their search was completely selfless, with no personal advantage to themselves. It was unlike Naaman, who made a search for His personal healing (II Kings 5). There are many stories in the New Testament of those seeking after Jesus, but all derived something from their search. These wise men simply came, worshiped and returned home.

The TREASURE they left behind was an act of their worship (Matthew 2:11). The indication is this was not a small token of their adoration, but the cost to them was expensive in time and travel. They gave sacrificially of themselves and their gifts. The fact that men of their position (wise men) came and fell at the feet of this Christ child is amazing in itself, but to extend to Him their wealth shows the depth of their sincere seeking.

Then there is the subject of their THEOLOGY. Their seeking of the Kingly Messiah in the Jewish context was a radical shift from their traditions and normal belief system. They sought truth beyond their present knowledge and accepted traditions. The sincerity of their seeking had such depth; they adjusted everything they held dear. They followed the Truth wherever it took them. They risked everything with a radical openness. They re-evaluated everything in their lives in light of the search.

This is all evidence of their seeking. The lengths to which they went to find the new King shows the sincerity and depth of their seeking. Perhaps this should cause us to examine our personal evidence of seeking. How TOTAL is our focus upon Him? What TROUBLES can we point to which indicate our sacrifice for the sake of seeking? Where are the TREASURES sacrificed at the feet of the new revelation of His being? Where has our THEOLOGY stretched and expanded in light of the revelation of His person? If these questions are hard to answer, perhaps not much seeking is taking place in our lives.

## The Seeking Flow

The flow of their seeking is found in the word, ***worship.*** ***And when they had come into the house, they saw the young Child with Mary His mother, and fell down and worshiped Him. And when they had opened their treasures, they presented gifts to Him: gold, frankincense, and myrrh,*** (Matthew 2:11). Contained within the picture of this word is the idea of falling down or being prostrate before Him. It has to do with a dog licking his master's hand in submission and love.

This describes the seeking of the wise men. From the beginning to the end they submitted to their passion of finding Him. Their example holds spiritual truth. They submitted to God's revelation of a new King. This was not their idea. God revealed it to them. The prevenient grace of God came to their lives. God initiated this, and the wise men responded. Further revelation came through the prophets (Matthew 2:5). They responded in submission, the revelation expanded, and the star appeared to guide them (Matthew 2:9), leading them to the location of the new King. When they beheld the baby King, they submitted in worship and sacrificially gave of their wealth (Matthew 2:11).

As the wise men responded in worship and giving, they were ***divinely warned in a dream that they should not return to Herod,*** (Matthew 2:12). The grammar structure indicates the warning was a result of their seeking and responding. Because they were seeking, and they responded to each revelation from God along the way, He warned them to take another way home. God used them again to protect the new King.

What a message Matthew gives us! We come to a problem and cry out to God. We expect Him to reveal a way out for us, even when we do not respond to Him in the consistent, daily submission. On the other hand, if we live in the submission of the seeking flow, we can with confidence expect Him to warn and protect us through the situation at hand. The key is found in the constant and consistent response of seeking.

# Matthew 2:1-2

## Seeking the King

***Now after Jesus was born in Bethlehem of Judea in the days of Herod the king, behold, wise men from the East came to Jerusalem,*** (Matthew 2:1). The Greek word translated, ***Now,*** does not necessarily indicate time, or even establish a contrast, but it is used to introduce a new section. It is a distinctive word used in chapters one and two to mark out the four narratives of the Christmas story (Matthew 1:18; 2:1; 2:13; and 2:19).

At the conclusion of the genealogy of Jesus Christ (Matthew 1:1-17), Matthew begins the first narrative (Matthew 1:18-25). We have titled it "The Emerging of Jesus." This narrative tells Jesus' story from His conception to His birth. Matthew writes from Joseph's viewpoint, allowing you to see the struggle of Joseph in regard to the pregnancy of Mary, but also his obedient submission.

***Now*** marks the beginning of the second narrative. We have titled it "The Entrance of the Wise Men" (Matthew 2:1-12). Matthew raises issues which are not the main theme, but they bear some importance in the overall message of the book. Matthew establishes the time period. It is not the exact date of Christ's birth, but he documents the historical period in which it takes place. He footnotes that Jesus was born ***in the days of Herod the king.*** Herod ruled over Palestine from 37 B.C. to 4 A. D.

Matthew describes Herod the king as coming to the ***chief priests and scribes of the people*** (Matthew 2:4). This was very important to the Jews to whom Matthew is writing. The chief priests and the scribes validate the location of the birth of Jesus Christ in their sacred Scriptures. Matthew highlights prophecy in each narrative. He does so here (Matthew 2:6). The birth of Christ fulfills the long range plan of God.

The wise men come seeking the new king. This gives credence to what the Jew's know. Christ is born into an atmosphere and context of world expectation. It is as if the whole world is sitting on the edge of their seats, looking for a new leader. We can only imagine that expectation. It would parallel our expectation of the immediate return of Jesus Christ. Do you remember what it was like as we awaited the entrance of the year 2000? We expected something unusual to affect every area of life, religion, finances, technology, and transportation. Every television and radio newscast and every newspaper told us to expect major upset. So it was at the time of the birth of Christ.

Everyone ***in the days of Herod the king*** had a prevalent expectation that some remarkable person was about to appear in Judea. The Jewish world anxiously anticipated the coming of the Messiah. Their scholars knew the period of His appearance was approaching. They computed the time mentioned by the prophets (Daniel 9:25-27). They were looking for a military leader who would deliver them from Roman domination. The Jewish population had spread all over the world, many living in Egypt, Rome, and Greece. Others had migrated to Eastern countries. They helped spread the expectation for the appearance of someone special. Suetonius, a Roman historian, is reported to have said, "An ancient and settled persuasion prevailed throughout the East that the Fates have decreed some one to proceed from Judea who should attain universal empire." Tacitus, another Roman historian, said, "Many were persuaded that it was contained in the ancient books of their priests, that at that very time the East should prevail, and that some one should proceed from Judea and possess the dominion." Josephus and Philo, two Jewish historians, make mention of the same expectation. It is in this atmosphere and context that the wise men join in the seeking of the new King.

Matthew is focused in his writing to the Jews. There are three aspects to the theme in this narrative. We will now look at them together.

## Jesus is King
## Matthew 2:1-2

***Now after Jesus was born in Bethlehem of Judea in the days of Herod the king, behold, wise men from the East came to Jerusalem, saying, "Where is He who has been born King of the Jews? For we have seen His star in the East and have come to worship Him,"*** (Matthew 2:1-2).

The emphasis of this passage is on the Kingship of Jesus. Matthew gives us the genealogy of Jesus, proving He is in the lineage of King David (Matthew 1:1-17). He must have the right to sit on the throne of David. Jesus passes the first qualification for this expected person.

In the second narrative, Matthew focuses on the Kingship of Christ. It is the context of the passage. The wise men are SEARCHING for the new King. They are the first in Matthew's account to acknowledge Christ as the new King. Later we will discuss who the wise men were, but for now you must know their function was connected with kings. God broke through their false religion and inspired them with the reality of the King of Kings. Their generous gifts expressed their excitement in finding the Christ Child (Matthew 2:11). They were certain this Baby was the new King. They submitted to and worshiped Him (Matthew 2:11).

The STAR announced the King. Any obsession with the star and its composition misses the impact of the message. God designed this supernatural phenomenon to grasp the attention of the wise men, alerting them of the birth of a King. As astronomers, they were aware of the appearance of a new star. They were willing to follow it as it led them to the King.

Matthew is definite about the location of the birthplace. The SETTING of Christ's birth proclaims His Kingship. ***Jesus was born in Bethlehem of Judea,*** (Matthew 2:1). The word, ***Bethlehem***, means "House of Bread." How significant that the Bread of Life would be born in the House of Bread! The last half of the name, lechem, also signifies the flesh which is applied to the part of the sacrifice which was burnt upon the altar (Leviticus 3:11-16; 21:6). Bethlehem can be considered the "House of Flesh," or the "House of the Incarnation," which is the place where God is manifested as the King. Bethlehem identified Jesus with the history of His human ancestry through Ruth, who married Boaz in this very town. She was the ancestress of King David (Ruth 1:5-6), who was born in Bethlehem and was anointed King by Samuel.

This Kingship is the cause of the STRUGGLE and upset both in Jerusalem and in the heart of Herod. ***When Herod the king heard this, he was troubled, and all Jerusalem with him,*** (Matthew 2:3). A new king would certainly threaten this ruler. When Jesus appears, all other authorities claiming kingship feel the pressure of His presence and authority.

The SEDUCTION of this narrative springs from the issue of Kingship. Men tell lies and form plots (Matthew 2:9). Deception comes to the forefront. It all revolves around this new King.

The SUBMISSION of those who respond to the revelation can only be explained in terms of the new King (Matthew 2:11). The wise men worshipped from their hearts as they ***opened their treasures.*** They recognized the presence of the King.

What does the revelation of His Kingship do to your life? What is your response? Is His Kingship the central issue of your life? Do we have any other issue that matters? This is the ultimate question. Every thing which flows from our lives is a response to the revelation of His position as King.

## Jesus is the Universal King

## Matthew 2:1-2

The beginning of this narrative has an ironic twist. Matthew writes to his people, the Jews, several years after the crucifixion. He establishes the right of Jesus to assume the throne of David, and he gives an explanation of the virgin birth. Then he presents a narrative where people are actually proclaiming His Kingship. But the group proclaiming His Kingship is not Jewish. They should have been! The Jews had the ability to discover the time period in which the Messiah would come. According to the narrative, they knew the place of His arrival. They should have been the ones to discover the star and ask the questions concerning His birth.

The second narrative is about the GENTILES from the East who have been captured by the Divine revelation given through a star. They have set aside their self-interest and their schedules to seek the new King. Instead of the Jews announcing the birth of the King of the Jews to the Gentile world, the Gentile world is knocking on the door of Judaism with this startling revelation.

Matthew announces that Christ is a universal King. The narrative takes on the tone of the greatness of the reign of this King. This is not a minor historical happening in a minority race of people called Jews. This King is broad in His ruling, and it affects our lives this very moment. The end of the age will be under His control. ***When the Son of Man comes in His glory, and all the holy angels with Him, then He will sit on the throne of His glory. All the nations will be gathered before Him,*** (Matthew 25:31-32). This Kingship is on such a high level there is nothing above it. He is not one King among many in the land. This King is King of Kings indeed. Matthew highlights the GENTILES involvement, making Jesus a universal King.

The GALAXIES are involved, which expands the universal thought in this narrative. The birth of Jesus Christ, the King, has affected the heavenly universes. The stars are now revealing this truth.

A star, sudden in its appearance, and large enough to command the attention of the astrologers of that day, catches the attention of the wise men. There seems to be no definite knowledge about who these wise men are, so I do not want to speculate. But everyone agrees they were high ranking in their world. They had come to Jerusalem with an entire army, following the revelation of the star.

This Kingship of Jesus is so huge the GOVERNORS of this world are disturbed. No one feels secure in his position when the King is announced (Matthew 2:3). Herod, in this narrative, is Herod the Great. His authority is strong. He simply gives the command and baby boys in Bethlehem and its surrounding districts are slaughtered. But this new King supersedes the authority and territory of Herod the Great. Jesus is the universal King.

His Kingship is high and His dominion vast. God Himself protects it. This is a major theme in these Christmas narratives. Repeatedly, God intervenes as He protects the ruling of the new King. God thoroughly approves of this new King. Christ is placed in this position by the sovereign act of God. Jesus is a universal King.

Surely this speaks to us. Is there any way to set yourself outside the dominion of the King? Is there any way to assume His desires and plans do not apply to you? Is there any way to decide you can rule yourself? Surely there is no way to allow any area of your life to remain outside His universal rule! The right choice is total surrender to the Jesus, the universal King.

## Jesus is the Only King

### Matthew 2:1-2

Jesus is the only King. This statement needs some clarification. All would agree there is no other King but Christ. We realize that ultimately He will rule over all people. Everything and everyone comes under His control, both in heaven and in hell. He is the only King. But do you see how far removed that is from our lives? This concept of Kingship puts Him in control of the great issues of the Kingdom. We are affected by these issues even though they are far from us. But will we allow Him to have direct involvement in the intimate course of our lives?

The Kingship of Jesus has never been focused on earthly thrones or the domination of known civilization. His Kingship is in the Kingdom of God. The Kingdom is always focused on God's rulership as He empowers and enhances our lives. This Kingship is widespread, and yet concentrated. He reigns within each individual as if His rulership is only within that individual. This ultimately is not a threat to the governmental structures of our world, but a substantial threat to the kingship of our individual lives.

***Herod the king*** is the perfect symbol of this. He is a type of the carnal mind which is self-sovereignty within the individual. All other kings will accept our self-centeredness and utilize it for their own benefit, thus politics is born. It is a game to see who can exert the most power and manipulate the most people. The rulers of this world do not care about our personal selfishness as long as it serves their best interest. They will cater to it in order to control and use us for their own ends.

But the Kingship of the newborn Christ is very different. It threatens the rulers of this world, as well as our own personal desires and sovereignty. He is not a carnal king using carnal avenues to bring about his personal desires. The King of the cross style calls everyone who will be in the Kingdom of God to the loss of their lives. This is the elimination of all carnal, self-centered patterns. Politics cannot exist in the Kingdom of God due to the very nature of the King.

In the narrative, ***Herod the king*** is the perfect type or symbol of the self-centered carnal mind. The atmosphere of his person and the actions of his being embodies the heart of carnality. In this narrative, it is the announcement of the Kingship of Jesus which reveals the terrible stench of the self-centered carnal mind. The wise men come to Jerusalem and ask the people in the city, ***"Where is He who has been born King of the Jews? For we have seen His star in the East and have come to worship Him,"*** (Matthew 2:2). The moment Herod heard of their seeking, ***he was troubled, (***Matthew 2:3). The actual Greek word for ***troubled*** paints a vivid picture. It means to stir up or to agitate. It has to do with causing one inward commotion and distress. It has the idea of DEPRESSION contained within its definition.

The announcement of the Kingship of Jesus, which should bring rest, relaxation, and peace to the human heart, has produced the opposite. How can it be explained except for the self-centered carnal mind? The Kingship of Jesus is a threat to our personal lordship.

The Kingship of Christ is revealed. Herod is DISHONEST. Herod is a descendent of Esau, which means he is a half Jew. He tries to convince himself and the Jewish people, he has a legal right to set upon the throne of David. But he is not a rightful heir through the ancestry of King David. Herod has usurped the throne for himself. Upon the announcement of the rightful heir to the throne, he reveals his hypocrisy.

Self-centered carnality has usurped the throne of our lives. We were not built by God to rule ourselves, but to be dependent on Him. His Kingship is an immediate threat to our self-sovereignty. Playing a role we were never intended to play exposes our dishonesty.

The element of DECEPTION is present in this narrative. Herod lies to the wise men. He pretends to join them in their search for this new King as he says, ***"I may come and worship Him also,"*** (Matthew 2:8). See how cunning self-centered carnality really is? It will do anything to survive. It will put on the appearance of sincere worship. It is not against being religious, but above all, it must maintain control.

As one traces this self-centered carnal symbol through the narratives, the solution becomes apparent. It is DEATH. There is only one possible answer to the Herod like nature of self-centeredness. It must come to death (Matthew 2:19). This nature cannot be corrected or tamed. One cannot gradually grow out of it. The provision of the cross is death to all we are in our nature of sin. Jesus cannot rule in our lives until we die to our self-centered carnal mind. His Kingship confronts us with a call to respond to crucifixion. It is our only way out.

# Matthew 2:1-2

## Revelation for the Search

***Where is He . . . ?*** (Matthew 2:2). It is the universal question of all generations. Every religious ceremony, meditation, prayer, and ceremonial sacrifice shouts this question. It is the same age old challenge offered by Elijah to the four hundred and fifty prophets of Baal (I Kings 18). ***"Then you call on the name of your gods, and I will call on the name of the Lord; and the God who answers by fire, He is God,"*** (1 Kings 18:24).

Religion cannot tolerate a god who is silent. It violates the purpose of religion itself. The ritualistic dancing and cutting of the flesh of the prophets of Baal (I Kings 18:28), and the quiet prayer of a single prophet (I Kings 18:37), purpose to locate God. God must be found or religion is a failure. Does your religion bring you intimacy with God? Has He entered into relationship with you and made Himself known? Is He available to you? If "no" is the answer to these questions, then you have the wrong religion. You must cease what you believe, drop your religious practices, and look elsewhere. Any religion that does not bring intimacy with God is a waste of time.

In the midst of the terrible tragedies of life, this same question appears. ***Where is He . . . ?*** is voiced by mothers and fathers who have lost their children, and by husbands and wives who have lost their spouses. It would have been so easy for God to intervene in the situation. Does He not care? Everyone faces this. Religion cannot tolerate a god who is silent. Does your religion bring His presence into the circumstances of your life? Does your god speak to the great questions you are asking? If not, perhaps you need to search for a new god.

God planted this question in the heart of man. Mankind cries out for intimacy with God. The twist in the life of man comes when he substitutes other things for relationship with God. As Paul describes the condition of the pagans, ***Because, although they knew God, they did not glorify Him as God, nor were thankful, but became futile in their thoughts, and their foolish hearts were darkened,*** (Romans 1:21). While the substitutions seem to be numerous, they all have one thing in common. They have ***. . . exchanged the truth of God for the lie, and worshiped and served the creature rather than the Creator, who is blessed forever. Amen,*** (Romans 1:25).

Every defeat we experience is because of improper relationship with God. The lack of serenity spells separation from Him. As we see the Gospel story unfold, we realize the goal of God for each of us. All of God's action from the beginning to redemption was to bring us back into intimacy with Him. Every virtue of Christianity is explained in terms of His presence. This relationship is described not in terms of simply knowing about Him or even knowing Him. It is seen in words like intimacy, oneness, closeness, and completeness.

In the Old Testament Hebrew language there is no word for "presence." There is no way to express that someone is in the presence of God. The word used translates into the English, "in His face." To be in the presence of God is to be so close one can sense His breathing, feel the heat of His body, and smell His cologne.

The cross, resurrection, and ascension blend together in the minds of the Gospel writers. They view them as one powerful event. The climax is the outpouring of the Holy Spirit at Pentecost. Everything builds to this one purpose. God wants intimacy with man by indwelling Him. The expressions of God and man become the same. Each lives life for the other. The New Testament expresses this relationship in terms of marriage, one flesh. We are the bride of Christ.

The wise men express the heart's cry of each individual in every generation, ***Where is He . . . ?*** I cannot imagine the despair we would experience if there were no answer! There is an answer and it comes from God Himself.

## Revelation

God is not hiding! He is revealing! He is coming close! He does not withhold from us, but consistently pours out in our direction. God knows the only possibility we have of knowing Him is for Him to come to us. He aggressively removes every barrier in order to embrace us. He gives us His revelation.

In writing to the Jews, Matthew emphasizes the revelation of God comes through the VOICE OF THE PROPHETS. Herod the king sensed enough to call ***all the chief priests and scribes of the people together,*** (Matthew 2:4). It is from their knowledge of the prophets they discover the location of the new King (Matthew 2:6). Hundreds of years prior to the actual event, the knowledge of this place was spoken (Micah 5:2). God revealed His presence to us.

God chose to bring the revelation to the Jewish world. They lacked no knowledge or information. It was contained in their traditions and ceremonies. They handled it every day of their lives, and perhaps that was their problem. They became so accustomed to it they no longer saw it. The traditions which were to keep the vision alive became the distraction which hid His face. They heard the voice of the prophets and became accustomed to the message.

But God was not finished with His revelation. He spoke to them through the VOICE OF THE PAGANS. The wise men came to Jerusalem and asked, ***"Where is He who has been born King of the Jews?"*** (Matthew 2:2). The Greek grammar construction indicates they went up and down the streets asking everyone they met. Evidently they assumed if they, as outsiders, knew of the birth of the new King, surely the people of Jerusalem would know the details of this great event. They were surprised when no one knew where or even that He had been born. The pagans from the East, who had none of the traditions of the Jews, and had not heard the voice of the prophets, came to announce to the people of Judea the news of their new born King.

Perhaps this is a warning to us. Could it be the message has become so common, and the traditions taken for granted, that we have lost the passion for the vision of His presence? What was to have highlighted His intimacy in our lives has become a distraction to us. We have come to value the form more than the presence. Will those outside our tradition come and reveal His presence to us again?

How did the wise men come to know of His presence? It was the VOICE OF THE PLANETS. As they questioned the inhabitants of Jerusalem, they said, ***"For we have seen His star in the East and have come to worship Him,"*** (Matthew 2:2). How did the star communicate the birth of this new King? We are not told. We assume they were students of astronomy, however, there is as much speculation about the identity of these men as there is about the star's appearance. The indication is the wise men did not follow the star to Jerusalem, but assumed this main city of Judea would be filled with the excitement of this event. Once they were told of the prophesied birthplace of the Messiah (Matthew 2:5-6), the star reappeared and guided them not only to Bethlehem, but to the exact location ***where the young Child was*** (Matthew 2:9).

The apostle Paul reminded us it would be this way. ***For since the creation of the world His invisible attributes are clearly seen, being understood by the things that are made, even His eternal power and Godhead, so that they are without excuse,*** (Romans 1:20). God will not allow us to miss His presence. He will penetrate our lives with the revelation of Himself. The voices declaring His location are so many, they cannot be missed or quieted. If you do not live in intimacy with Him, it is because you do not want to! His revelation has come to you! God will not allow you to miss His message.

## Record

The answer to ***Where is He . . . ?*** is found in the record. The ***chief priests and scribes of the people*** had full knowledge of where the Christ was to be born. They found it in their Scriptures (Micah 5:2). Perhaps to the wise men the knowledge of the birth of a new King was a news flash, but only to them. It was clearly a matter of record for the Jews. A star appeared that had never before been seen. A search was conducted from the East looking for something brand new. But it had been foretold. How tragic it is that the keepers of the record lost the passion of the revelation and kept this announcement quiet. The record demands to be shared!

Hundreds of missionaries have told the stories of nationals crying out, "Why hasn't someone told us this before now?" The news of Christ is startling. How can it be kept a secret? Yet, it has been told. It is a matter of record. It is in the Scriptures! However, we must not think of them in terms of information contained within a book. The Scriptures (the record) are really the life of the person Himself. The Written Word has the life of the Living Word, and it is powerful in its impact. So the news is not new, but God is revealing Himself in a constant flow. It is a matter of His personal record. He is not hiding or withholding from us. He is revealing and giving. The revelation is not just information, but the Person of Christ. He is the record.

The answer to the great need of our lives is not something new. God does not need to invent a new cure for this new generation. It is a matter of record. The answer has been there all the time and is being revealed afresh to every heart. There is no problem. There is an automatic answer flowing from the record. Every conflict in our society, regardless of how new we might think it is, has its answer in the up-to-date record. What an amazing truth! The answers to your life's problems are already recorded. It is in the record, Jesus Himself.

## Respond

If the answer is already recorded, why do some not seem to know? The answer to, ***Where is He . . . ?*** is found when we respond. It is obvious in this story. The wise men received revelation from God. The star appears and the record is revealed. Their schedule is interrupted and the financial cost is high, but they respond. They seek with great determination because of the greatness of the revelation. As they seek, the Scriptures are revealed (Matthew 2:5). The revelation of God brings them directly to the location of the new born King (Matthew 2:9). They cannot possibly miss the King if they keep responding. God's revelation sees to their guidance.

***The chief priests and scribes of the people*** have also received revelation, even clearer than the wise men. They know the exact town in which the new King is born. What keeps them from responding to the news of the wise men from the East? Why would they not lead them to Bethlehem? Why would they not join in the search? Herod calls a meeting; the leaders of Israel research the matter; the question is answered. They simply return to the matters at hand. After all, they must maintain their traditions and oversee their church organization. They have no time or interest in seeking after the revelation of God's presence among them. Matthew's Gospel account shows the revelation of God coming to them repeatedly. To the very end they refuse to respond and seek.

Herod is a bit different than the leaders of Israel. He is interested in seeking and finding, but only for the purpose of destruction. He does not respond to the revelation as God proposes it. He is not willing to seek for himself, but sends someone else (Matthew 2:8). His words are deceitful for his ultimate goal is to destroy this new King.

This lesson has a deep reality. The heart of our responding must come from our being. We cannot rely on the seeking of others; it must burn within our hearts. We join the group who has received revelation from God and has the established traditions and patterns of seeking. But if our hearts are not open, we settle for forms which look like seeking, when in reality, we do not hunger and thirst for his presence in our lives.

There must be no deception in our seeking. It is easy to shift the motive with a hidden agenda. In Herod's case, it is the motive of murder. It does not have to be that severe to be destructive. We seek in order to go to heaven, or to be prosperous, or to be accepted in a certain group. The list of motives goes on and on. But beware! Anything other than His presence is a deception! We must seek Him and Him only.

A strong message of the Scriptures is that blindness takes place when we do not respond or if we seek with a wrong motive. Herod the king did not find the Christ child. He became blinded by his rage and insecurity (Matthew 2:16), committing an unthinkable crime. Paul speaks to the terrible condition of the heathen who sees revelation and will not respond to it. ***Therefore God also gave them up to uncleanness, in the lusts of their hearts, to dishonor their bodies against themselves,*** (Romans 1:24). To another group of people Paul tells of those who will not respond, ***whose minds the god of this age has blinded, who do not believe, lest the light of the gospel of the glory***

***of Christ, who is the image of God, should shine on them,*** (2 Corinthians 4:4). Jesus certainly faced this with the leaders of Israel. Jesus began His parable ministry ***. . . ; because seeing they do not see, and hearing they do not hear, nor do they understand,*** (Matthew 13:13).

This story calls us to respond to the revelation which is in the record. Christ can be found! Intimacy with God can be ours! We can be one with Him! It is the discovery of simple hungering and honest seeking. Are you a seeker?

# Matthew 2:1-2

# A Christmas Response

It has been my attempt to discover the heart of the Christmas story through the eyes of the wise men. The story seems to bring us back to the aspect of seeking. The focus on seeking is found in, ***Blessed are those who hunger and thirst for righteousness,*** (Matthew 5:6). The wise men wanted to find the new King. It was the desire of their hearts. It was the passion and fire that drove them in an aggressive search. Their journey of seeking lasted for a year or more. Their story is a drama of searching.

Both the wise men and Herod the king were seeking the new King. The difference between the two is not in the object of their search. Though the search of the wise men and the search of Herod the king were both filled with passion, aggressiveness and relentlessness, there was a huge difference between them. The difference is found in the motive of their searches.

The wise men have a quality of life which is not found in Herod the king. I have referred to this quality as "response." If the Scriptures are true, then all of Christianity is a positive response to the action of God. The wise men did not initiate the search, but they responded to the Divine action of God. God planted the concept of the Messiah King in the heart of man through the heritage of the past. He caused a star to appear in the sky. He did not reveal everything to the wise men, but following the star was their next step in responding to God.

We want to contrast this with the activity of Herod the king. He is doing. God is speaking to him through the Gentiles (wise men) who have come to Jerusalem with the message of the new King. The wise men have delivered revelation to him. The wise men are in the mode of responding, but Herod is in the mode of doing. You can see this clearly in the tone of this passage. Notice what Matthew says about Herod! ***And when he had gathered . . .*** (Matthew 2:4). ***He inquired of them . . .*** (Matthew 2:4). ***When he had secretly called . . .*** (Matthew 2:7). ***He sent them to Bethlehem . . .*** (Matthew 2:8). These statements describe a man who is in charge and is aggressively doing as he sees fit.

Listen now to the phrases which Matthew uses to describe the wise men! ***When they heard the king, . . .*** (Matthew 2:9). ***When they saw the star, . . .*** (Matthew 2:10). ***And when they had come . . .*** (Matthew 2:11). ***Then, being divinely warned in a dream . . . , they departed . . .*** (Matthew 2:12). These statements describe the response of the wise men. The same reality of truth comes to the wise men and to Herod the king, but the reactions of both are very different. The truth produces a "doing" in Herod the king, while it produces a "responding" in the wise men. There is a drastic and measurable difference between the two. We want to learn this difference by looking deeper into the response of the wise men.

## Source

The difference between "doing" and "responding" has to do with the source. Doing is self-sourced. Statements like, "I did it!" immediately highlight the focus on self. Christianity is never self-sourced. Christianity is a close relationship with Jesus, and He is the source of our lives. We are involved, present, participating, and making choices, but it is all in the form of responding. The word, respond, creates the focus on a source which is beyond the one involved. We are not acting out of ourselves. Someone else is involved.

Let me try to demonstrate this with my favorite illustration. After having been gone for several weeks, my wife meets me at the airport. When I exit the plane, she runs to me, grabs me, and gives me a big kiss. I turn to someone standing nearby and say, "Did you see me kiss my wife? It was a powerful kiss!" No, I do not make such a statement. The reason being, I did not kiss my wife. I was certainly there. My lips were involved, I had my arms around her, and I enjoyed it. Our lips were pressed together, but still I was not kissing her. She was kissing me! But I was responding!

Some one seeing the incident might think I was kissing my wife. With our arms wrapped around each other, and our lips connected, it looked like I was kissing my wife. But I know, and she knows, she was kissing me. I was responding to her. This same scenario applies to the Christian life. You can look at the life of a fine Christian and wonder how they do it. They appear to be disciplined by the Scriptures in their daily life. They are faithful in spiritual matters. You can ask them, "How do you do it?" Their reply is, "I am not DOING this at all! I am responding." They are sourced by someone else deep within. The

Christian sourced by God is living beyond himself. He does what he cannot do, says what he cannot say, and loves like he cannot love. It is Christ sourcing him, and he is simply responding.

I am an evangelist. If I ever have the opportunity to return to the pastorate, I already have a plan. I want to plant a new church. I have no idea where or when this will take place, but I have already decided the name of the church. I plan to call it "Launch Me Jesus Church." This name comes from an experience of long ago. I was bending over to pick up something I had dropped only to have some big bully kick me in the appropriate place. I went flying through the air, landing several feet away. Everyone was laughing except me. I immediately tried to explain that the muscles of my legs had coiled. I had leaped into the air as if I were in the broad jump. Such an explanation was ridiculous. I certainly participated, was involved, flew through the air, but it was not by the muscles in my legs. I was simply responding. The kicker was the source of it all.

The opening of every service at the new church plant will start with the announcement, "Assume the position!" This will be the required position of all who wish to be called Christian in our church. We will daily live bent over. Christ will be the constant source of all our movements. We will not be doing, but responding.

This is a difficult concept because it is totally out of control. We are not in charge. We do not know where we will land. We have no explanation for what happens, because we do not know the complete plan. Christ is not obligated to explain anything to us. Our sole responsibility is to respond. The source of energy is the difference between "doing" and "responding."

We see this clearly in the contrast between Herod the king and the wise men. Both are seeking the new King. God has given them both the same information. Herod the king is doing; the wise men are responding. The explanation for this is not the information. Responding is not simply knowing the right thing to do and doing it. This produces a picture of God being a part of us while we do His will. The picture of responding is not just information given, but the internal resource being received from God. We are therefore not acting out of ourselves, but out of Him. An interaction takes place between God and the wise men which enables them. He is their source.

This is a foretaste of the glorious new covenant. The mystery of the Old Testament is revealed in ***Christ in you, the hope of glory,*** (Colossians 1:27). The Christ who had been outside the disciples will now come to be inside. As the Father demonstrated Himself through Jesus, the Man, now Jesus will live within and demonstrate Himself through man. God will source us. Let it be very clear! Christianity is not contained in doing the right thing. It is not a matter of discipline or control. It is not about us, but about Him. The central issue of Christianity is SOURCE.

## System

We must clearly state that "responding" or "doing" becomes the heart of the system of life. "Self-sourced" or "God-sourced" is seen in the structure of life. The issue under discussion is at the heart of the system. You cannot departmentalize responding in your life. You cannot self-source parts of your life and allow God to source the rest of you. It is all or nothing. Either you are entirely self-sourced or entirely

God-sourced. "Doing" or "responding" is like the leaven Jesus described. ***The kingdom of heaven is like leaven, which a woman took and hid in three measures of meal till it was all leavened,*** (Matthew 13:33).

The system is described in the contrast between Herod the king and the wise men. There is nothing in the lives of the wise men that is not a response to what God is doing in and through them. The journey into Jerusalem is in response to the star which has appeared and the internal wisdom God has given them about what the star means. The message they deliver to the Jews in Jerusalem of the birth of a new King is in response to the message that burns in their hearts. It was planted there by God Himself (Matthew 2:2). Their trip to Bethlehem is not due to the instructions of Herod, but God intervened through the star (Matthew 2:9). The wise men respond in ***exceedingly great joy,*** (Matthew 2:10). Their response of worship is directly related to what God is doing in them as He opens their eyes to the truth of the new King (Matthew 2:11). God enables them to give the gifts that will be Mary and Joseph's financial resource for their flight into Egypt. When the wise men return to their own country, they travel out of their way to avoid Herod the king! From our previous study we learned this was a result of their seeking the mind of God. He answered them with instructions and insight (Matthew 2:12). This is the pattern of their lives. Their system is dominated by the flow of responding.

Herod the king is also dominated, but it was with "doing." Everything he does is self-sourced. The self-centered carnal heart is in charge. Herod lives, reacts, and thinks out of himself. Deception underlies his actions. It is the pattern of his life. How can anyone order the destruction of all the baby boys in Bethlehem and the surrounding districts? It comes from his focus on himself. Secret meetings (Matthew 2:7), use of the Scriptures (Matthew 2:4), and internal distress (Matthew 2:3) come from the source of self. There is nothing in Herod's life which is a product of God enabling and empowering him. "Doing" dominates his life's system.

These examples should make it simple for you to define what is sourcing your lives. You do not have to search for the answer. "Doing" and "responding" are not hiding from you. One or the other is in every area of your life, dominating and controlling your actions. Will you look honestly at what is controlling you?

## Sequence

Everything in this story is in succession. One thing follows another. But this should not surprise you if the subject at hand is the heart source of the system of life. Herod the king, upon hearing of the birth of the new King, is immediately distressed (Matthew 2:3). His self-sourcing takes control. The story from Herod's view unfolds in a sequence. He searches for the location of the baby King through the leaders of Israel (Matthew 2:4). This leads to a secret meeting with the wise men (Matthew 2:7). When they did not cooperate with him, he ***was exceedingly angry,*** (Matthew 2:16). One thing follows another, and it is all traceable back to the self-sourcing of his doing.

We all understand this principle. One lie always leads to another lie. Cheating once leads to cheating again. What horrified us at one time often becomes acceptable. The limits on our doing at the beginning are soon stretched and we establish new limits. Self-sourced doing is always expanding its actions.

We also see this principle in the wise men. They respond. God enables them from the beginning through a star and the wisdom to understand its meaning (Matthew 2:2). As they respond to this, they come to Jerusalem where further insight is granted to them through the Scriptures (Matthew 2:5). Soon they follow the star as it appears again and gives them direct guidance to the new King (Matthew 2:9). The result is they actually come into the presence of the baby King (Matthew 2:11). This expansion of relationship brings them to special Divine guidance in the crisis hour (Matthew 2:12). The kind of relationship we long to experience with God only comes through continual response. It is a result of the heart change from "doing" to "responding."

You start by examining the results of your life. Is the sequence of your story moving to intimacy with God? Has closeness come between you and God, until He can give Divine warnings to you? The answer to this investigation will lead you to examine the inner source of the patterns of your life. Are you "doing" or "responding?" Are you "self-sourced" or "Christ-sourced?"

# Matthew 2:7

## Seeking and Deception

There are many portions of Scripture which are very familiar to us. This can be a problem when it comes to clearly seeing the truth the passage has to reveal. The story of the wise men seeking the baby Jesus is one such passage. It is hard to come to this with a fresh approach, but it is necessary.

If you were reading the story of Matthew 2:1-12 for the first time, you would no doubt be impressed with the diligence of searching found in both the wise men and Herod the king. The only ones spoken of in this passage who are not intense about searching for the new King are the chief priests and the scribes of the people. They are the ones you would expect to be excited and thrilled about His arrival. This is the strange twist of the message.

As the story progresses into the rest of the chapter, there is a revelation of the twisted, carnal, evil motives in the heart of Herod the king. He is not searching with the same sincerity of the wise men. He is deceptive in his search, but his desire looks good on the surface. At first glance it appears Herod should be applauded for his seeking and openness to the arrival of the new King, but his deception is soon revealed.

The deception is revealed by an ANGEL of the Lord. ***Now when they had departed, behold, an angel of the Lord appeared to Joseph in a dream, saying, "Arise, take the young Child and His mother, and flee to Egypt, and stay there until I bring you word; for Herod will seek the young Child to destroy Him,"*** (Matthew 2:13). God knows what is happening in the life of Herod the king. Herod conceals his real motive from the wise men, but he cannot conceal it from God. This is old truth to us who are a part of the church. We can fool our family, friends and associates for a while, but we can never fool God.

There are two verses in the Book of Hebrews which we would like to note at this time. ***For the word of God is living and powerful, and sharper than any two-edged sword, piercing even to the division of soul and spirit, and of joints and marrow, and is a discerner of the thoughts and intents of the heart. And there is no creature hidden from His sight, but all things are naked and open to the eyes of Him to whom we must give account,*** (Hebrews 4:12-13). The author begins with ***the word of God*** and describes its dividing and revealing power. He then quickly moves to ***there is no creature hidden from HIS sight.*** It is as if the Word of God and the all knowing God are so closely related, they are the same. The Word of God in the hand of God is the instrument which cuts and exposes our lives to Him, so He knows. Even in this story, Herod the king is exposed to the Word of God as written by the prophets. His deception cannot stay concealed in light of God and His Word.

Herod's deception is revealed by his ANGER. ***Then Herod, when he saw that he was deceived by the wise men, was exceedingly angry; and he sent forth and put to death all male children who were in Bethlehem and in all its districts, from two years old and under, according to the time which he had determined from the wise men,*** (Matthew 2:16). When Herod ordered the destruction of the young boys, it resulted from his anger that his deceptive plan had been hindered. Our attitude always reveals our deception, and it always climaxes in anger, hatred and bitterness. When there is deception in your soul, you cannot conceal it. You express it in your attitude and relationships.

Herod's deception is also revealed by his ACTION. What was the great sin of Herod? Was it the mass murder of young boys, or was it the internal deception of his heart? Your actions give proof of the condition of your heart. There is a moral principle that our actions display what is in our hearts. When you shake the container, what is inside will come out. The only thing which spills from your life is what is within your life. Our actions always expose us. Herod the king is the perfect example. The raging dishonesty and deception of the heart will drive us to do things of which we never dreamed ourselves capable.

Contained in the core of Herod's deception are some basic elements which are common to all deceptions. It will do us well to investigate them.

## Element of Hiding

### Matthew 2:7

Matthew puts a great emphasis on Herod's actions. ***Then Herod, when he had secretly called the wise men, determined from them what time the star appeared,*** (Matthew 2:7). It is difficult to discern from the text if this is a secret meeting that no one else knew about, or if this was simply a meeting where no one else was present. Either way, there is a definite sense of cover up. But that is always the heart of deception. If everything is exposed and made known, there is no deception.

Herod did not want to publicly commit himself to acknowledging the new King. He was concerned about his image. How would it look to the leaders of Israel if he openly made known his desire to locate the new King and then worship Him? Then there was the possibility that word might reach the parents of the new King that he was taking a dangerous interest in their newborn. None of this would produce the image Herod the king desired to maintain, so he hid these facts in his deception.

Is this the pattern of all deception? We cannot be open and sincere because of how it might look to others. We must maintain our image. Do you see how this destroys seeking? This is the strong emphasis of this passage. The very nature of seeking reveals a lack in my life. If a certain revelation would hurt my image, I hide in my deception to protect what others might see. But this destroys any correction God might want to make in my life. This eliminates all revelation of new truth which might expand me, taking me from where I am to the next level. Therefore I become stale, stagnant and maintain my deception.

The opposite of seeking is non-seeking. The opposite of openness is to be close-minded. This is deception. If you are not seeking Him then you are automatically deceived. Regardless of how far one has come in the reality of truth, deception naturally takes place when the door is closed. In order to maintain the truth we have, we must seek. Hiding is damning to the soul.

It is very easy to hide behind our past. I cannot be open because of the way I was raised. I explain my reason for being closed by saying I am just a private person. It is my personality type. The call of the new King is to step out from behind our excuses and openly seek Him, regardless of where it takes us, or what it might do to us. We need a radical openness of heart. All deception must cease and there must be no more hiding.

## Element of the Heart
## Matthew 2:7

***Then Herod, when he had secretly called the wise men, determined from them what time the star appeared,*** (Matthew 2:7). Matthew clearly states the purpose of the secret meeting between Herod the king and the wise men. Herod ***determined from them what time the star appeared.*** The Greek word translated ***determined*** is very strong. It means "to know accurately or to do exactly." It is often translated "to inquire diligently." It has the idea of careful investigation and carries with it the desire to be very accurate. This word is only used two times in the New Testament and both of them are related to this actions of Herod the king.

In this story Matthew states the intent and motive of Herod's heart. Herod drills the wise men concerning the time of the first appearance of the star. When Herod realizes the wise men are not returning, he is very angry. ***He sent forth and put to death all the male children who were in Bethlehem and in all its districts, from two years old and under,*** (Matthew 2:16). Matthew clearly reveals how Herod determined the age bracket of two years and under. He says it was calculated ***according to the time which he had determined from the wise men,*** (Matthew 2:16).

Herod carefully sought information from the wise men. He was seeking the location of the new King. In fact, He was seeking the new King Himself. But while seeking for the right thing, he was seeking with the wrong motive. He did not want to worship Him as he said, but he wanted to destroy Him as revealed by his actions. Deception springs from the wrong heart motive. Deception is always related to the condition of the heart! It is not a misunderstanding of the mind, nor a sickness of the past. It is not a personality trait. It is an expression of the carnal heart.

Jeremiah found himself crying out against the deceit of the heart.

***The heart is deceitful above all things,***
***And desperately wicked;***
***Who can know it?*** (Jeremiah 17:9).

Immediately the answer came thundering back.

***I, the Lord, search the heart,***
***I test the mind,*** (Jeremiah 17:10).

This is the reason why seeking and openness before the Lord is so important. There is absolutely no chance for us to live above deception without the searching of the Lord in the heart. Deceit in the heart will hide the very deception from us. We will go on being deceived and not know it unless we seek after Him. Christ alone can expose the heart condition. We must have total heart openness to the One who is truth. It is an inside heart problem.

## Element of the Hostile Forces
## Matthew 2:7

***Then Herod, when he had secretly called the wise men, determined from them what time the star appeared,*** (Matthew 2:7). The appearance of the star is only one indication of what is found at the basis of the Christmas story. A war is taking place. Two different and contrary plans are being carried out, and this is creating conflict. The enemy is exerting aggressive action against the unfolding revelation of God's Messiah. This narrative expresses two parallel forces. God is bringing about the restoration of all He has dreamed, and Satan is doing all within his ability to stop it.

This is not a mythological story of the past. It is not an ancient view without any reality in the present. It is the correct view of the world we see and the world we cannot see. We are in the midst of the battle of the ages. ***For we do not wrestle against flesh and blood, but against principalities, against powers, against the rulers of the darkness of this age, against spiritual hosts of wickedness in the heavenly places. Therefore take up the whole armor of God,*** (Ephesians 6:12-13).

This is not a general war taking place in the sky. It is a conflict raging in our personal lives. It affects every aspect of life. We are the battle ground for the conflict. It is bigger than the war between good and evil. It is not a battle between forces, but between personalities. It is a war between God and Satan. This means you cannot measure the acts of war by what we might consider good or evil. We must go to the very heart of the war to understand the conflict.

The artillery in the battle is attitude and motive. The most powerful missile on the demonic side is deception. This means the most important weapon on the side of righteousness is truth. This is a war between truth and deception. The truth is that Satan has already been defeated. God has already punished him and thrown him out of heaven. The cross rendered him powerless with no chance of future victory in our lives. How can he possibly combat this? What weapons does he have at his disposal? There is only one. It is deception.

Jesus highlighted this when addressing the Pharisees. ***"You are of your father the devil, and the desires of your father you want to do. He was a murderer from the beginning, and does not stand in the truth, because there is no truth in him. When he speaks a lie, he speaks from his own resources, for he is a liar and the father of it,*** (John 8:44). Satan's only weapon is his lies. His method is deception. How does he maintain control over your life? How does he keep you in defeat? He convinces you that you cannot live as God intends. He lies to you and tells you that you are bound by your habits and cannot have freedom. It is just the way you are. Only the truth can set you free.

Deception cannot tolerate openness and seeking. Once you commit to know the truth regardless of what it does to you, the bonds of deception are broken. Freedom of truth begins to draw you into victory. God expands you into His dreams. Nothing can stop you. But remember Satan is very deceptive. You may not recognize his presence. You may go on in your religious practice, aggressively denying any possibility of deception. The real test is, "are you seeking?" Are you open to the expansion of God's truth within you? Will you risk the consequences of what His truth will do to you? Will you embrace the embarrassment of His exposure of who you really are?

# Matthew 2:10

## Dancing With God

Joy is the delight of the mind. It is a positive consideration and mental condition. When moderate, it is called gladness. When it is raised to the highest degree, it is exultation. When our desires are limited by our possessions, and we surrender, it is contentment. When our highest desires are accomplished, it is satisfaction. When battles rage, and we win victory, it is triumph. When joy has possessed our minds for so long it has settled into a pattern of the inner heart, we call it cheerfulness.

It is striking to study this concept in the context of the New Testament. There is a remarkable absence of the idea of happiness. The state of blessedness as described in the beatitudes of Jesus (Matthew 5) seems to be completely beyond the level of happiness. The idea of joy and rejoice do not compare to being happy. The thrust of being happy seems to be a self-centered focus which is self-destructive. The desire to be happy destroys any possibility of being happy. Happiness seems to be a temporary emotion of the moment. It wavers with the circumstances of life. It seems to be connected with chance or luck. In fact, we make statements like "happy-go-luck." Happiness is equated with no responsibilities, which actually breeds the opposite.

Now joy is something different. It is not dependent on circumstances or luck, but is a temperament of the heart. What takes place in the wise men when they see the star again is an acceleration of what they have already been experiencing. Obviously they come to a state of exultation. Matthew uses words like "exceedingly" and "great" to express the joy of the wise men (Matthew 2:10).

The use of the words "joy" and "rejoice" in the Old Testament is very revealing. The most frequently used Hebrew word is translated into the English as "joy," "gladness" or "mirth." It is used in the Book of Proverbs in a powerful statement. The author writes,

***The light of the righteous rejoices,***

***But the lamp of the wicked will be put out,*** (Proverbs 13:9).

Here it properly means "to be bright" or "to shine." Joy is connected with righteousness and the demonstration of the brilliant glory as it is lived out. There are other Hebrew nouns which are translated "exult," "rejoice," "joy" or "shouting." They actually come from the root word which is a verb meaning "to go in a circle," "to be excited" or "to dance around for joy." In the Hebrew language the idea of joy is expressed in a full body demonstration.

I want to investigate the concept of joy as highlighted in the lives of the wise men. A familiar contrast takes place in this passage. It is the comparison between Herod the king and the wise men. It is the same view we see in their searching, their motives for the searches, and now in their state of minds. Herod is ***troubled, and all Jerusalem with him,*** (Matthew 2:3). The Greek word which is translated ***troubled*** has to do with being agitated. It is the picture of a washing machine. The instrument in the middle of the machine which is in constant motion back and forth, simply agitates the clothes to be washed. This is the condition of Herod's heart. It is the opposite picture of joy. Fear and uncertainty are included in the picture. There is no contentment or peace. Insecurity has permeated his entire life.

This agitation will become the basic explanation for all of the actions of Herod in the rest of the passage. Why has he gone to the chief priests and scribes of the people (Matthew 2:4)? Why has he lied to them about His true motives (Matthew 2:8)? Why has he ordered the destruction of all male children two years of age and under (Matthew2:16)? It all springs from the internal trouble, the agitation, he is experiencing.

The opposite of this is the condition of the wise men. ***When they saw the star, they rejoiced with exceedingly great joy,*** (Matthew 2:10). Their condition is not momentary. They first saw the star appear nearly two years ago, it brought them joy, and that joy has increased to a high level. This joy is the explanation of the aggressive searching they have undertaken. It has kept them going when it would have been easy to quit. Herod sets the obstacles of hatred and evil before them, but that does not stop them.

A part of the investigation of this study is to view our inner condition. Where do you and I fit into the contrast between Herod and the wise men? Are we troubled or filled with joy? There may be degrees of expressing the inner condition, so we will have to search carefully. We have all known people who simply live in a state of anger. Everything upsets them. We have all known a few who seem to press on delightfully through every obstacle. Where are you and I in this process? Could we learn from the wise men?

## The Source of Joy

Where does joy come from? We need to be careful in our investigation lest we give the wrong impression of joy's source. There is no desire to disrupt the focus on Jesus. Everything in the passage keeps coming back to Jesus. Jesus is the source of all joy. He is the reality of truth. Outside of His person, there is no joy. We are not discussing a temporary emotional feeling of happiness. Joy is about Jesus.

With this as our context, let's look carefully at the passage. Joy is connected with the wise men seeing the star again. ***When they saw the star, they rejoiced with exceedingly great joy,*** (Matthew 2:10). Joy is not mentioned in their actual entrance into the house or in seeing the Christ Child. ***And when they had come into the house, they saw the young Child with Mary His mother, and fell down and worshiped Him. And when they had opened their treasures, they presented gifts to Him: gold, frankincense, and myrrh,*** (Matthew 2:12). When they see the Christ Child, they fall down in submission and worship, and they give generous gifts. Joy is present before all this happens.

Joy is distinctly connected with the search. In the passage, joy is not connected with the conclusion of the story, or the final solution of the search, but is connected with the journey itself! Joy is found in the search. It may be difficult to distinguish between joy as a product of seeking or cause for the search. Joy was the temperament which drove them on in the discouraging times. The anticipation of actually seeing the new and powerful King brought joy to their hearts. Each new sign indicated they were closer to the discovery of His location, and this brought them joy. When the star appeared, it was a reassurance of the first message they received nearly two years previously. They never abandoned it.

Joy is found in the stretching, growing, seeking, learning and expanding to discover the experience. The comfortable, traditional, secure, self-interest, play it safe experience does not produce joy. Joy is in the journey itself. It is not by accident. God designed it this way. Joy does not end when the task is accomplished. Without Christ as your focus everything grows old, and you are left with the feeling of finality. God made us to investigate. When we seek Him Who is just beyond our grasp and bigger than what we see at this moment, there is no end to joy in Christ.

Will heaven bring us to the conclusion of our journey? NOT so! Heaven is only the beginning of the unfolding dream God has for us. His plan is not limited to the seventy years of living on this earth, but for eternity. Think of the joy we shall know when the accelerated pace of learning is experienced in heaven. We will then investigate, learn, seek, and change in unhindered ways. The joy is in the journey.

Joy is what liberates you from your own security, pleasure and self-interest. Joy has to do with being possessed by someone greater than you! When a man is consumed with his career, he may find happiness. But his career is only temporary, for he quickly gets old and is forced to retire. The athlete finds pleasure in the preparation and development of his physical abilities. He is ecstatic when he achieves his sport's record. But then the young man kneels at the altar weeping because the tendons in his ankles have been stretched. He cries out that his life is over and all happiness is gone. It is so temporary. The father gives himself to financial gain and finds satisfaction in his accumulation of wealth, only to have a major loss when the stock market goes down. Even if it does not go down, he faces the end of his life with nothing beyond. He is empty of joy. The search must be for that which is greater and bigger than ourselves and this life. Where else can we go but to Christ?

Matthew highlights the joy found in the search of the wise men. We must clarify the joy is found in the search for the new King. The search is not for joy, but for Christ. Joy is not something to be sought. You and I must forget about it. If we focus on it and attempt to grasp it, it will disappear because the source is gone. There must be no other focus but Christ. He is the source of joy. If we focus on joy then we become preoccupied with our own security, pleasure, or self-interest. Freedom only comes when we are caught up in something great enough to give meaning and purpose to all of life and every relationship. Christ alone is the only adequate center for our existence. Joy is found in Christ.

## The State of Joy

There is an incredible discovery we can make from the word "joy." The original language of the Bible is the Greek language. The Greek root word for "joy" is "chairo." It is a verb, and is translated "rejoice." This is significant because it is also the Greek root word for "charis." This word is translated "grace." Joy and grace both come from the same root word. Does this not tell us there is an intimate connection between joy and grace?

This does not appear to be right. It would seem that "charis" (grace) should have been the root word for "chairo" (rejoice) and for "chara" (joy). We could then propose that grace produces joy and rejoicing. But now we are forced to consider the fact that "chara" (joy) and "charis" (grace) come from the verb "chairo" (rejoice) which means joy and grace come from rejoicing. There is a deep action running throughout the character of God. He is in the constant state of rejoicing, even though you can find passages in the Scriptures where God weeps. The action of rejoicing is not a temporary, light, emotional response to circumstances. The act of rejoicing is the flow of the inner spirit of God which affects everything He touches. When God touches something, the principle of rejoicing spills forth with grace.

Grace, as you know, is unmerited favor, which is granting something to someone who does not deserve it. The inner action of rejoicing enables God to manifest grace. God lavishes grace upon us because He is rejoicing. We do not have time to investigate this thought in relationship to God, but we must think about it for our lives. We will never be able to pour mercy and grace to our world if we are not in the state of rejoicing.

This deeply affects the lives of people all around us. Ministry to others does not come because we are trained to do it. It is not the result of certain talents. It is a result of the inner state of rejoicing, which automatically touches others with grace. Forgiveness, love, mercy, and compassion are all a part of the circle of grace. It is these attributes which win our world.

Most of us know this to be true, but we are unable to perform such attributes on a consistent basis. This produces hypocrisy and inconsistency for which our worldly friends severely criticize the church. It is simply impossible for us to produce grace. Oh, to seek Jesus alone for the answer! It is in our total focus on Him we are able to rejoice. This allows Jesus to flow through us with His grace and mercy. We join Him in His very nature of rejoicing. His joy becomes ours, and thus, He bestows His grace through us. Let us join the wise men in seeking the Christ Child.

# Matthew 2:11

## Jesus in the Aorist Tense

***And when they had come into the house, they saw the young Child with Mary His mother, and fell down and worshiped Him. And when they had opened their treasures, they presented gifts to Him: gold, frankincense, and myrrh,*** (Matthew 2:11).

Matthew's presentation of this verse was no accident. The statement is so bold, it is impossible to miss. The difficulty for us is that we see what he says in our context and language. We need to see it through Matthew's eyes, but we are blocked by the English language and our cultural thought process.

He begins with the word, ***And.*** It is a primary particle, which has a joining effect, but it also has something of a cumulative force. What takes place in verse eleven is not isolated, accidental or just happening. It is the climax or the next step in the progression or effect of the cause or the build up of a long series of events.

You can see this clearly in the context of the passage. The wise men did not get here by accident. Their journey is cumulative. Their decisions and choices brought them to this place of worship. Other passages have revealed there was at least six hundred years of influence which contributed to this moment. The Babylonian Captivity was a result of disobedience, but is now used by God to open the door to the entire Gentile world.

Think of the first time they saw the star and the investigation which brought them to the conclusion that a new King was born. Do you suppose there were other wise men who thought this was a crazy idea? Could this believing group of wise men have been labeled and scorned for the suggestions they made. After all, what happened did not fit their pattern and was not culturally acceptable. They were the makers of kings, and now they were searching for a King they did not make. He is One who is greater than anyone they have encountered, and they are submitting to Him!

Consider the family demands and involvement the wise men had to work through. What were the financial ramifications involved as they planned the journey? How long were they going to be gone? Did they think it would only be a couple of months, or would this task take a year and a half or two years? How can they justify the unending search with no real assurance they will discover the fulfillment of their dream?

Surely they sense the disturbance of their question when they arrive in Jerusalem (Matthew 2:2). As learned as they were, they must have sensed hesitation and something strange about Herod the king. They had to continue making hard choices. Immense involvement has brought them to this moment. No wonder Matthew starts this verse with ***And.***

Have you ever opened your eyes and wondered how you got where you are? How did your life arrive in this set of circumstances? How did you end up with the tendencies and patterns you have? How did the habits of your life get so strong? From where did the broken relationships come? How did life become so complicated?

This is a message to all young people. Carefully guard your choices now! You are going someplace! Where will you be five years from now, and what will you be like? You will not accidentally become that person. You will get there on purpose, and it will be all by yourself!

During my days of seminary training I was a pastor in Georgia. There was a wonderful elderly lady in the church named, Miss Willie. She never had children of her own, but she mothered the entire community. She was a retired school teacher who had reached the age of eighty years. She was a true saint! The presence of God and sweetness of the Holy Spirit was constantly flowing from her. As her pastor I went to call on her to encourage and help her. It never seemed to work out that way, for I always came away different and better because of being with her. It dawned on me as a young man that she did not accidentally wake up on her eightieth birthday and suddenly become sweet, kind and filled with God. She had been working at this for a long time. This was a result of seeking His face, living in His presence, and trusting Him in the difficult times. If I had any chance of being like Miss Willie, I had better start right then.

We want to kneel at the altar of prayer and have God eliminate forty years of aggressive living with all of its consequences. It took a long time to get where you are, and it will take some time to become what you want to be. We certainly believe in a crisis experience with

God which changes the very heart and inner soul of the individual. But we also know the pain of working that change through long years of experience, patterns and habits.

To some of us it is discouraging to think of these things. Is there no answer? This verse contains the answer to it all, encouragement for the moment, and clear instructions. But it is here where the difficulty of our English language and culture come into view. Matthew presents this verse (2:11) in a strong statement. The strength of the statement is based upon the fact that he uses six verbs in the aorist tense. ***And when <u>they had come</u> into the house, <u>they saw</u> the young Child with Mary His mother, and <u>fell down</u> and <u>worshiped</u> Him. And when <u>they had opened</u> their treasures, <u>they presented</u> gifts to Him: gold, frankincense, and myrrh,*** (Matthew 2:11).

Matthew did not place these six aorist verbs in one verse by accident. He attempts to communicate a truth to us which can bring us to the very heart of the wise men and what they were expecting. Again the difficulty is our thought process. It is shaped by our language, and it has no ability to think in terms of the aorist tense.

Harold Lamb wrote a biography of Alexander the Great, who conquered the world by the age of thirty. He describes the upset and dismay the Greek army felt as they followed Alexander across Asia Minor. The only maps they had were Greek maps. These maps showed only a part of Asia Minor. The rest was a blank space. They discovered their march had taken them off the map.

Wouldn't it be something if this is exactly what we are called to do? The answers we are looking for, oneness with God and the solutions to our conflicts, are all found off the map. They will not be discovered in the way we have always thought. We will not find the answer in the confines of our language and our culture.

If you are to grasp what Matthew is trying to communicate in this verse, you will have to march off the map. The chief characteristic of the aorist tense is its emphasis on punctiliar action. This means the verb is to be considered without regard to the past, present or future. There is a past, present and future, but this is not under consideration in the aorist. In this verb tense, you are to think outside these boundaries. I find it almost impossible to do this. Everything in my language and culture is in regard to the past, present and future. How do you go outside of this?

The aorist tense does not regard the past as when a thing has started, and it does not regard the future as when it will end. It only views the moment. The moment being viewed is not necessarily the present moment. It is a moment outside the past, present and future. It is such an intense focus of the event itself that time seems to have no relevance. How can it be?

This may be the closest we have in our language to the eternal state of our God. I have been asking for "the mind of Christ." Could this be the atmosphere of that mind? It is difficult to place ourselves in this perspective, but visualize God in His eternal state. He is high above the time zone. He is not touched by all that envelops us. We live on a line called "time." Where ever I stand on this line, it is called "the present." What lies ahead of me is called "the future." I know little about it. What I do know is strictly guesswork. I have not been there yet. If I look behind me, there is nothing but "past." What I know of it is contained in my memory, which is not as good as it once was. I will never be there again. I walk on this time line a second at a time, always living in the present. But God lives above the time line. He has no past, present or future. He lives in the "eternal moment." Is this what God is calling us to? Is this His dream for us in the fullness of the Spirit of Jesus?

I am not sure this is as far fetched as it may appear! A young man sees a young lady across the hall and is attracted to her. He begins the search to find out who she is and where she is from. He finally orchestrates an introduction and the getting acquainted process begins. The first date is set for the week end. There is a second, a third and a fourth date. There are then too many to count. He has fallen head over heals in love with her. Marriage is proposed and they join in the union of one flesh. In the years to come they have children born into their home, and they are busy about the responsibility of raising them.

There is a past, a present and a future. But what sustains the marriage is not the past. Anniversaries are celebrated and remembered. The marriage is not successful because of the present, for there are good times and bad, and all is experienced in the now. The foundation of the marriage is not the future, for no one knows what that may hold, and death is approaching. The key to this marriage is "the eternal moment." It goes beyond the past, the present and the future. It is the forever moment of love which has become the dominating focus of his life. Somehow this couple has stepped into the aorist tense of focus and intent. The embrace of love has become so dominate it has gone beyond time. It controls how they view their past. It shapes their present memories, and it will dictate the events of their future. They are living in the aorist tense.

Let us now return to our passage of study (Matthew 2:11). I have been troubled, not with the appearance of the wise men in the Christmas story, but by their disappearance. According to verse twelve, they receive the Divine warning from God and return to their country without seeing Herod. The account of the wise men ends here. I wanted a footnote which tells me they went home to get their families, and returned to Palestine to follow the new King. But we hear nothing about them after this. Surely an experience this profound could not end so abruptly. How can they simply bow in worship, and then walk off as if it meant nothing to them?

This may be the reason Matthew placed all of these verbs in the aorist tense. This moment for the wise men is an eternal moment. This moment of worship becomes the focus moment in which they will live for the rest of their lives. It shapes their future and dominates their past. It controls their present. Yet, it is not past, present or the future; it is aorist. The new King has engulfed them, so captivated them, so touched them, they will live permanently in the atmosphere and happening of that moment; it is an "eternal moment."

This is the cry of my heart! Oh, to focus, to embrace, to experience Him in the aorist tense. I want to go beyond the past, the present and the future into the eternal now! I want to live in Him and Him in me, until the eternal moment affects how I view my past, controls the events of the present, and dictates what takes place in the future. I want to live in the eternal moment, until my past, my present and my future does not affect my relationship with Him. I want the eternal moment to affect my past, my present and my future. I want His presence to consume, dominate and capture me until there is nothing else. It is the fullness of the Spirit of Jesus that brings Him in me and me in Him. It is there that I have my being.

What does He need to do in my life to bring me to "the eternal moment?" Whatever that is, I welcome His eternal activity!

# Matthew 2:11

# The Eternal Moment

There is much to comprehend in this one powerful verse. Listen to it again! ***And when they had come into the house, they saw the young Child with Mary His mother, and fell down and worshiped Him. And when they had opened their treasures, they presented gifts to Him: gold, frankincense, and myrrh,*** (Matthew 2:11).

The language in which we think forms the boundaries of our culture. The Scripture we are dealing with comes from a different culture and a different language. The culture of the Greek language has great depth. The Greek language embraces philosophy and theology in a greater way than our English language.

The aorist tense is heavily used in our text of study. Six times it appears in Matthew's description of the wise men worshiping the Christ Child. Let me highlight it for you again. ***And when they had come into the house, they saw the young Child with Mary His mother, and fell down and worshiped Him. And when they had opened their treasures, they presented gifts to Him: gold, frankincense,***

***and myrrh,*** (Matthew 2:11). Matthew describes something beyond the action of the verbs themselves. The message is penetrating and forceful. It is a description of an encounter with God.

There are six different kinds of verbs in the aorist tense. Three of these are very rare and probably do not need to be discussed. However, there are three different aorist tense verbs which may well apply to this verse. There is the "historical aorist," which is also called the "punctiliar aorist." It focuses on the action of the moment without regard to the past, present or future. There is the "inceptive aorist," which focuses on the point at which the action began, also without regard to the past, present or future. The third is the "cumulative aorist," which focuses on the point at which the action may have ended, also without regard to the past, present or future.

What makes this difficult for Bible scholars is that the different usages of these three aorist tenses are a matter of interpretation. There is no proof which one Matthew may be indicating. You have to look carefully at the context and judge which one of the various kinds of aorist may fit what the author is writing at the moment. One cannot be dogmatic concerning their usage.

As we begin our study of the content of verse eleven, I want to make some suggestions concerning the six verbs which Matthew presents. I am not being dogmatic, but only attempting to discover the truth of the passage.

## The Eternal Moment

The first, fifth and sixth verbs in the sentence are in the historical aorist. Matthew begins the sentence with this emphasis and ends it with the same. The first aorist verb introduces the entrance of the wise men into the house and the presence of the new King. He uses the phrase, ***they had come.*** The last two aorist verbs focus on the offering the wise men give in worship to the new King, ***they had opened*** and ***they presented.***

With these verbs in the historical aorist, Matthew colors the action of the verse. The wise men search for the new King, and their search is climaxed in their encounter of the Christ Child as seen in light of the historical aorist. Here the aorist merely states that something has happened relative to the speaker, with no particular focus on its beginning, end or progress. It is difficult for us to think in these terms. It is not that there is no past or future. The issue is the focus of the verb. The experience, the encounter with Christ, is all consuming. Wouldn't it be something to have an encounter with Christ so strong and consuming that the beginning fades and the future rewards do not matter? If that happens, the focus of your life becomes Him and the reality of His presence. Your embrace with Him becomes an eternal moment!

There is always a past, a present and a future. But when your life becomes consumed with Jesus, you live in the moment forever. Your embrace with Him determines how you view your past. Your interaction with Him dictates how you respond in the present. His presence manifests itself in the plans for the future. You live dominated and controlled alone by the eternal moment of His presence.

Matthew further indicates this by the actual Greek word he uses for the coming of the wise men. The Greek word translated ***they had come*** is the most frequently used verb denoting either "to come, or to go." The focus of the verb is on the act. There is another Greek word which would be used if the focus was on the arrival or on the start of the journey. The Greek word used in verse eleven ignores the beginning or end; it focuses on the experience or the act itself. When this is placed alongside the aorist tense, the message becomes very loud. Can you imagine an experience with Christ so all consuming we live in the embrace alone. Everything else is secondary to Him. He determines everything both past, present and future.

Matthew closes this eternal moment with the same aorist tense. He gives us two verbs which are a part of the offering the wise men give to Christ. He says ***they had opened*** and ***they presented.*** The historical aorist gives us the sense of the eternal moment in this presentation. The focus is not on the beginning or ending of the offering, but upon the act itself. It is as if the wise men live in the act of opening and presenting. The offering they give is not viewed as completed or sufficient. The focus is beyond the past, present or future. We see the all consuming openness and offering.

As the encounter of the wise men and Christ is an eternal moment, we also see an eternal moment in their offering response. It calls us to the opposite of duty, law or accomplishment. There is no sense of meeting your obligation. There is no satisfaction in having given enough or doing a good thing. Think of the significance of living in the eternal moment of openness and response to Him. "Having arrived" is never in the picture. He completely enthralls us, and we live in total response to Him! Our past, present and future are dominated by this obsessive eternal moment. It is the call of the Gospel.

The eternal moment is also verified by the Greek word translated ***they presented.*** This verb seems to lay stress on the persons to whom and by whom the offering is made. Matthew highlights the close proximity between the wise men and the Christ Child. When the wise men encounter the new King, a connection of relationship takes place. Couple this with the eternal moment and the impact is doubled. What takes place in the lives of the wise men when they see the new King is beyond the past, present or future. They live in this moment for the rest of their lives. It is not that this moment influences them in the future, but the moment of the encounter is so focused they live in its embrace and relationship forever.

Oh, to have an encounter with the new King like this! When we embrace Him in such intimacy, everything else fades. The tightness of that embrace will never be relaxed! It becomes the atmosphere in which we live all of life! Yes, there is a past, present and future, but Christ brings them into the aroma of the eternal moment. Christ is the all consuming factor!

## The Expanded Moment

There is a second use of the aorist tense in this verse. Matthew writes that the wise men came into the house and ***they saw,*** (Matthew 2:11). Because of the Greek word in the sentence and its usage, we judge the aorist tense used in the cumulative aorist. Sometimes the aorist will yield a meaning that is almost identical with that of the perfect tense, and may even be used as a substitute. When this takes place, it is the cumulative aorist.

The perfect tense has to do with something which happened in the past and has results in the present. This immediately gives us an expanded view of the verb ***saw.*** The aorist tense demands the consideration of the verb be without regard to the past, present and future. As one moves into the eternal moment, we see the emphasis of this verb as something which expands and unfolds in our living. Matthew describes an action in the lives of the wise men which expands their consistent unfolding influence. It is a powerful eternal moment, and they live in its unfolding.

Matthew enforces this concept with the usage of the Greek word translated ***saw.*** It refers to the idea of inside knowledge. Often, it is translated "to know." It includes much more than a simple act of physical seeing. It describes an internal understanding and comprehension. Matthew links this verb with the aorist tense, and paints a vivid picture of the encounter between the wise men and the Christ Child. All the dreams and desires of the wise men are climaxed in this encounter. Their passion to find the new King has driven them to this moment. What is the encounter like? How will He be? When they see Him, they view their past, present and future from the perspective of this eternal moment. They understand the depth of their systems. All questions are answered in this experience. Life begins to make sense to them. They embrace the eternal moment, and it unfolds and expands in its impact.

Oh, to have such an encounter with Christ! Oh, to see Him in such a way! A clear vision of His being will bring anyone to this dwelling place. No wonder Paul reminds us of the blinding process of the Devil's influence, (2 Corinthians 4:3-4). Satan must do all in his power to hide us from the greatness of Christ's person. If we push everything aside, we will come into the house where He dwells. If we make it into the house, we will see Him in an expanded moment in the aorist tense. He will consume us with Himself in an unfolding manner which will never release us. This eternal moment will affect our view. The past, present and future are not eliminated or deemed unimportant. When Christ embraces us, that encounter supersedes everything else that happens to us. He becomes the center of the reference point. We finally experience the hub of the wheel. All of life keeps whirling by, but it now rotates in order and sense because we dwell in the eternal moment. It is a wonderful place to dwell!

## The Experienced Moment

Matthew uses two more verbs in the aorist tense. When they entered the house and saw the Christ Child, these men had a proper reaction. Matthew writes ***. . . and fell down and worshiped Him,*** (Matthew 2:11). As you see these aorist verbs in their context, it becomes apparent they are "inceptive aorist." This means the author uses the verbs to focus on the beginning of the experience without regard to the past, present or future.

It is not hard to understand this focus. Those who find Christ fall down before Him; they adore Him, and they submit themselves to Him. He is their Lord, and they worship Him. What other response can there be? See this in light of the culture and experience of the wise men. They are the chief officials of their country. They are used to the refinement and glory of the setting of kings. They have just come from the palace of Herod the king. They spent time in a secret meeting with him. He gave them the mission to seek out the new King.

Their search ends in an unexpected location. It is a humble cottage. The only attendant to the new King is His mother. He is not surrounded by refinement. The only gold this King has will be what they give Him. This did not seem to shock them. There was something about the presence of this new King which overshadowed any of the surroundings. The moment of impact was not created by the glory of the dwelling, but the power and presence of the person. Christ captured them.

The response of the wise men was they ***fell down.*** The Greek word translated is used for a descent from a higher place to a lower place, or it is used for a descent from an erect position to a prostrate position. Connected with this is the fact they ***worshiped Him.*** This Greek word has the meaning "to kiss, like a dog licking his master's hand." Perhaps the proper approach to understand the emphasis is to be captured by the attitude and atmosphere of the action of these verbs. Matthew describes the wise men as being submissive to the new King.

Matthew paints a picture of the wise men moving into an eternal moment. The Christ Child becomes the all consuming focus of their lives. Everything in the past, present and future is seen through the eyes of this relationship with the new King. It will not be a stagnant moment, but an unfolding moment. The expansion of the relationship will take place within this focus. They will live in the eternal moment of His presence, awe struck and in submission to Him. Their submission will expand as the eternal moment grows in their lives.

This is the call of holiness. An all consuming intimacy with Christ must take place in us. This is beyond an experience in the past, or even something we look forward to in our future in heaven. He captures us with His presence in the eternal moment. This must expand in our lives. We have not arrived or experienced the depth of submission and worship as He wants to reveal it to us. Oh, the joy of the unfolding revelation of oneness with Him.

# PART FOUR

## Matthew 2:13-16

Tragedy at Christmas

# Matthew 2:13

## His Initiative – Our Response

Matthew makes a statement in the narratives which is too obvious to ignore. He constructs a sentence that proposes a truth which is relevant to our lives. We know this has high priority in Matthew's mind, because he uses it in three of the four narratives. He does not propose an instruction for something we are to do, but shares with us a concept. This concept gives us an attitude to live by. I discovered it in the study of the first narrative (Matthew 1:24). His presentation is so forceful that I dedicated an entire study to it. I had no idea it would appear again. Matthew uses the same sentence construction again to begin the third and fourth narratives.

In each case an Angel of the Lord speaks to Joseph. There is something present in Joseph's character and attitude which attracts me. I want this same quality in my life. The second narrative is the story of the wise men. They come to Jerusalem seeking to locate the new King. Herod receives word of their search and is deeply distressed (Matthew 2:3). He immediately begins to plot a method by which he can locate and destroy the new born King. He lies to the wise men to encourage them to return with the details of the new King's location. His deceptive purpose is ***that I may come and worship Him also,*** (Matthew 2:8).

The wise men are total opposites of King Herod. They are in an attitude of seeking and request guidance from God. God warns them in a dream, through an Angel of the Lord, that they should not return to Herod. As the third narrative opens, the same Angel of the Lord who appears to the wise men, appears to Joseph in a dream, probably during the same time period, saying, ***"Arise, take the young Child and His mother, flee to Egypt, and stay there until I bring you word; for Herod will seek the young Child to destroy Him,"*** (Matthew 2:13).

The grammar structure of this sentence in the English is not the same as it is in the Greek. There are some remarkable differences which we need to highlight for the sake of truth. The sentence has an assumed subject. It is "you." In the context of the verse, this refers to Joseph. The reason for this assumption is the three main verbs are all in the imperative mood. This is a command given by the Angel of the Lord to Joseph. The command is ***take, flee,*** and ***stay.***

The opening word of the angel's command is ***Arise.*** In the Greek language, this is a verb in the participle form. It acts like an adverb in that it gives content to the main verb or verbs. Each of the main verbs, ***take, flee,*** and ***stay,*** are modified and shaped by the action of ***Arise***. ***Arise*** is in the passive voice. This means the subject is NOT responsible for the action of the verb, but is being acted upon. It would be better to translate ***Arise*** as "having been aroused." Everything which is going to happen in each of the main verbs is going to be in response to the action which takes place in Joseph. He does not initiate the plan. He does not send out spies to see what Herod is going to do. Joseph is acted upon by the Angel of the Lord, who is the resource of God's plan.

This brings us back to the basic premise of the Word of God. It is the fundamental and primary teaching of the Kingdom. We are not, never have been, and never will be, the source of Kingdom living. The Christian life is never a product of "doing," but is always a result of "being." God calls upon us to respond to His Divine action. This is difficult for us, because it means we are not in charge. We become a product of the Divine Life. This requires patience on our part, and that is hard for us. We have to wait upon the action of God. We have enough difficulty waiting on others; now think of waiting upon God. His timing is crucial in the fulfillment of His plan. If Joseph and his family leave for Egypt too soon, they will miss the visit of the wise men. The timing of their departure is very important to them and to God's plan. The wise men have the necessary financial support Joseph will need to support his family in Egypt (Matthew 2:11). If Joseph flees to Egypt too late, Herod is going to make an aggressive move upon Bethlehem and the surrounding districts, and the Christ Child will be in grave danger (Matthew 1:16). Therefore, God acts upon Joseph, when the Angel of the Lord arouses him in a dream, and he makes the journey.

Matthew, and the other Scripture author's, state and restate the principle of the Kingdom throughout the Gospels. Jesus gloriously manifests this throughout His life. The epistles call us to the radical experience of being sourced by God. This is the only acceptable life style for Kingdom people. We must resign all doing, self-initiated action, and self-sourcing. Regardless of how good our performances are, or how much applause we receive, it is not legitimate if God does not produce it.

Once again God acts upon Joseph, through the Angel of the Lord, and calls upon him to respond. The response is threefold. He is to ***take, flee,*** and ***stay.*** We want to look at each action separately.

## Embrace

## Matthew 2:13

The Angel of the Lord arouses Joseph from sleep and instructs him to ***take the young Child and His mother,*** (Matthew 2:13). The Greek word which is translated ***take*** is much deeper in meaning than it appears. Joseph is not asked to simply transport Mary and the Christ Child to Egypt like a cargo of goods. He is to take them from one location to another, but the request is much greater that this. There is a depth of relationship which God requires of Joseph. He is expected to respond with caring and concern. God calls upon Joseph to embrace the Christ Child.

There are other places in the Scriptures where the same word is used. In the first narrative (Matthew 1:18-25), the Angel of the Lord uses this same word to instruct Joseph. He confronts Joseph in a dream with these words, ***"Joseph, son of David, do not be afraid to take to you Mary your wife,*** (Matthew 1:20). The idea of ***take to you Mary*** in marriage, as your wife, is much deeper than transporting her from one place to another. This involves all the love which should be present in a marriage. This even involves the becoming of one flesh as marriage is described in the Scriptures.

This same word is used to refer to the kind of relationship we are to have with Jesus and the experience of being in the Kingdom. ***He came to His own and His own did not receive Him,*** (John 1:11).

This negative statement shows that Jesus' own people did not receive Him. Jesus said to His disciples, "***And if I go and prepare a place for you, I will come again and receive you to Myself; that where I am, there you may be also,"*** (John 14:3). In both of these Scriptures the idea of receiving is much greater than just taking something to transport as cargo. It is deeply relational and an unquestionable embrace. In speaking of the second coming, Jesus tells the disciples, "***Then two men will be in the field: one will be taken and the other left,"*** (Matthew 24:40). In the context of all we know about the second coming, and the method of how Jesus is going to receive us, we know this is more than a simple transport.

The Angel of the Lord arouses Joseph, acts upon him, and the purpose is his participation in the plan of God to ***take*** his family to safety. God sources Joseph in this mission. This is an imperative verb, in the active voice, which is being modified with a passive verb participle. In other words, Joseph is not expected to initiate this, only participate in carrying it out. God calls him to respond. The response God calls him to is relationship, embracing and acting as a father to a child who is not his natural son.

I have no problem seeing myself in this scene and applying this truth to my life. God has come to my life to arouse me. He has taken the initiative. I have not stimulated Him to move; He has come and quickened me to response. He calls me to relationship. I am to receive or ***take*** Him. It is not like transporting cargo, but it is the embrace of marriage, the intimacy of Kingdom life, and the sharing of who He is. What an opportunity!

## Escape

## Matthew 2:13

The second main verb is ***flee,*** which is also an imperative and is in the active voice. But again it is modified by the participle adverb "having been raised." Joseph did not initiate this. He responded. He is to ***flee to Egypt,*** (Matthew 2:13). This was not uncommon for that day. Egypt was somewhere in the vicinity of sixty miles away. There was large segment of Jews in one of the main cities, just across the border.

This word has the idea of seeking safety in flight. It has the thrust of avoiding danger by fleeing. It is the instruction of Jesus concerning the last days, ***"then let those who are in Judea flee to the mountains,"*** (Matthew 24:16). Jesus gave similar instructions to His disciples as He transferred His power to them and sent them out to minister. ***"When they persecute you in this city, flee to another,"*** (Matthew 10:23).

In this context, God is acting upon Joseph through an Angel of the Lord, and He is asking Joseph to respond to the movement of God by embracing the Christ Child as his own and physically relocating Him to safety. The Angel of the Lord gives an explanation for this action by saying, ***for Herod will seek the young Child to destroy Him,*** (Matthew 2:13). This involves a complete upset in Joseph's life. Everything is affected, his carpenter's business, his home, friends, customs, traditions and possessions. Joseph is fleeing from everything normal in his life. The only thing remaining will be his relationship ***(take)*** with the Christ Child.

This is the heart of the Gospel! There is no safety in clinging to what has been, even though it is not wrong. This is not an issue of right and wrong. It is always an issue of response to being aroused by the Divine God. It is a call to lose control and be changed. It is a life to be lived in response to the fullness of the Holy Spirit, who wants to live within you. God is arousing us from our ministry, our living and our doing. Just because we label it "all for Him" does not justify our self-centered actions. He calls us to flee from all we are, and all we have been, and totally respond to Him.

## Exist
## Matthew 2:13

The third main verb is ***stay.*** The Angel says, ***"and stay there until I bring you word;"*** (Matthew 2:13). The Greek word can be translated "you be." It comes from the word which is translated "I am." It highlights a state of being. It has an adjective, which is the word ***there.*** The idea is to maintain a state of being in a particular spot, in this case Egypt. This verb is also an imperative, in the active voice, which is motivated by the adverb participle ***Arise.*** You are to be actively involved. God is not going to do this without you. He expects you to participate wholeheartedly, but you are not going to initiate anything. God will act upon you both, in your going and in your coming. Will you respond to Him? What do you want me to do? That is the wrong question. God calls you to a state of being. He brings you into the middle of redemption for the entire world. It is not your plan or design. He initiates and moves the circumstances; God calls you to ***stay there,*** just be there.

This is the most difficult issue in Christianity. Being in charge for us means we are in control, and we are doing. We fix, manipulate, plan, offend, divide, build, destroy, etc. We do it all in the name of ministry and for the sake of the Kingdom. In the meantime, God actively attempts to raise us up and bring us to a place of total response. He wants us to come to crucifixion so He can manifest His live alone. All that is required of us, in the state of being, is to "be there."

It is the opposite of our personal reasoning. The old thought process says, "Nothing is being accomplished." The urge of the old self is to protect, guide, and guard. But there is only one place where things get done and where safety is experienced. It is to ***stay there.*** Once you see it, you will want this to be your constant abiding place. Do not ever stray again.

# Matthew 2:13-18

# Kingdoms At War

Matthew paints a significant picture in the context of these four narratives. It is a picture we seem to forget in the normal flow of our daily lives. The reason we forget is that it frightens us, and we ignore it so not to be bothered. We are in a state of denial. It is the raging conflict which takes place between the kingdom of Satan and the Kingdom of God. We are forced to recognize this in the scene of the third narrative. Matthew expresses great pain in this passage. Herod is in an evil rage, and he pronounces this edict. ***He sent forth and put to death all the male children who were in Bethlehem and in all its districts, from two years old and under, according to the time which he had determined from the wise men,*** (Matthew 2:16).

Listen to the cry in the prophecy:

***"A voice was heard in Ramah,***

***Lamentation, weeping, and great mourning,***

***Rachel weeping for her children,***

***Refusing to be comforted,***

***Because they are no more,"*** (Matthew 2:18).

The above quotation is taken from Jeremiah 31:15, and it was stated nearly six hundred years prior to the event in Bethlehem. The original purpose of the prophecy was to describe the sorrowful departure of the ten tribes of Israel into captivity after the conquest of Jerusalem by Nebuzaradan, captain of the guard. All the captives were gathered in Ramah. Jeremiah himself was in chains. There the fate of those who had escaped the destruction of the city was decided at the will of the conqueror (Jeremiah 40:1). The nobles had been slain; the sons of the king had been murdered in his presence; the eyes of the king had been put out, and the people were then gathered at Ramah in chains. They were to start on their mournful journey as slaves to a cruel monarch, leaving behind them all that was dear to their lives. The sadness and grief of the scene is well expressed in the language of the prophet.

Rachel was the symbolic mother of Israel and was weeping over her sons. Did it not continue even to this destruction? Josephus, the great Jewish historian, did not include Herod's edict to destroy the baby boys in his account. This is not surprising in light of the many evil acts Herod committed. Nazareth was a small town, and the number of families with baby boys, two years of age and younger, would not have been many. The number is estimated to be between twenty and fifty. But one baby boy, slaughtered by Herod's evilness, is too many and certainly worthy of the pain expressed in this prophecy.

How can we cope with such an evil deed taking place in the midst of such a glorious scene as the birth of the Savior of the world, if we do not see it as an expression of the war taking place between two Kingdoms? Let it be clear this is not an isolated scene. Repeatedly in the unfolding story of the New Testament, the Satanic Kingdom raises its head. Satan appears with strength in the temptation of Jesus (Matthew 4:1-11). The devil did not send one of his angels to attempt the destruction of the Messianic influence. He came himself. It is a picture of the tremendous focus of the Satanic Kingdom on destroying Christ and all He proposes.

The devil recognized this was not one minor aspect of the movement of God in a small, unimportant section of the world. This is not the local church soft ball league losing one of its games and has no major significance to the satanic plan. What is happening in the person of Jesus is major, the heart, and the key focus of the plan of God. If Satan is ever going to get out of bed and exert his energy, he had better do it now against this one event. He dare not slack off concerning the birth and maturing of the Christ Child. He declares war on a high level!

There is a parallel between this emphasis and your life. Perhaps your life does not have the same prominence in the plan as did the life of Christ, BUT certainly the life of Christ indwelling you does. We must not ignore the attack of the demonic force to our personal lives. Should not Joseph and Mary consider the slaughter of the baby boys of Bethlehem and its surrounding districts as a direct result of satanic planning? Were they not in the midst of a major war where things were happening to them which were completely beyond their understanding? Were the events taking place in connection to their lives of monumental importance to the redemption of the world and very significant for eternity?

Herod the Great, in some ways, was the most forceful leader the Jews had ever experienced under Roman domination. He did many things which placed him in popular favor with the Jews. In the thirteenth year of his reign, during a severe famine, he spent all his resources and sold valuable works of art to import grain from Egypt for the relief of the people. Still more did he win popularity by rebuilding the temple on a magnificent scale, equal to that of Solomon; yet with such scrupulous care that it seemed a restoration rather than a new building.

But Herod had a self-induced insanity. There was an evil about the man which would make anyone wonder about demonic possession. At the beginning of his reign, with the help of Rome, he conquered Jerusalem (37 BC). He slew his leading adversaries, including the entire Sanhedrin with the exception of two members. There was a constant string of murders flowing through his family. He put to death Hyrcanus, his wife Mariamne's grandfather. Mariamne herself was murdered, though Herod declared her as the only woman he ever truly loved. The two sons from their relationship, Alexander and Aristobulus, were executed as well. Just four days before his death, Herod signed the order for the execution of his bitter accuser, his oldest son, Antipater. At last, seized with a fatal disease in the stomach and bowels, he became crueler than ever; he ordered that the nobles, whom he had called to him, should be slain immediately after his decease, that there might be no lack of mourners at his death. It was during this time period he ordered the destruction of the baby boys in Bethlehem. Is this not a man under demonic influence, maybe even demon possession?

War is declared! Two kingdoms clash in the unseen world, and there is a physical eruption and evidence of the upheaval. Did Joseph have any idea of the depth of that in which he was involved? Did Herod know he was simply a tool in the hands of demonic power? Would we not be overcome with total dismay, if we did not see these events in light of the spiritual war expressed by Paul? ***For we do not wrestle against flesh and blood, but against principalities, against powers, against the rulers of the darkness of this age, against spiritual hosts of wickedness in the heavenly places,*** (Ephesians 6:12).

How do we apply this to our lives? Could this give us insight into the events in our living? There is a major war in the spiritual realm. How do we live in light of the activities, seen and unseen, which are a part of this major war between the Kingdoms? Are we not in one Kingdom or the other? Perhaps the answers to all of these questions are given to us in the life of Joseph. Joseph had no greater insight into the battle of the unseen, spiritual world than you and I do. He was ignorant of the depth of both the danger and the long range influence of what was happening. There were things happening which were completely beyond his realm of knowledge and understanding. Is this not true with us? In every sense of the truth, Joseph was not in charge of anything happening to him. It was as if he was a stage upon which the war between the Kingdoms was playing out, yet, he played a vital role in the success of the Kingdom of God.

In the previous study (Matthew 2:13), Joseph did not initiate any of the action taking place. God was acting upon him, arousing him from sleep in the middle of the night. The instruction given by the Angel of the Lord was to ***take the young Child and His mother, flee to Egypt, and stay there until I bring you word; for Herod will seek the young Child to dcstroy Him."*** But this instruction is preceded with ***Arise.***

This is a verb form which is a participle, aorist, and passive. As a participle, it gives content to the main verbs and colors their action. It is passive, which means the subject is not responsible for the action of the verb form; he is being acted upon. Joseph did not set an alarm in order to awaken in the middle of the night. He did not plan an escape route, because he had spied on Herod the king and knew his evil plot. Joseph is totally ignorant of all the details of the massive war between the Kingdoms, but finds himself thrust in the middle of the conflict. The Angel of the Lord acts upon Joseph and calls upon him to respond.

I believe this is just as true for you and me! We can choose to live with strictly a physical view, where everything can be explained in terms of nature, or we can open our eyes to the conflict which is beyond us. The problem with doing this is the powerful responsibility to respond. It puts us into a war which we cannot control and certainly of which we have very little knowledge. It draws a very strong and straight line which demands our choice. Will we surrender to the Captain of the Host and respond to His direction?

I want to suggest three principles of this conflict as revealed in the life of Joseph and in our lives as well. First, the success of the redemption of the world hangs on one man being acted upon, and his response to that action. Is there any question this is true concerning Joseph? Joseph plays a key role in the drama which will affect not only all generations to come, but all generations in the past.

What would have happened if Joseph had not responded to the Angel of the Lord? God moved upon him in the midst of his moral difficulty (Matthew 1:20). He did not have to be obedient at this point. The Angel of the Lord again moves upon Joseph while they are in

Bethlehem (Matthew 2:13). He did not have to be obedient then either. God could have saved the day another way. He probably had many methods by which to save His Son. But this is a mute question, because Joseph did respond to the call of God.

I am absolutely committed to the truth of the Scriptures which constantly communicate God's creation to each one of us as special, calculated and purposeful! God did not create us and then discover how to involve us. He dreamed a great plan! In the middle of His dream was a tremendous need. You were created to fill that need. You were born out of the dreams of God! You play a key role in fulfilling the dream of God for all generations, both past and future. As Joseph did not know the details of his tremendous involvement in the dream of God, so you also lack that knowledge. But this does not mean it is not true. We know more about Joseph's involvement now than he did then. This will be true for you in the future as well. But the test for your life is this, will you respond to what you cannot see and fully know?

I am very frightened by the thought of getting distracted by minor issues of this life and missing the opportunities to respond to God. However, I have discovered you and I cannot miss His call. God will awaken us in whatever fashion necessary. He might choose to use an Angel of the Lord in the middle of the night, just as He did with Joseph. He will act upon you in clear terms, and then the choice is yours to respond to Him.

The second principle of truth is this: the success of saving one family hangs on one man being acted upon, and then his response to that action. Do you see how critical Joseph's response to the angel's action was to his family? Unless God intervened another way, the fate of the baby boys two years old and under, would have been the fate of the Messiah if Joseph had not responded. Think of what it would have been like for Joseph to have had to live with the knowledge that God had spoken to him and he did not respond. A life time of grief and guilt beyond degree would have been upon him. The entire family, and future of that family, was at stake.

I am dedicated to the Biblical idea that your family is as important to God as were His dreams for Joseph's family. Just as He came in the night hour for Joseph, so He will come for you. You cannot for one moment consider that you are one in the crowd, unnoticed by God. Hey Dad, God speaks to you as clearly as He did to Joseph. You do not understand the deep details of the revelation any more than Joseph did, but the call to respond is still there. The same can be said about you, Mom. The war is raging, and like it or not, your family is in the middle.

The success of saving one man hangs on his being acted upon and responding to that action. This is the third principle. The eternal destiny of both Joseph and Herod hangs in the balance of their responses. These two men will be viewed by history, and the unfolding plan of redemption is determined in this passage. Their lives are the stage for the action of the war of the ages.

Joseph did not choose, or volunteer, to play this key role in the redemption process. He is not qualified by his education, financial ability or leadership position. He has little knowledge of what is happening, and what part it will have on his personal redemption. Maybe his response to the angel at the night hour is a response which will secure his personal redemption. His response is not for his personal redemption, but he is playing a key role in bringing about that redemption.

The picture of Herod is the same here. This man is doing everything he can to destroy his personal redemption. The Christ Child is the only chance he has in light of the evil which lurks within him. If he knew the truth, he would protect and foster the Christ Child, for Herod's fate is sealed in Him.

This is true for you also. Is not your life the stage of action through which the redemption of your own soul is going to pass? Your response is the key to the success of that redemption. I have seen it in the lives of senior adults. They set before me and earnestly speak of revival, and how they long for the "good old days" when people got blessed and conviction fell upon sinners. Yet, that same group sits in the back pews and does not respond to the Angel of the Lord who comes to them repeatedly. They give no expression to the presence of the Lord, and no response to the truth, by kneeling at an altar of prayer. Their lack of response is the death of the very revival for which they say they long.

Our lives are the stage upon which God fights the redemptive battle. It affects our world, our families and our personal lives. It is not about knowing the details, only the call. Will you respond?

# Matthew 2:13

## Sin at Christmas

We are studying the four Christmas narratives. Matthew uses them to paint vivid pictures through word studies and contrasts. We see God's involvement through the particular elements Matthew interjects into the narratives. Prophecy is one of these elements, which reveals God's long range involvement. The appearance of the Angel of the Lord reveals the immediate concern of God.

A major war is raging. It is a time when spiritual forces raise to their full height. The Kingdom of God and the Kingdom of Satan battle on the stage of this world for the souls of man. Each Kingdom uses the full extent of measures available. The battle seems to focus on two men. Others are involved and affect the war, but the heat of the battle seems to display itself in Joseph and King Herod. The drama is overwhelming. How can something so wide spread, as to cover all eternity, affecting every past and future generation, take place in a small section of the world through the life of an obscure peasant man?

Matthew writes the Christmas story through the person of Joseph. His involvement is the central focus of the narratives. He seems to know very little of his importance in the unfolding redemption of the world, and yet, he is the symbol of surrender and submission to the interaction of God upon his life. Even at the outset we are told, he is ***a just man,*** (Matthew 1:19).

The counterpart to Joseph is Herod. All evil seems to reside in him. He is the total expression of the Kingdom of Satan. As Joseph is spokesman for all that is good, Herod is the symbol of all that is evil. Joseph is the extended hand of God to accomplish the birth and safety of the Redeemer, and Herod is the instrument of the devil to do all that can be done to prevent it. Both are willing instruments, yet neither knows the depth of their participation.

In a previous study we described some of the evil deeds that come from Herod's hand. These deeds illustrate a complete disregard for all life except his. At the beginning of his reign in Judea, he had all the members of the Sanhedrin murdered except for two. There was a constant string of murders taking place among his family members as Herod eliminated any one he perceived as a threat. It was a dangerous thing to be born a son of Herod the Great. These other crimes were so horrifying in comparison, Josephus, the Jewish historian of that day, does not mention the slaughter of the baby boys of Bethlehem and its surrounding districts.

The killing of the baby boys was horrific, but Matthew writes of something else in this narrative that we must not miss. Matthew points out the deeds of sin Herod committed, but he strongly highlights the very nature of sin which dominated Herod. Through the accumulation of his deeds, and his interaction with the wise men, we quickly see the depth of evil which overpowers the man. We again discover the two fold nature of sin in our lives. It is internal and external, deed and nature, attitude and action, doing and being.

The Angel of the Lord recognizes this as he warns Joseph in the night hour. The Angel announces to Joseph, ***"Arise, take the young Child and His mother, flee to Egypt, and stay there until I bring you word; for Herod will seek the young Child to destroy Him,"*** (Matthew 2:13). In the original language of the Scriptures, the angel uses three verbs to describe Herod. These are an expression of what Herod will do, for this always comes from being. But the intent of the words used paint a deeper picture. They show us what Herod is!

## Motive
## Matthew 2:13

The first word used by the angel is translated ***will.*** It has to do with intent. It means Herod's action will be the result of no momentary emotion, but of premeditation. It highlights the idea of certainty, compulsion or necessity, to be certain to act, and in addition. We see this in the grammar of the Greek verb. It is a present, active, indicative verb. It is present tense in Herod's life. This is not what he once was, or what he is going to become; this is what he is now. This is an active verb, which tells you the subject is responsible for the action of the verb. Herod is not being acted upon or responding, but is acting out of his own nature. It is indicative, which reminds us it is a simple statement of fact. It could not be any other way because of the nature within Herod.

I find this Greek word fascinating. It occurs one hundred and ten times in the New Testament. In the King James Version there are seventy-four translations of the Greek word. It is translated ***shall*** twenty-five times, ***should*** twenty times, ***would*** nine times, ***to come*** nine times, ***will*** seven times, and ***things to come*** four times. That leaves thirty-six times the word is used in the Greek. Three of those times the word is not translated at all, and miscellaneous words are used in the other thirty-three translations.

Let me quote one of the verses from Matthew. ***But when he saw many of the Pharisees and Sadducees coming to his baptism, he said to them, "Brood of vipers! Who warned you to flee from the wrath to come?"*** (Matthew 3:7). This is one of the nine times it is translated ***to come***. It has the idea of absolute certainty. This is the same Greek word the angel uses concerning Herod. Joseph is not to flee to Egypt just in case Herod might decide to do something to destroy the Christ Child. It is absolutely certain the Christ Child is in danger, and it is coming from the nature which dominates and drives King Herod.

Herod's will is under the domination of predisposition. Herod has yielded to it until he has become its slave. The power of the predisposition is strongly influencing him; he has become dominated and controlled by it. We quickly see the problem is far beyond a deed done. Herod did not lack information; therefore he made a wrong choice in his action. The destruction of the boys is not the result of intending to do the right thing, but making a mistake due to wrong counsel. Herod's action is predetermined by the yielding of his inner will to the self-centered carnal mind which now controls him.

It is important to understand that we are not born this way. We believe at birth each person contains the carnal nature, but it gains control of us only when we yield to the self-centered carnal mind. No one is made to become, or begins as, the slave to the selfish disposition. It is a warning to us of what we can become. To some degree, has it not happened to all of us? Have we not yielded to it? Are we not driven by our own selfish wills? Do we not protect our private turf? Do we not want to cry out with Paul when he said, ***"O wretched man that I am! Who will deliver me from this body of death?"*** (Romans 7:24).

## Movement
## Matthew 2:13

***Seek*** is the second verb spoken by the angel concerning Herod. This word in the Greek language also has something to say to us. It is used one hundred twenty times in the New Testament. Most often the subject of this verb has to do with man. When one views the use of this word only in religious references, it is used to state man's general philosophical search or quest. Paul relates this concept in his writings, ***For Jews request a sign, and Greeks seek after wisdom;*** (1 Corinthians 1:22). In speaking to the men of Athens, Paul refers to their concept "To the Unknown God." He spoke of this God as the creator who made man ***so that they should seek the Lord, in the hope that they might grope for Him and find Him, though He is not far from each one of us;*** (Acts 17:27). In the instructions in the Sermon on the Mount, Jesus spoke of worry concerning something to eat, drink or wear. ***"For after all these things the Gentiles seek,"*** (Matthew 6:32). However, Christians are to ***". . . seek first the kingdom of God and***

***His righteousness, and all these things shall be added to you,"*** (Matthew 6:33).

That which takes place in Herod's life is much more than just the seeking of an object. The search to destroy the Christ Child comes from a deep internal spiritual realm. His religious and spiritual life is being exposed in this search. His philosophical search, or quest for purpose, meaning, and security for life, is found in his seeking. Do you sense the desperation of the search? He will go to whatever extent necessary to find the answers he wants for his own life. He will do whatever he has to do to get what he wants, and he will remove whatever is in his way. His search is intense!

Herod is on a quest to find the Christ Child. He has no idea that this Child is the only one who can bring him fulfillment. The motive of his search is to destroy the baby. He cannot lose His position to this new King. Though Herod is seeking, just as the wise men are, his motive is destruction. The Christ Child is the answer for his life, but this new King cannot fulfill Herod's life because Herod is in control. Do you see the huge conflict present within him? He is driven to search, only the very manner in which he searches destroys any finding.

This is always the deception of self-centered carnality. It enslaves us and drives us, only to leave us empty and unfulfilled. The young man desires fulfillment in marriage. He wants love, home and companionship. But his self-centered carnality drives him to the selfish abuse of his mate. The home becomes the stage of battle and conflict, and the marriage is quickly destroyed. He loses everything. The search is proper, but the motive becomes dominated by self-centered carnality. Everything is lost.

The local church, the body of Christ, wants love, fellowship, and the experience of God in their midst. Each member is searching for this fulfillment. Organization is established to help secure the involvement of each person in these endeavors. Competition, envy, and power struggles quickly become the center of the search. Self-centered carnality raises its ugly head. In an attempt to secure love, fellowship, and the experience of God, selfish motives arise and destroy the body. The search is proper, but the motive becomes dominated by self-centered carnality. Everything is lost.

This picture can be drawn repeatedly. The search is present. Nothing is wrong with the seeking. God put a common drive within us, but we become dominated by our own self-centered carnality. It does not have to be this way, but that is how we become. We do not begin with this domination, but it develops as we yield to it. We become enslaved. Who knows the depth of evil of which we are capable?

## Motif

## Matthew 2:13

There is great strength in the statement of the angel, ***"For Herod will seek the young Child to destroy Him,"*** (Matthew 2:13). The intent is not to keep the Christ Child from being King, not to injure Him, not to enslave Him, not to discredit Him, but ***to destroy Him.*** The Greek word means to put out of the way entirely, abolish, put an end to, or ruin.

We live in a more tolerant age. Each person has the right to express themselves as long as it does not infringe upon the rights of others. Your sexual preference is your personal choice. We will tolerate your choice and think nothing less of you for it. While this may be the attempt of people in our day, it is an allusion. The end result is always and consistently ***to destroy Him.*** It simply does not matter how broad we may paint the picture, the final decision is ***to destroy Him.*** Herod the king gathered the wise men together in a secret meeting. He broadly stated his desire to find the Christ Child for the purpose of worship, but it was deception. He has one clear goal, ***to destroy Him.***

Let it be clearly known to everyone, this is always the end result of self-centered carnality. The battle between the Kingdoms is always a fight to the death. Total destruction can only be the final outcome. Self-centered carnality cannot, and will not, tolerate Christ. The very nature of who Christ is so threatens the existence of carnality, it must be eliminated. There is no chance of tolerating, utilizing, taming, controlling or mixing self-centered carnality with Christ.

This is why holiness has always sounded the radical note of "crucifixion." We must come to death. Self-centered carnality so masters us, the only deliverance is for our self-centeredness to be crucified. It is out of control. We have no power over it. It is woven into the story lines of the third and fourth narratives. The Christ Child is protected in Egypt until Herod dies (Matthew 2:19). Upon Herod's death, the Christ Child's presence is restored to the land of Israel.

Will you die that He might live in you? The patterns of self-centered control have become so strong; you must take sides with Christ against yourself. It is your only hope. You can continue on to destruction as Herod did, or you can accept the hope provided for you. Search carefully, with the help of Christ, for every evidence of self-centered carnality. Do not leave any remnant of it behind. If you do, you have spelled ultimate destruction for yourself.

# Matthew 2:15

# The Safety of Egypt

Matthew presents the material of his first four chapters in a remarkable way. It is clear in its purpose and startling enough to demand our attention. He does this from the genealogy (Matthew 1:1), through to the Sermon on the Mount (Matthew 5, 6 and 7). He centers almost every paragraph on at least one text in the Old Testament, explaining some event in the life of Jesus from the Scriptures.

Matthew commonly uses the word ***fulfilled*** in the four narratives of the Christmas story (Matthew 1:22; 2:15, 17 and 23). Each usage is connected to a prophecy of the Old Testament coming to pass. The actual definition of the Greek word translated ***fulfilled*** is "to complete, to render full, and to fill up." In some cases it means "to fill up to the top" (Luke 3:5). It contains the idea "to carry through to the end, to accomplish, carry out" (Luke 7:1).

God has a dream He will accomplish or fulfill. We do not know the details, nor do we know the end result. It is a dream which is beyond our knowledge. But our knowledge, in comparison to what the Old

Testament prophets knew, has been greatly expanded. The Old Testament prophets had no idea of the magnitude of their prophecies. In comparison to the greatness of the plan, we are in the same position. We are like an Old Testament prophet who holds the sacrificial lamb, and wonders what the full extent of the sacrifice might be. It is beyond our investigation to this point, but God is expanding our knowledge. This is the adventure of the Christian experience.

The expansion of God's plan in these days is on an accelerated rate. In the coming of Christ, and the fullness of the Spirit of Christ within us, we reach another stage in the rocket of revelation. God is unfolding His plan in rapid progression. He has placed grace upon grace, which brings a depth to our understanding of His Word. Where will all of this take place? Perhaps all of heaven will be a continual unfolding of the revelation of God!

The expanding plan of God in our lives is a reality. At the same time, it is a reality that things are being ***fulfilled.*** The definition of the word is "to complete, to render full, and to fill up." The indication of this verse (Matthew 2:15), is that the escape into Egypt, the slaughter of baby boys, and the following return of Christ to Egypt at Herod's death, all play a part in the filling up, completing or rendering full the plan of God.

Let be boldly state that we do not believe God caused baby boys to be killed in order to fulfill His plan. If we wanted to blame someone for this evil act, it would not be God. Satan, in his evil ways, is always the instigator of such things. This simply shows us how great God is! He has calculated into His plan every evil plot of the devil. He has utilized it for His own glory and to fulfill His plan. He redeems the activity so sufficiently; it is as if He has planned it Himself.

Perhaps your response to this is like mine in the beginning. I could not reconcile the slaughter of baby boys, two years of age and younger, with the completion of the plan of God. It was too horrible, senseless and evil. I was repulsed by it, because I had forgotten the basic principle of the Gospel. Matthew presents the Gospel of the cross style. "Life" is in the midst of "death." The way to "win" is to "lose." The way "up" is "down." The way "in" is "out." This is the principle of the cross style. When redemption takes place, the principle of the cross is in operation.

Please do not think we are reading something into this event. Matthew makes a bold statement, doing so by the means of prophecy. The completion of the prophecy is the filling up of the dreams of God. The Old Testament statement is very short; it hardly seems like a prophecy. Matthew writes, ***that it might be fulfilled which was spoken by the Lord through the prophet, saying, "Out of Egypt I called My Son,"*** (Matthew 2:15).

This quotation is taken from Hosea (11:1). Think about the context of the statement. God's heart is broken over Israel once again. He is reaching out in redemptive love. In a wild plan to communicate this love, He decides to use Hosea. The prophet of God is instructed by God.

> ***"Go, take yourself a wife of harlotry***
> ***And children of harlotry,***
> ***For the land has committed great harlotry***
> ***By departing from the Lord,"*** (Hosea 1:2).

God shows a desperate means of action. In obedience, Hosea marries a prostitute by the name of Gomer. Please understand this was not a token obedience. He genuinely loved her. They had three children, each named by God. They had special significance in the message which was to be delivered to Israel.

But the ways of prostitution were very strong in Gomer. She soon returned to her old life style. Hosea was broken hearted and devastated. It was at that moment God delivered His message to the heart of Hosea. God communicated to Hosea that the way he felt about Gomer was the exact way God felt about Israel. Now Hosea knew how God felt towards His people. The message came clearer still as God said, ***"Go again, love a woman who is loved by a lover and is committing adultery, just like the love of the Lord for the children of Israel, who look to other gods and love the raisin cakes of the pagans,"*** (Hosea 3:1). Hosea immediately obeyed. He found Gomer as she was about to be sold on the auction block as a slave. She was sick, abused and used. He bought her back, only paying a couple of dollars and eight bushels of barley. Hosea nursed her back to health with his love.

Against this personal background, Hosea was able to give an adequate prophecy to Israel. The tears of God flowed down his cheeks, and the voice of God sounded through his lips as he pleaded with Israel to return to God.

How do you feel about this story? At first I was repulsed by it. Why would anyone want to do such a thing? But again, the answer is found in the principle of the cross style. How does redemption come? Someone gives themselves away. Someone has a broken heart and loves so much they pay the price at the auction block. Redemption is always surrounded by this atmosphere. God extended His hand of redemption to Israel through the prophet Hosea.

Hosea was a prophet with a broken heart, pleading with Israel. ***"Out of Egypt I called My Son,"*** (Matthew 2:15). This is a statement from God, spoken through the prophet Hosea. Now Matthew brings it to light in this narrative of the Christmas story. He goes back seven hundred years to Hosea, who goes back seven hundred years to another event involving Egypt. The details of the story fill many pages.

Joseph was the favorite of his father, Jacob (Genesis 37:3-4). He was the object of jealousy for his brothers. Jacob gave his favorite son a coat of many colors. Joseph told his brothers his dreams, which told how he would someday rule over them. This only drove them to hate him more. One day the brothers found the opportunity to kill him, but Reuben saved Joseph's life by insisting they sell him to the Midianite traders who would take him to Egypt. The evil brothers took Joseph's coat, tore it, and poured the blood of an animal on it. They gave the coat to their father, telling him that Joseph was dead.

Joseph was sold as a slave to Potiphar, an officer of Pharaoh, and a captain of the guard in Egypt (Genesis 37:36). Joseph refused to sexually compromise to the temptations of Potiphar's wife, which consequently landed him in prison. Here his ability to interpret dreams through the power of God became known. He was eventually summoned to interpret the dreams of Pharaoh. He interpreted Pharaoh's dream with the message of seven years of plenty and seven years of famine (Genesis 41). Pharaoh immediately put Joseph in charge of the preparation for the time of famine. Joseph became so powerful he was put next in authority to Pharaoh himself.

During the famine, Joseph's brothers found themselves in great need. Their father, Jacob, sent them to Egypt to purchase grain (Genesis 42). There are many details to this story, but the ultimate outcome was reconciliation between Joseph and his family. Here is the encounter of Joseph and his brothers when Joseph reveals who he is: ***"Please come near to me." So they came near. Then he said: "I am Joseph your brother, whom you sold into Egypt. But now, do not therefore be grieved or angry with yourselves because you sold me here; for God sent me before you to preserve life . . . And God sent me before you to preserve a posterity for you in the earth, and to save your lives by a great deliverance,"*** (Genesis 45:4-7).

Joseph's entire family eventually moved to Egypt. Jacob, the father, passed away. The brothers were afraid with their father gone, Joseph would turn on them in hatred. His brothers fell down at his feet and said, ***"Behold, we are your servants,"*** (Genesis 50:18). In tears, Joseph responded to his brothers, saying, ***"Do not be afraid, for am I in the place of God? But as for you, you meant evil against me; but God meant it for good, in order to bring it about as it is this day, to save many people alive,"*** (Genesis 50:19-20).

How do you respond emotionally to this story? Do you shift back and forth as I do? I see the hatred, jealousy, and sinfulness of the brothers, and I want to cry out for judgment and punishment. I see the ***fulfilled*** plan of God and want to rejoice. The chosen family was saved through the means of Egypt. God was going to call His son, Israel, out of Egypt in order to redeem the world. How does redemption come? Someone gives themselves away. Someone has a broken heart and loves so much they are willing to pay the price. Redemption is always surrounded by the atmosphere of the cross. The brothers of Joseph, without knowing it, were completing the dreams of God for the world. God used all of the evil, which was intended to ruin and destroy the life of Joseph, to fill up His redemptive plan.

The terrible treatment and horrible evil which came to Joseph was simply filling up the dreams of God to redeem the world. The tragic events which surrounded the marriage of Hosea and brought such heartache to his home, were simply filling up the dreams of God to redeem the world. The slaughter of baby boys, two years of age and under, did not catch God by surprise. God calculated it all into His plan. This, too, would help fill up, render full, and complete the dream of God to redeem the world.

In case you might feel like God is taking unfair advantage of the lives of people, might I remind you of the unfolding story in the Book of Matthew. God will soon allow His Son to come to death for the redemption of the world. The crucifixion event, with all of its surrounding evils, will render full and complete the dream of God to redeem a world. The Jews in all of their black mailing of Pilate, Pilate in all of his cowardice, Rome with all of her cheap treatment of life, will all play a part in the ***fulfilled*** plan of God.

Dose this not scream at you and I about our lives? Why would God allow this to happen to me? How can the abuse of my childhood ever be looked upon as having any value? The evil of my own activities, which have brought so much pain to my life and the lives of others, is horrible in my sight. So it should be! How can I ever view it as filling up, rendering complete, the dreams of God? It is the principle of the cross. You must grasp the heart of the Kingdom of God. It is in the midst of death, we find life. In the midst of brokenness, we experience wholeness. It is the in the middle of complete loss, we find everything. What a Kingdom!

# Matthew 2:16

## Better to be a Hog than a Son

There is a quotation which appears in many commentaries regarding the slaughter of the baby boys at Christmas. It is so common, you are forced to consider it carefully. Macrobius lived during the conclusion of the fourth century. He reported a statement made by Augustus, the emperor of Rome. Apparently he heard about the slaughtering of the baby boys, two years of age and under, and Herod's murder of his own son at the same time. Augustus reportedly said, "It is better to be Herod's pig than his son." In the Greek language, there is a word play between "pig" and "son." There is only one letter difference between them. He was making a joke.

Herod was professing Judaism. While he was an Edomite, he was at least half Jew. He professed Judaism in an attempt to have a better relationship with those over whom he ruled. Herod has knowledge of Judaism. It is interesting that he knew exactly how to find out where the Messiah was to be born. He immediately called on the chief priests and scribes (Matthew 2:4). Herod knew the Scriptures would reveal the answer. No doubt he did enough religious observance to be accepted by the leadership.

However, there was certainly no heart in his religion. It was one of convenience and self-promotion, yet, it was his profession. As a professing Jew, he could not kill swine, or have anything to do with their flesh. Therefore, pigs were safe from Herod, but sons were not, whether they were his own or from Bethlehem and its surrounding districts. Did the Jewish faith take a lesser stand on murder than they did on the defilement of swine?

This is not the first, or the last time, this concept has arisen. Do not become encumbered with the details, but focus on the concept. It is easy to be strong in one aspect of our faith, because it is convenient or helpful to what we want, while other points of what we say we believe are easily set aside. Far too often our "pigs are safer than our sons." One can find numerous occurrences in the Scriptures where this takes place. Matthew highlights this concept repeatedly.

There is an intriguing story in the Galilean ministry of Jesus (Matthew 8:28-34). Jesus had fallen asleep in the boat as He and the disciples were crossing the Sea of Galilee. A storm arose suddenly, tossing the boat about with strong waves, and the disciples were panic stricken. In their fear, they awoke Jesus. After questioning the disciples as to why they were so fearful, Jesus rebuked the storm and ordered the sea to grow calm. The storm had taken them off course, and they ended up in the country of the Gergesenes or Gadarenes. The people in this land were Israelites from the tribe of Gad.

Their history is significant to this story. Before the conquering of the Promised Land, Israel had settled on the far side of the Jordan River.

When it came time to march into Canaan and possess the land, the tribe of Gad did not want to go. They preferred to settle right where they were. There is a significant spiritual lesson to be learned from this desire alone. They wanted to stop short of all that God had promised them. They were content with a partial fulfillment of the journey and the dream. They had grown content with where they were. Moses gave them permission to do this on one condition. Their young men were required to go with the rest of the tribes of Israel and fight the battles necessary to conquer Canaan land (Numbers 32).

They had now lived on the wrong side of the Jordan River for hundreds of years. As Jews, they had backslidden to the position where the chief income was raising pigs. Their herd numbered at least two thousand, in the event which occurs. Matthew records Jesus' encounter with two demon-possessed men. When Jesus cast the demons out of the two men, the demons asked Jesus if He would allow them to enter the swine. When the demons entered the pigs, ***the whole herd of swine ran violently down the steep place into the sea, and perished in the water,*** (Matthew 8:32). Those who tended the herd immediately ran into the city and told the owners of the swine what had happened. Evidently all of the town's people had ownership of the herd for ***behold, the whole city came out to meet Jesus. And when they saw Him, they begged Him to depart from their region,*** (Matthew 8:34).

Jesus delivered two men from demons, made them whole, and restored them to their families. But in doing so, He destroyed the town's herd of pigs, thus destroying their economy. This made the town very angry. The pigs and the financial benefit they had to the city were far more important to these people. How easy it is to fall into this trap. Our faith tells us people are most important. Our mission statement is focused on evangelism and the growth of the Kingdom of God. BUT – BUT – as with one church, we become totally upset with a woman who brings fifteen children from the community to the revival services. They track mud on the carpet in the entrance of the church. In another church, we see the enthusiasm of the young married couples dampened by criticism of their more contemporary style of worship, even though they are reaching out to the lost. Many churches are far more concerned with maintaining their comfortable positions than embracing the poor and homeless who are sleeping on their church steps.

Do you realize how easy it is to slide into this way of thinking? Our hogs become of greater value than our sons. Our careers, from which we receive our self-worth, become of higher value to us than our families. But the bottom line is Christ Himself. We lose sight of Him as we are distracted into the thousands of things which demand our time. We begin to protect our hogs instead of our sons.

There is another occasion when this concept appears in Matthew. The scribes and Pharisees come to Galilee, all the way from Jerusalem. It is a trip of eighty to one hundred miles. Their chief concern is ***"Why do your disciples transgress the tradition of the elders? For they do not wash their hands when they eat bread,"*** (Matthew 15:2). Their concern was not germs from dirty hands, but their prejudice concerning Gentiles. Their traditions dictated that anything which had been touched by a Gentile would defile a Jew upon contact. Blowing dust had no doubt touched the Gentiles. Before a Jew could eat, he had to ceremonially wash his hands. If he did not, the food or drink which he consumed would defile him inwardly, thus their concern that the disciples were not washing their hands.

Jesus confronts them boldly because they care more about their laws concerning their hogs than they care about their sons. ***He answered and said to them, "Why do you also transgress the commandment of God because of your tradition?"*** (Matthew 15:3). He quotes to them the commandment about the honor they are to have for their father and mother. But they twist that commandment, through the means of their tradition, to escape the financial obligation they have toward their parents. They are just like Herod. In their case, it is better to be their hog than it is to be their parents. They worry so about what is going into their mouths, which might defile them, that they are completely overlook what comes out of their mouths. Their words reveal their hearts. To them, tradition has become of greater value than heart purity. They value their hogs much more than they do their sons.

At the close of His ministry, Jesus preaches a powerful sermon. It is His final public pronouncement. The first of the sermon appears to be heated and filled with anger. However, as you read the entire sermon in light of its closure, you view it differently. Jesus is broken hearted. He cries out, ***"O Jerusalem, Jerusalem, the one who kills the prophets and stones those who are sent to her! How often I wanted to gather your children together, as a hen gathers her chicks under her wings, but you were not willing!"*** (Matthew 23:37). Do you feel His Spirit and the deep anguish over how lost they are?

The first of Christ's sermon pronounces the "seven woes" to the scribes and the Pharisees. In one of these woes, Jesus highlights the concept we are talking about. It is much better to be their hog than their son. These religious people are so concerned about such minor, legalistic issues that they miss what really matters. The Pharisees are very serious about paying their tithes, one tenth of everything they possess. In every Pharisee's back yard is an herb garden. Herbs are grown in small plants, and each herb is about the size of your little finger. In their legalistic manner of paying their tithes, they would take a knife and cut off ten percent of the herb. Jesus tells them, ***"Woe to you, scribes and Pharisees, hypocrites! For you pay tithe of mint and anise and cummin, and have neglected the weightier matters of the law: justice and mercy and faith. These you ought to have done, without leaving the others undone,"*** (Matthew 23:23).

I am afraid we repeat these kinds of actions hundreds of times in our modern day lives. My father was a pastor, and in one of the towns where we lived was a town drunk. My father was out calling one day, and he dropped in on this man. During their conversation, this man readily admitted that he swore too much, drank too much, beat his wife, and that he never came to church. When my father felt it was about time to leave, he prayed for the man. As he was leaving, the town drunk followed my father out of the house, onto the porch, while saying, "You are right preacher! I need to get right with Jesus and come to church. But I want you to know, I never eat meat on Friday!" He was taking care of his hogs, but killing his sons. This kind of thing is difficult to recognize in our personal lives. Jesus often said, ***"Blind guides, who strain out a gnat and swallow a camel!"*** (Matthew 23:24).

It is not hard to see the problem of the Pharisees. Their concern was their outward appearance. They focused on their position, their ratings among the people, and how they compared to others. It was always an issue of power and finances. Perhaps it is the same with us. We compare ourselves against others with the measuring stick of our authority and how much money we have. Do the issues over which we are concerned focus on intimacy with God? Is it about getting closer to His heart? Do our concerns spill from a passion to know Him, and do we find our lives flowing from Him? If we cannot answer "yes" to these questions, then we are protecting our pigs and killing our sons. Jesus said it plainly, ***"Woe to you, scribes and Pharisees, hypocrites! For you cleanse the outside of the cup and dish, but inside they are full of extortion and self-indulgence,"*** (Matthew 23:25).

We can see the same concept appearing in the life of Pilate. He was under heavy pressure during the trial of Jesus. The leaders of Israel were blackmailing him. His wife was sending him notes to leave this Jesus alone. Caesar was going to get involved if Pilate did not handle this situation carefully. On top of all this, there were strong religious ramifications to what was taking place in this trial of Jesus. Pilate's religious beliefs told him that there were many gods he might worship; it was very likely some of them, at times, would appear on earth. One never knew when he would actually be dealing with "a god." Jesus had admitted to Pilate that He was a King. But Jesus assured Pilate, ***"My kingdom is not of this world. If My kingdom were of this world, My servants would fight, so that I should not be delivered to the Jews, but now My kingdom is not from here,"*** (John 18:36). This statement from Jesus must have shaken Pilate to the depths of his soul. Could he be confronting a god? What is he to do?

Pilate fails miserably at every point. We clearly see his compromise, and there is no way to excuse it. He tries every conceivable way to escape his responsibility. He appears as a little child, pushed around by the bullies of his day. His actions leave him with no possibility of holding his head high. Jesus is crucified, and a sign is placed on the cross. It states, ***"This is Jesus the King of the Jews,"*** (Matthew 27:37).

Pilate infuriates the Jews again. They are very upset by this sign. They come to Pilate and demand a re-writing of the sign. They cry out, ***"Do not write, 'The King of the Jews,' but, "He said, 'I am the King of the Jews,'"*** (John 19:21). While Pilate had comprised on every issue of the past several hours, he refused to give in on this point. He squared his shoulders and would not allow the Jews to push him any further. He said, ***"What I have written, I have written,"*** (John 19:22). Though Pilate has compromised on the major issues in the Jews' treatment of Jesus, on this minor issue, he draws a line and stands firm. He killed his sons, but he would not touch his hogs.

I will leave the application to your life in the hands of you and the Holy Spirit. I simply know that the evangelical church has never devoted more money to religion. We have never had better buildings, more adequate education, and more printed material than we have now. Yet, the divorce rate within the church is slightly higher than it is outside the church. In regard to premarital sex, there is no difference between the teens in the church and those outside the church. Somewhere we have missed the focus. Our hogs seem to be more important to us than our sons. God forgive us!

# Matthew 2:16

# Living Out of Anger

There is an incredible book which I have recently read. It is **<u>The Spiritual Guide</u>** by Michael Molinas. He was a fascinating person of the sixteen hundreds. If the church had not interfered with Mr. Molinas, he would have most likely been the leader of the Protestant Reformation before Martin Luther. His whole emphasis was to lead people into an intimate relationship with Christ. It was not that he was against counting beads or prayer books, but they were unnecessary in his opinion. Perhaps for the beginner these tools could aid a person's communion with God, but for the open hearted individual there was an intimate communication far beyond ceremonies.

The people of the church embraced his teachings. They began a massive reformation. The leaders of the church councils also proclaimed their approval. After examining his teachings, they found no heresy, or even disagreement. But this did not last long. Eventually they found reason to lie, accuse and finally remove Michael Molinas as a teacher.

Was it a theological disagreement? The one who offers a brief view of Molinas' life as an addition to the book declares, "NO!"

Molinas simply stated that divisions and upheavals seldom, if ever, take place in the church because of theological differences. However, they are always offered as the excuse. Rather they are a product of grabbing for power and money within the organization. The beginning reformation of Molinas was the reducing of bead sales and discounting the unquestioned authority of the priests. If allowed to continue, he would have altered the entire church system. The leaders could not let this happen. They felt compelled to do whatever necessary to keep the present power system in place. Thus, Michael Molinas found himself in exile for the rest of his life. All of his writings were destroyed except for the book to which I have made mention.

You can see this pattern in the life of Christ. Was it the miracles Jesus did that upset the leaders of Israel? Were they disturbed by the large multitudes repenting and becoming better Israelites? No! They were upset by the constant insistence of Jesus that the oral traditions were not as valuable as the laws of God. He consistently proposed the idea that what is inside of man is more significant than his outward appearance. The final blow came when Jesus declared the dismissal of the sacrificial system, because He was the fulfillment of it all. This would greatly revolutionize the Jewish system, and the financial and personal power of the leaders would be diminished. They must crucify Jesus.

We see this played out in the life of King Herod. The list of dead bodies as a result of Herod's commands, are lying everywhere. Many of them are members of his family. His pride and personal security drive him to protect and guard his position and authority. Can you imagine the turmoil within him when he becomes aware of the new born King of the Jews? Not only can he not find the new born King, but the wise men have deceived him. ***"Then Herod, when he saw that he was deceived by the wise men, was exceedingly angry; and he sent forth and put to death all the male children who were in Bethlehem and in all its districts, from two years old and under, according to the time which he had determined from the wise men,*** (Matthew 2:16).

The Greek word translated ***deceived*** expresses the idea of mocking. It is the same word which expresses the actions and words of those around the cross of Christ (Matthew 20:19; 27:41; Mark 15:20; Luke 22:63; 23:11). The root meaning of the word is "to play like a child." It is focused on making sport of or jesting. Can you see how this threatened Herod's authority?

What is the natural result of this? It is anger. We want to focus on the anger spoken of in this verse. The Greek word is a strong word, which is made even stronger by the addition of another word, which is translated ***exceedingly.*** It means to be extremely angry, even to the point of being in a rage. I realize there are others kinds of anger. Jesus expresses anger when He cleanses the temple (Matthew 21:12). We are going to limit our discussion to the kind of anger Matthew reveals as coming from the life of Herod. We will call it "rage."

I have heard of rage my entire life. In the college scene, the study of psychology highlights rage as the cause of many major problems in life. There are people who live in rage. They are not always throwing fits of anger, or expressing it the way King Herod did, but still rage dominates their lives. We have so many home problems, dysfunctional families, abusive situations, we have become dominated by rage, and we do not recognize it.

When I was a young teen, my younger brother did something to me, which made me very angry. I will never forget the emotion that erupted from me at that moment. I think it would be right to call it rage. I was totally out of control. I reached out, grabbed a small board, and threw it at him as he ran away. I put all my weight behind propelling that board. If it had hit him, as I intended, it probably would have killed him. What would that have meant to my family, to my brother, and to my own life? It was rage. Hey, I was in the same category as King Herod. What was the difference between him and me? I soon recognized there would be terrible consequences as a result of such rage. King Herd did as he pleased, but I was going to take a different course. I curbed the expression of my rage, but it affected my attitudes, actions and relationships.

I am not simply interested in recognizing rage in my life. I do not want to just deal with it. I want to know where it comes from and what creates it!

## Anti-Truth

Rage is a product of anti-truth, and there is something unreal about it. At the heart of all rage is untruth. If you know the truth and embrace it, there will be no anger. This is not the only time we find rage in Herod. This is the pattern of his life! He lives in anger. At the root of it all is untruth. This automatically makes the devil the cause of this kind of anger. Jesus said of the devil, ***"You are of your father the devil, and the desires of your father you want to do. He was a murderer from***

***the beginning, and does not stand in truth, because there is no truth in him. When he speaks a lie, he speaks from his own resources, for he is a liar and the father of it,"*** (John 8:44).

If you seek and embrace the truth, you will not be angry. We see it plainly in the life of Herod. He has no clue as to what is happening. Matthew expresses this by giving us Herod's view of what the wise men are doing. He thinks they are playing him as a fool! He thinks they are tricking him, and that brings his anger to a boiling point. No one is going to do this to him. The reason he thinks like this is because this is exactly what he is doing to them. He judges everyone by the measuring stick of himself.

In the situations where you express rage, could it be because you do not understand the whole truth? You know bits and pieces of it, and you have come to your own conclusions, but you have not seen it through the eyes of God. Is this not the circumstances of King Herod? He has no awareness of the Angel of the Lord appearing in the night hour. He certainly has no knowledge of the kind of Kingdom the Christ Child will establish. If the Angel of the Lord appeared to the wise men because they asked him to, would not the same Angel of the Lord appear to King Herod if he had been seeking the truth? Is it not true for all of us as well?

We have returned to the subject of "seeking." Oh, we must have openness and sincerity in our lives. Rage does not live in the person who is passionately seeking after Christ. Jesus will bring light and dispel the darkness. He said, "***And you shall know the truth, and the truth shall make you free,"*** (John 8:32). Have you read the verse which immediately proceeds this verse? ***Then Jesus said to those Jews who***

***believed Him, "If you abide in My word, you are My disciples indeed,"*** (John 8:31). The obvious truth is that which Jesus discusses in His Word. Who will seek? Who will passionately allow the Word of God to reveal itself? There is a way out of rage.

I am simply not interested in recognizing rage in my life, and then attempt to deal with it. I want to know where it comes from and what creates it!

## Against God

Rage is a product of being against God. This is one of the great tricks of the devil. He camouflages the issue. He gets us focused on a minor thing, and we miss the major activity of God. Rage is not about the circumstances in which we find ourselves; it is about God and what He is doing. You can see it clearly in this passage. What brings Herod's rage to the surface on this occasion? ***Then Herod, when he saw that he was deceived by the wise men . . .*** (Matthew 2:16). As we have described earlier, this word has to do with "to play like a child," "to make sport of or jest." This is not what is taking place at all. Matthew writes from Herod's viewpoint. The wise men have no motive to undermine Herod, or to make fun of him; they are simply listening to God. Therefore, Herod's rage is not against the wise men. His rage is against God, who is directing the events.

This is a dominate teaching throughout the New Testament. We see it clearly in the life of Jesus. It may be the secret as to why Jesus could express such forgiveness at the cross. Rage could have easily possessed Him. He could have expressed extreme anger at His own people, the Jews. The leaders of Israel have plotted and lied to bring

Him to the cross. They broke the law in order to bring Him to crucifixion. He could have expressed rage at the Romans, who seem to have no concern about human life, except their own. Seeing that the disciples have deserted Him should have brought a response of rage. Judas betrayed Him with a kiss; Peter denied Him three times. None of the disciples have remained faithful.

But Jesus knows something beyond all of this. He knows ultimately neither the Romans, nor the Jews, or even His disciples are responsible for what is happening to Him. His Father is fulfilling a great plan. Peter understood this and expressed it in his sermon on the Day of Pentecost when he said, ***"Him, being delivered by the determined purpose and foreknowledge of God,"*** (Acts 2:23). God is acting in the midst of the crucifixion. To be outraged at the Romans, the Jews, or the disciples would have been, in reality, a rage against God. This is His plan.

In an earlier study we found the same truth about Joseph in Egypt. His brothers hated him because he was the favorite of their father. They sold him into slavery and told his father he was dead. When Joseph was promoted to the leadership of Egypt, they had to come to him for grain during the famine. Should this not have been a moment of outrage in Joseph's life? At last his horrid brothers were standing before him, and he had control over their lives. He should have hated them for what they did to him. But Joseph had the insight that God was in charge of a great plan. He said to his brothers, ***"Do not be afraid, for am I in the place of God? But as for you, you meant evil against me; but God meant it for good, in order to bring it about as it is this day, to save many people alive,"*** (Genesis 50:19-20). Why should he be mad at them when God was fulfilling His plan through their actions? To be enraged at them would have been to be enraged at God Himself.

Can you apply this to your life? Would it be fair to conclude that all rage is ultimately against God, who is really in charge? The realization of this truth will eliminate all rage. It will bring you into the confidence and security of God's presence. I find rest in knowing the circumstances of my life are in His hands.

I will never be interested in recognizing rage in my life and attempt to deal with it. I want to know where it comes from and what creates it.

## Authoritative

Matthew gives us some interesting insight into King Herod's life. ***Then Herod, when he saw that he was deceived by the wise men, was exceedingly angry;*** (Matthew 2:16). Again the Greek word for ***angry*** is a very strong word, which is made even stronger by an additional word, which is translated ***exceedingly.*** This Greek word for ***angry*** is in the passive voice. This tells us Herod had lost control of his passion. He was now completely controlled by it. His senses, and what little judgment he may have had, were blinded by his rage. It is what we call "blind rage." It can be spoken of as "to be so angry as not to be able to think."

Oh, I weep for us in our blindness. How will any of us have the clarity of thought to see truth and respond to it? It will take God Himself to break in upon our lives in revelation. Did He not do this with Herod time and again? Herod saw the same star the wise men saw. He looked at the same revelation of Scriptures many others had looked at. Rage reached the level of control in his life where he could no longer see revelation.

It parallels the situation with the leaders of Israel. Jesus spoke to them in parables (Matthew 13). He said to His disciples, ***"Therefore I speak to them in parables, because seeing they do not see, and hearing they do not hear, nor do they understand,"*** (Matthew 13:13). It is a fulfillment of the prophecy given by Isaiah. Even as Isaiah spills forth in prophecy there is this awareness that something has taken over the people. Something has been turned loose in their lives which have become bigger than life itself. The people surrender their ability, which then becomes their inability. It is a dangerous thing to do. Once they could see. Now they cannot see. Rage is like that.

Would you seek with me for the truth of God? Can He break in upon us one more time? Can openness and responsiveness overwhelm our hearts once again? Can we see anew?

# PART FIVE

## Matthew 2:19-23

## The Return Home

# Matthew 2:19-23

# The Moses' Story

As we approach the last section of the Christmas story it is absolutely necessary for us to go back to the original theme of Matthew's writings. He presents Jesus as the Kingly Messiah in forceful narratives. He establishes this basis with the "Genealogy of Jesus Christ" (Matthew 1:1-17). He clearly delineates four distinct narratives to trumpet the birth of Christ. East narrative begins with the same coordinative, continuative conjunction. Let me list these again for you:

The Emerging of Jesus – Matthew 1:18-25

The Entrance of the Wise Men – Matthew 2:1-12

The Escape to Egypt – Matthew 2:13-18

The Excursion from Egypt – Matthew 2:19 23

These four narratives are intimately linked together by several dominant factors. First, each narrative has a consistent Divine initiative. God moves upon the scene to warn and direct. No one could accuse God of being an idle bystander to these activities. He is definitely directing His plan. Joseph is commanded to take Mary as his wife (Matthew 1:20) to legitimize the birth of Christ. The Wise Men are warned to return home without regard to Herod (Matthew 2:12) in order to hinder Herod's plan of destruction. Joseph is warned to flee to Egypt (Matthew 2:13) to protect the Christ child from Herod's plan. Now Joseph is instructed to return to the homeland (Matthew 2:19) to bring proper foundation for the coming ministry of Christ.

In the second place, Matthew consistently highlights the fulfillment of prophecy. Each narrative's significance is found in the words of the prophets. God has either caused or included the event into the heart of His plan. He has successfully redeemed it until every event helps produce the redemption of the world, which is the fulfillment of His plan. The prophets foretold the events of God's plan hundreds of years before they happened.

I have ignored the third factor in the study of these narratives to this moment. It is the element of typology. As we approach this fourth narrative, it is impossible to ignore any longer. I have downplayed this truth because it is easy to be misled by typology. However, the entire fourth narrative is governed by a certain correspondence with the story of Moses and the Exodus. Both Jesus and Moses are threatened by the political leader of the region who slaughters many innocent children to protect their own positions. A narrow escape is experienced by both Jesus and Moses. In response to a Divine command, both return to the land of their birth. The wordage of the command as given by God in both cases is very similar (Exodus 4:19; Matthew 2:20). There is one element I want to highlight concerning the typology found in the life of

Moses. When we have finished I hope you will be able to see it is the dominant idea. We will make our approach in two distinct steps.

### Intervention Equals Purpose

I have a problem with any Divine intervention which does not have a purpose contained within the revelation. If there is no purpose then I judge that it is not a Divine intervention. This is not a recent conclusion, but has been building and boiling in my being for years. While it may not be the conclusion of a single Scripture, the tone and atmosphere of the Word of God highlights this truth. God does not act just for the fun of it, or because He just feels like it at the moment. The actions of God are always a response to His dreams. They contain great purpose.

If God speaks to me, it is because He has a plan and my response is required. Not to respond is more than just disobedience against His momentary call. It is to declare war against the fulfillment of the plan of God. There are no insignificant responses just as there are no insignificant calls. At the heart of every call is great purpose! A psychic appears to have information about my past experiences and relationships which come to him through the means of the mystical world. Why? What is the point? There seems to be no great purpose. I want to hear from the heart of the ONE who has the plan.

In the story of Moses, the nation of Israel was in Egypt through the influence of Joseph. Several generations have now passed and a new Pharoah is over Egypt ***who did not know Joseph*** (Exodus 1:8). The Hebrew people had grown to be such a large and powerful group, the new Pharoah felt threatened. He set taskmasters over them to afflict them and make them slaves (Exodus 1:12). Yet, they continued to grow and multiply. The king instructed the midwives to kill every baby boy as he was being born. But God reduced the pain of childbirth so the Hebrew women were delivering their babies without midwives (Exodus 1:19). Therefore, Pharaoh commanded, ***"Every son who is born you shall cast into the river,"*** (Exodus 1:22).

A Levi baby boy was born who was hidden by his mother. When she could no longer hide him she made ***an ark of bulrushes for him,*** (Exodus 2:3). They hid him in the reeds by the river's bank. His sister hid in the distance to see what happened to him. Pharaoh's daughter came to the river to bathe and saw the ark. Upon discovering the baby boy, she took him as her son (Exodus 2:10) and ***she called his name Moses, saying, "Because I drew him out of the water"*** (Matthew 2:10). Moses' sister came out of hiding, approached Pharaoh's daughter, and asked if she could get a nurse from the Hebrew women. Pharaoh's daughter agreed and paid Moses' natural mother to raise him. Moses was educated and trained in Pharaoh's court.

This story is full of Divine interventions. God produced a man for His people who would take them out of Egypt, deliver the law of God to them, and guide them to the land He had prepared for them. God set into the motion the fulfillment of the Messianic promise which would bring salvation to the world. Is there any question? This is Divine intervention with a great purpose.

In the story of Jesus, Herod the Great is threatened by the news of a new born King (Matthew 2:3). The wise men are certain of His birth and the scholars of Israel have located His birthplace (Matthew 2:5). In great deception the insecure Herod requests that the wise men return to give him the exact location of the new King so he can personally worship Him also (Matthew 2:8). A Divine intervention warns the wise men ***that they should not return to Herod,*** (Matthew 2:12). Upon their departure God intervenes again. And angel of the Lord warns Joseph to immediately depart for Egypt ***for Herod will seek the young Child to destroy Him*** (Matthew 2:13). Herod realizes he has failed with his plot and is furious. He immediately orders the destruction of ***all the male children who were in Bethlehem and in all its districts, from two years old and under,*** (Matthew 2:16). Another Divine intervention takes place at the death of Herod and the young Child is called back to His homeland (Matthew 2:19-20).

It is very evident that there is a great purpose to Divine intervention. God is protecting His plan. If He was so forceful in His activity with Moses would He not be much more forceful with His Son? If Moses was a key to the fulfillment of the dreams of God, is not the Christ absolutely necessary? God would protect Moses from the slaughter of the baby boys by Pharaoh's order, so He would protect the destruction of Jesus from the slaughter of baby boys by Herod's order. As the Divine plan survived Pharaoh's puny life, so ***when Herod was dead,*** (Matthew 2:19) God's plan continued. This is Divine intervention with a great purpose.

If you will kindly give me a moment of your time, I would like to tell you the Manley story? There was a church camp called Epworth Forest in northern Indiana. My father was a pastor and had taken his family and the young people of the church to the youth camp. It was on a beautiful lake with a lovely beach. There were designated times for swimming on the schedule. My father had spent most of that time with me in the shallow water. At two years of age, I was an attention demanding swimmer. Near the end of the scheduled swimming time, my father asked a teenage girl to watch me while he went for a swim in the deeper water. He made his way to the end of the long pier and dove off into the water. As he entered the water, the Lord spoke to him urging him to return to the shore. He immediately turned around and swam to shore. He could not find me or the young girl. Frantically he began to go through the shallow water and found me sitting on the bottom of the lake with the top of my head slightly under the water. He rescued me with no serious consequences.

Who could dispute this Divine intervention? I have never made this story known to any group of people for fear of being misunderstood. I am certainly not on the level of Moses and my story is not equal to Jesus'. This is not an attempt to elevate or inflate who I am. But does God intervene without distinct purpose? Would it not be proper for me to feel important to the fulfillment of the dreams of God? Was it only once He intervened in my life or was the above story an illustration of another hundred events scattered throughout the course of living? The evidence of Divine intervention is so compelling; I am driven to yield to the purpose of the intervention. How could I even count my life as my own?

This is the truth of His Word to me? ***Or do you not know that your body is the temple of the Holy Spirit who is in you, whom you have from God, and you are not your own? For you were bought at a price; therefore glorify God in your body and in your spirit, which are God's*** (1 Corinthians 6:19-20). Were not the Moses story and the Jesus story for the sake of the Manley story? As the Moses story was for the distinct purpose of the fulfillment of the Jesus story, so the Jesus story is for the distinct purpose of the fulfillment of the Manley story.

Are you feeling left out? Let us consider "your" story. You might say, "I have no such story in my life. I know of no Divine intervention in my childhood. Even if there was, I cannot prove it was any more than simply fate. I am not sure it means anything at all." You are certainly right in your assessment. Absolutely nothing can be proved! But eternity is going to be so much fun. You and I will be able to see all of the happenings of our lives and we will know the plan and understand the events. As we look back on the Moses story and the Jesus story, so will we look back on "your" story. We will see the hundreds of times God healed your body and you were not conscious of it. As a teenager you should have been killed a dozen times, but you were not. God saved you from a multitude of accidents. Above all He enabled you to see the purpose of His interventions.

Divine intervention equals distinct purpose. God has not gone to the trouble of involvement in your life without great purpose in mind. I will not and cannot accept the fact it was fate and coincidence. The intervention is too distinct and planned. You are no longer your own! Rights no longer belong to you. Time and energy are not for you to spend. You are under orders. Christ claims you!

## Purpose Equals Christ

If you even remotely agree with me regarding this truth, there is a question which begs to be answered. What is the purpose? While the details of His purpose may differ with every life, there is a fundamental thrust at the heart of the purpose. In reality, there is only "the purpose" not many! Perhaps He has called you to preach, to be a missionary, a teacher, or a worship leader. All of these callings are only incidental details of "the purpose." The danger is to see these details as dominant and overshadowing "the purpose." If you will focus on "the purpose" then the incidental details will be of little concern.

Investigate with me "the purpose" of the Moses story. It is a marvelous story of Divine intervention. When all Hebrew baby boys were to be destroyed, Moses was rescued safely. The marvel of his rescue is that Pharaoh's daughter took him into the very home of the one responsible for the destruction of the Hebrew boys. She paid Moses' real mother to raise him during the most formative years of his life. His real mother taught him about his heritage as a Hebrew and God Jehovah never allowed him to rest in the courts of Pharaoh. Though he was educated as an Egyptian and received recognition as a skilled Egyptian general, still Moses' heart identified with the bondage of his own people. He attempted to deliver them by secretly killing an Egyptian guard (Exodus 2:12). When his life was threatened by Pharaoh, he fled for his life and went into hiding for twenty years.

***Then the children of Israel groaned because of the bondage, and they cried out; and their cry came up to God because of the bondage*** (Exodus 2:23). God heard their cry and answered, but it was not because of their personal suffering, the method of their prayers, or the sacrifices they offered. ***God remembered His covenant with Abraham, with Isaac, and with Jacob*** (Exodus 2:24). It was His plan! He confronted Moses in the wilderness through a burning bush (Exodus 3:2). Moses played a key role in fulfilling the life of Christ, the Redeemer of the world. Because God had a great purpose for Moses, He Divinely intervened in his life. The purpose was Christ.

The leaders of Israel condemned Jesus. They held Moses in high esteem and trusted him, but rejected Jesus. Jesus said to them, ***"Do not think that I shall accuse you to the Father; there is one who accuses you – Moses, in whom you trust. For if you believed Moses, you would believe Me; for he wrote about Me. But if you do not believe his writings, how will you believe My words?*** (John 5:45-47). The purpose of Moses was Jesus. Moses had no focus but Jesus. God revealed many details of His plan in Moses' life, but "the purpose" was the life of Christ.

Now let us return to the Jesus story. The plotting, deception, and demonic response of a political king could not stop the fulfillment of the birth of a new King. Slaughtering of baby boys in Bethlehem and its districts could not touch Him. Divine intervention took place repeatedly. An ***angel of the Lord*** was on the scene rescuing the circumstances and protecting the Divine plan. All that had been dreamed was prepared through Moses and now would come to pass through the life of Christ. The Divine interventions were for a great purpose and that great purpose was the life of Christ. All things are focused on Him. There are many details to the story with a variety of circumstances, but the focus is the life of Christ. Miracles were done and parables were told, but the focus is the life of Christ. Let nothing else be highlighted. Jesus is the fulfillment of the plan of God. There is no other provision. Nothing can be added to Jesus. Contained within His person is the total design of God. Divine intervention is with a great purpose and the great purpose is Jesus.

Now let me tell you of the Manley story. Some Divine interventions I have recognized and others I have not. I have received some with gladness and often complained about others. I have been very grateful for such a privilege, but I have griped over the inconvenience. But this I know, these Divine interventions have always had a great purpose. The purpose is the life of Christ. God wants nothing for me but the nature and Spirit of Jesus living His life through me. He has never wanted service, money, or periodic moments of worship. I was built to be the body of God.

I have often substituted religious activities for His purpose. I have produced a form of godliness which may have looked good to my peers, but it was not Him. My legalistic pattern was accepted by the church, but it was not His life. I disciplined and controlled myself by my own spirit, in order to produce a security which allowed me to rest, but He was not the source. He has consistently intervened in my life for the purpose of bringing me solely to the life of Christ. There is to be no other source. My life is to be a product of Him alone. The Moses story was for the purpose of the fulfillment of the Jesus story. The Jesus story is for the purpose of the accomplishment of the Manley story. It is only accomplished when He lives through me.

What about "your" story? Are you any different? All of this has been for you! He is bringing you to the fulfillment of His life within you! No substitute will satisfy. No amount of religious activity will be sufficient. This is not a mere experience. It is not a membership enrollment plan. God's dream is fulfilled when He is living and producing through you. It is your shift from self-sourced to Christ-sourced. This is not a call to do the best you can, but a call to allow Him to be the best He is in you. Only then can "your" story be known!

## Matthew 2:19

## Herod Was Dead

How does history see you? When we look back how will you be remembered? Perhaps you feel you will not be thought of at all since you are not a famous person. You will never be in the history books. No doubt this is true with all of us, but someone will think of you. Someone will look back and reflect on you. What will they remember?

I became specifically interested in how the plan of God will remember me. It is one thing for secular history to view my contributions, but more important is my value in the dreams of God. Some of us believe that real history is "His Story" as contained in the Scriptures. Here is the real scene of reality. Therefore I am really interested in how God sees me!

Matthew forms a contrast between two statements in the beginning of his book. One is in the passage which is our focus (Matthew 2:19) and the other is back at the beginning of the chapter (Matthew 2:1). One is the opening statement of the second narrative and the other is the opening statement of the fourth narrative. One gives us great insight into the person of Christ and the other states something very significant about Herod.

## The Contrast

Matthew creates three different contrasts. There is the overall contrast and then two contrasts within this structure. On the one hand is the birth of Christ as seen in the first narrative (Matthew 1:18-25). It is a picture of acceptance of the message of God. It is a picture of faith and openness to all God wants to do regardless of what the complications might be. An angel of the Lord intervenes and the obedience of Joseph saves the day. Christ's birth is legitimized and God's plan moves forward. All of this takes place in the midst of an extreme moral dilemma. Joseph anguishes over the situation of Mary. All of his dreams have been ruined. He cannot possibly marry his betrothed Mary. He would be identifying with her sin as if he was guilty. There is no right thing to do. It is beyond the understanding or the reasoning of man. All is lost! BUT this dilemma does not stop the sovereign plan of God for redeeming His world. In the midst of the moral dilemma Christ is born. Miracles take place. Thus Matthew writes, ***Now*** (But) ***after Jesus was born.***

Then the picture shifts to Herod the king. God used wise men from the East to announce the birth of Christ to Jerusalem. It was plainly in their Scriptures if the Jews would have listened. The prophets foretold the location of His birth and where He would dwell (Matthew 2:5). This announcement does not cause wickedness within the heart of Herod, but it certainly reveals it. From his nature spills forth nothing but evil, deception, murder and destruction. Herod fights to maintain his security, position and control. His life's history reveals a pattern of self-centeredness. Every action seems to be sourced by the demonic nature of the carnal mind. There is no extreme he will not go to protect himself. He will kill innocent baby boys without a thought (Matthew 2:16). He appears invincible because of His authority and power. BUT Matthew writes, ***Now*** (But) ***when Herod is dead.***

Now these two separate contrasts blend into a single contrast. On the one hand ***Jesus was born.*** It is a picture of complete response to the plan of God. Everyone involved in the fulfillment of this plan is simply responding to the sourcing of God. Jesus coming to earth in the great incarnation is a response to the plan of God. The sacrifice, surrender, and total abandonment of Himself to the Father are displayed throughout the entire story. The wise men are in a state of response to God even though they would be considered pagans in contrast with the Jews. They are outside of the circle of Messianic prophecies and influence. God communicates to them through a star (Matthew 2:2). Surely their peers scorned them for running off on such an uncertain journey. But they respond to the vision God gives them. Joseph and Mary respond to the sourcing of God. Every action Joseph takes is against the logic of a well planned life style. He embraces a young lady as his wife though he thinks she has been unfaithful to him. He runs to Egypt in the middle of the night for fear of his life. It is impossible to miss the tone of dependency, surrender and openness. It is a picture of generosity (Matthew 2:11), embracing (Matthew 1:24), and seeking (Matthew 2:2). It is in the midst of this atmosphere the redemption of the world comes. ***Jesus was born!*** God is enabled to move in the fulfillment of His great plan. An entirely new covenant is given to mankind. God sits the struggle of the old covenant aside. He breaks His four hundred year silence in the greatest communication of all times. Indeed, ***Jesus was born!***

The story of Joseph is contrasted with a very different picture. Herod the king exemplifies self-seeking. He fights, protects, controls and defends. He is doing everything possible to maintain control. He tries everything to keep things as they are. He acts in anger (Matthew 2:16), deceit (Matthew 2:8), and evil (Matthew 2:16). There is no limit to what he will do. The very depth of the inner depraved soul of man is revealed in him. Satan's best work is being displayed. If self-centeredness is ever going to win, this will be the time. BUT ***Herod was dead.*** All his self-effort brings him nothing but death. The cause is lost! Self finds nothing but destruction in the midst of all it attempts to conserve.

We see the same contrast at the other end of the life of Jesus. What took place at His birth also happens at His death. Jesus protects nothing. He offers no resistance. He sets the stage for the action of the cross. He comes to Jerusalem and makes Himself available. He does not draw His sword, but rebukes one who does (John 18:10-11). There is an attitude and atmosphere of surrender, response and openness. Surprisingly Jesus uses no miracle power to bring any kind of relief to the terrible circumstances of the crucifixion. He loses everything. His ministry is over. The Kingdom of God is not established. His disciples are scattered. Nothing lasting is accomplished. He is crucified. BUT He is raised from the dead! Everything He lost is won, plus more. He sits at the right hand of the Father in power as King of the Kingdom. In dying, He lives; in losing, He wins. In humiliation, He is exalted.

The leaders of Israel rejoice over what they have accomplished. It has taken a lot of meetings, toil, and effort, but it has been worth it. Jesus is finally crucified. After all it is better for one man to die than for all of Israel to be destroyed. They must protect and guard their great traditions. If Jesus had His way everything would have changed. The oral tradition which has been more binding than the actual law of God would be set aside. The Gentile world will be embraced as brothers. The economy of the temple would have been lost, and they would have ceased to buy and sell in the court of the Gentiles. Worship in the temple would never be the same again. The leaders of Israel have no choice but to guard, protect, and preserve the traditions of Israel. They fight with all their energy to save the cause. Jesus has to die.

BUT the temple is destroyed. It is but a few brief years after all their efforts of saving the day, the temple is destroyed. Not one stone is left on top of another. It is like a plowed field. All of their self-effort saves nothing. Holding on to their traditions brings utter destruction to all that has been. The Jewish nation is scattered to the four winds and will not be recognized as a nation again until the mid-twentieth century.

It is a parable of strong teaching for our lives. Only as we surrender, die and yield can God enable us to live. When we protect, guard, and try to save we bring ourselves nothing but destruction. It is in loosing our lives we find our lives. It is in dying we live! This is true in our home, our jobs and all of our relationships. We must embrace the death of Christ. It is the style of the cross. Losing our lives must be the style of our living.

## The Confirmation

Matthew uses these two parallel phrases to present a strong contrast and project truth upon us. ***Now*** (But) ***after Jesus was born*** (Matthew 2:1) and ***Now*** (But) ***when Herod was dead*** (Matthew 2:19) are so similar in grammar construction our attention is drawn to the contrast. Each statement begins with the contrasting conjunction ***Now*** (But). The primary translation of this Greek word is "but" which suggests the contrast. There are some other remarkable similarities between the two phrases. A strong focus on the event itself is found in the aorist tense of both verbs. Both of these statements are participle phrases which serve as adverbs giving content to the main verb. ***Now after Jesus was born*** gives the time when the wise men came to Jerusalem from the East. ***Now when Herod was dead*** gives the time when an angel of the Lord appears in a dream to Joseph in Egypt.

There is only one difference between these two contrasting statements. It is in the voice of the verbs. The verb referring to Jesus ***(was born)*** is in the passive voice and the verb referring to Herod ***(was dead)*** is in the active voice. The difference between these two types is in the responsibility of the action of the verb. The emphasis is upon Herod's responsibility for his condition of death. However, Jesus is not responsible for His birth, but is being acted upon. Jesus is responding to the activity of God who is producing Him, while Herod is aggressively destroying himself with his own selfish acts.

This is a reinforcement of the contrast Matthew establishes between Jesus and Herod. We find life when we submit and surrender. This is the only attitude which does not produce death. The examples of this truth are so numerous in every area of life that these pages cannot contain them. Paul urges husbands and wives to submit to each other (Ephesians 5:22-33). It is the only possibility for marriage to maintain the high level of intimacy as portrayed between Jesus and His bride, the church. Self-centeredness brings destruction to the relationship and always divides. Children are exhorted to obey their parents (Ephesians 6:1). It is a command of God which promises life. Rebellion sows the seeds of death. Servants are to be submissive to those who are over them (Ephesians 6:5). In reality they are actually surrendering to Jesus.

The guiding principle in every area of life and in every conflict is the style of the cross. We must be redemptive. Do not think of yourself. Christianity does not urge us to think less of ourselves, but to think of ourselves not at all! It is the atmosphere of life. Everything else is death! The contrast between Jesus and Herod proclaims this truth. It is a life and death issue! As you plainly see in this illustration life or death goes beyond the single individual involved. The submission of Jesus brought about redemption for the entire world. It has spread to this very generation of time. Paul made this strong statement. ***Therefore, as through one man's offense judgment came to all men, resulting in condemnation, even so through one Man's righteous act the free gift came to all men, resulting in justification of life*** (Romans 5:18). As this was true about the submissive Jesus, so it is also true about the self-centered Herod. Listen to the cries of mothers and fathers in Bethlehem and its surrounding districts. No one can measure the depth of negative influence Herod had on Judah and the leadership of Israel at that time. Nothing was produced from his selfishness but death. This is but an example of your own life. Life or death is your choice. However, there is one more factor to study in this context.

## The Consummation

***Now*** (But) ***after Jesus was born*** is a phrase that brings nothing but rejoicing to the heart of the world. No wonder angels are singing in heaven. People from all corners of the world are involved (wise men). The lowest in cultural status to the highest among the rich are summoned by the glory of His birth. Shepherds are attracted and the mighty of Jerusalem are shaken. But what else could be the response?

This birth begins the climax of the long range plans of God. From the first Messianic promise (Genesis 3:15) God has been moving history in this direction. It has been a slow but steady process. Nations have been affected and miracles have been in abundance as God intervenes to conserve His plan. The birth of Jesus is the reaching of the summit. It has the sense of arrival about it. All the planning and work is now coming to fruition. It is accompanied with an air of excitement and thrill. The long wait is over. We have finally arrived.

But the atmosphere is totally different in the parallel statement. ***Now*** (But) ***when Herod was dead*** produces other sensations. Perhaps there is a bit of joy connected with his death. Finally the hindrance and threat are over. There is one less battle to fight; there is one less obstacle to overcome. However, any joy involved has the cloud of sadness covering it. What a tragedy! What a waste!

One wonders how his personal life will be viewed. The concern is not just the opinion of those close to me, but how God views my involvement. Am I a hindrance which He will be glad to see eliminated so His plan can go forward? Am I a fulfillment of His dream? Do I produce a sense of accomplishment for God? Do I hear Him wiping His hands as if He can finally take this obstacle off His list? Or is God sitting on the edge of His seat in anticipation? Am I a hindrance of fulfillment?

The difference between the two is not contained in talent, personality or effort. The difference is in response, openness, and seeking as contrasted with fighting, protecting and self-effort. The success of Joseph was found in his surrender and response to the Christ who entered his family. The tragedy of Herod was his resistance to the presentation of Christ at his very door. It is the cross style verses the self-style. What is your style?

# Matthew 2:19

## A Dream World

The time between the Old Testament and the New Testament is a period of four hundred years. A study of this time is very revealing. The main characteristic of the era is the lack of authentic prophets. There were many prophets and religious writings which were produced, but none spoke as the voice of God. It was a period of great silence! For many of us silence is very frightening. It leaves us with the sensation of emptiness. It appears nothing is happening. However, God was preparing to speak with a voice never before heard. He was going to bring about the greatest feat the generations would ever witness. He Himself was going to become man.

During these four hundred years without the speaking of God, man reverted to his own religious inclinations. Judah seemed to have been cured of her lust for idolatry through the Babylonian captivity. Never again would they run after foreign gods. There developed an almost intolerable spirit of exclusiveness. It appeared in the form of striving after legal holiness. A group of people who dedicated themselves to a strict observance of the law of God began to form. They became known as the Pharisees. They produced six hundred and thirteen oral interpretations of the laws of God. These oral interpretations became more important and sacred to them than the actual laws of God. The temple became the center of all Jewish life. The religious feast days were consistently observed. Men's lives were filled with religious observances and strict adherence to the law. When God is silent, one reverts back to his own doings.

The Gospel of Matthew is a record of God's breaking of the silence. He is speaking again! God had not rejected or abandoned man. He was simply preparing the scene for the greatest communication of all. The four narratives which begin the Book of Matthew give us the beginning of this revelation. Christ is born! However, it is not without its complications. Not everything goes smoothly, for there is an enemy. As we have noticed in the past, each of the four narratives highlights a Divine intervention. God rushes in to rescue the situation and preserve His plan.

There is a statement which occurs in three of the four narratives and is certainly indicated several other times. Each time it appears in nearly the same grammar form (Matthew 1:20; 2:13, 2:19). Matthew writes, ***Now when Herod was dead, behold, an angel of the Lord appeared in a dream to Joseph in Egypt,*** (Matthew 2:19). The same appearance is referred to in other places in the narratives (Matthew 1:24, 2:12, 2:22). Matthew highlights the importance of what is transpiring. This event is worthy of the full attention and intervention of God. Through the prophecies quoted we see the long range, detailed plan of God is at stake. God will not allow His plan for the redemption of the world to be thwarted. We need to understand the content of the statement, ***Behold, an angel of the Lord appeared in a dream.***

## Resound

The statement begins with the familiar word ***behold.*** This word appears two hundred and ten times in the New Testament. We read it often in the Scriptures, and it loses its effect on us. We need to be re-sensitized to its significance. It is a demonstrative particle. It can be translated "lo, behold, look, listen or pay attention." It serves to call attention to something external or exterior to oneself. It is a prompter of attention which serves to emphasize a following statement. It is the equivalent to yelling.

It is clear that is how Matthew is using ***behold*** in this sentence. The wise men had been carefully interrogated by Herod the king. They informed him of the exact date the star appeared which would be the very day the new King was born (Matthew 2:7). He had determined from the Scriptures that Bethlehem was the location of the birth (Matthew 2:5). All that was lacking was the exact location of His presence in Bethlehem. Herod insisted the wise men continue their search for the Christ child and simply return to give him the information. All of this was under the pretense of desiring to ***come and worship Him also*** (Matthew2:8).

But God had other plans. The wise men were warned in a dream by Divine intervention and instructed to go home another way (Matthew 2:12). When Herod the king received word of what had happened, he was ***exceedingly angry*** (Matthew 2:16). Without hesitation ***he sent forth and put to death all the male children who were in Bethlehem***

***and in all its districts, from two years old and under, according to the time which he had determined from the wise men*** (Matthew 2:16). But God was faithful with His intervention. ***Behold, an angel of the Lord appeared to Joseph in a dream*** (Matthew 2:13). Here is our statement recorded again!

Joseph responded immediately to the call of the angel. He left with Mary and the Christ Child in the middle of the night. They escaped into Egypt before the edict of Herod could be accomplished. A part of the warning given by the angel was to ***stay there until I bring you word;*** (Matthew 2:13). Waiting on God is always difficult. Should Joseph get a job? Should they rent or buy a home? How long will this waiting time be? Most Bible scholars consider this time to only have been about three months. The entire threat against the Christ Child was focused in the person of Herod. ***Now . . . Herod was dead,*** (Matthew 2:19). ***Behold*** is a proper statement. It is time for yelling. Put yourself in the position of Joseph and his family who have been waiting. What a relief! It is time to return! Praise the Lord!

Remember the definition of the word was to call attention to something external or exterior to oneself. Obviously Joseph is not in charge of what is happening. He does not know the timing of the plan. He does not even know the plan. Therefore the entire emphasis is carefully placed upon the activities and plan of God. The answer to the dilemma of Joseph's experience is found outside of himself. Joseph could act out of himself. He could take his family back to Judea at any time, but he would be acting blindly. He did not know the risks involved in the first place; he certainly does not know when the threat has passed.

The future of his family and himself is entirely out of his hands. He must focus on the Source which is beyond him.

It is the key lesson of life! ***BEHOLD!*** Listen closely to that which is beyond you. Do not live out of your own reasoning and resources. When life is reduced to our own personal body drives, the satisfaction of our personal lusts, the limits of our own thinking, and the control of our own discipline, we live in constant danger and turmoil. This is why we are yelling at you! You must seek beyond yourself. The answer is not found within your own resources. You need a personal Divine intervention from the One who is greater than you are!

You must not think, "Where should I go to find this intervention?" He will come to you. He has already come again and again. You must choose for Him against yourself. It is a significant shift in focus. The next statement in our verse describes the details of this new focus.

## Revelation

***Behold, an angel of the Lord appeared in a dream to Joseph in Egypt,*** (Matthew 2:19). In an earlier study of these four narratives, a description of ***an angel of the Lord*** was given. Let me repeat a significant detail of that information. This angel of the Lord is referred to in the Old Testament as the angel of Jehovah. The outstanding characteristic of this angel was his ability to experience the presence of Jehovah. There were occasions when God would actually fill and merge with this angel in such a way it would parallel the fullness of the Holy Spirit experienced in the New Testament. It is not that this angel was God dressed up in an angel's costume. This angel of the Lord actually existed and had purpose beyond the merger experience. But there were times God would fill and use the personhood of this angel to give expression of His own personhood.

Again the events of the narratives are so important to God; He has come to personally supervise the fulfillment of His plan. When the angel of the Lord speaks, God is actually speaking. The external happening which the word ***behold*** focuses on is the revelation of God. It is an old truth but so fundamental to our search. God comes to us; we do not come to Him. He initiates the contact. We have desires for Him because His appearance to us awakens within us these longings. God's significant plan gave birth to your very existence. You play a key role in the fulfillment of His dreams. You were born out of the dreams of God, thus He appears to you with revelation.

There is a key factor about the revelation which is worth our attention. ***Behold, an angel of the Lord appeared in a dream to Joseph in Egypt,*** (Matthew 2:19). The Greek word which is translated ***appeared*** is a verb in the middle voice. This refers to someone doing something in reference to oneself. This again highlights the concern God has for the fulfillment of His plan. He makes an appearance because He claims ownership in the Messianic plan. Christ is His! He has a personal stake in what is taking place. He appears to us for the same reason! He has invested Himself is our lives. The details of the dream accomplished in us are of great concern to Him. He Himself is willing to come to direct and guide.

What really fascinates me about this revelation is the meaning of the Greek word translated ***appeared.*** It is used in various places in the New Testament to mean "to manifest" or "to be visible." But there is a tone to the word. The basic word originates from the idea of "to shine." It is used in connection with the sun and moon. In describing the New Jerusalem, John says, ***The city had no need of the sun or of the moon to shine in it,*** (Revelation 21:23). The Greek word translated ***to shine*** is the same as the Greek word translated ***appeared.*** This same word is used this way in the second narrative in connection with the star appearing to the wise men. ***Then Herod, when he had secretly called the wise men, determined from them what time the star appeared*** (Matthew 2:7).

This is the same word Paul uses to describe what God wants to do in and through us. ***Do all things without complaining and disputing, that you may become blameless and harmless, children of God without fault in the midst of a crooked and perverse generation, among whom you shine as lights in the world*** (Philippians 2:14-15). In introducing the person of Christ to us, John begins his Gospel saying, ***In Him was life, and the life was the light of men. And the light shines in the darkness, and the darkness did not comprehend it*** (John 1:4-5). One does not have to study much of the New Testament to understand this Greek word is connected to brilliancy, light, glory and joy. But this is the context of the appearing of God through the angel of the Lord. We understand this from the shepherds who searched for the new born Savior. ***And behold, an angel of the Lord stood before them, and the glory of the Lord shone around them, and they were greatly afraid*** (Luke 2:9).

Does not God appear (shine) to us in order to give us truth? Is not truth what Jesus is (John 14:6)? The contrast used in the Scriptures between the Kingdom of God and kingdom of Satan is the contrast of light and darkness. The appearance of God will be in the context of light and glory. He manifests Himself to us to give us joy, truth, light, brilliancy and glory. If you want darkness you must stay away from Him. Men who want to hide and live in the shadows do not want the revelation or manifestation of the angel of the Lord. In our Christmas narratives, Herod the king did not see the angel of the Lord. We are not even sure he ever saw the star which led the wise men. In speaking of the coming of Christ, the prophet Isaiah said,

> ***"The people who sat in darkness***
> ***have seen a great light,***
> ***And upon those who sat in the***
> ***region and shadow of death***
> ***Light has dawned"*** (Matthew 4:16).

Are you seeking the Light?

**Rest**

Rest is the final element of our discussion. Matthew writes, ***Behold an angel of the Lord appeared in a dream to Joseph in Egypt,*** (Matthew 2:19). The other two times in the narratives when the angel of the Lord appears to Joseph are in dreams. I realize this means Joseph was asleep. Each time the angel of the Lord appears it is in the middle of the night. Matthew is not trying to give us any spiritual insight into the timing of the revelation of God to our lives. One would not want to establish a new theology of the idea that God only speaks at night when we are asleep. There are numerous times in the New

Testament when God speaks during other times of the day when people are doing a variety of different things.

However, the spiritual truth continues to communicate to us throughout the New Testament that God wants us to ***enter that rest*** (Hebrews 4:11). It is in the midst of resting in Him that God is able to speak to us. This is an inward attitude, not an outward condition. We hear the voice of God most clearly in a state of resting, not a state of doing. We see this in the call of the angel of the Lord upon the life of Joseph. In the third narrative, ***behold, an angel of the Lord appeared to Joseph in a dream, saying, "Arise, take the young Child and His mother, flee to Egypt, and stay there until I bring you word; for Herod will seek the young Child to destroy Him,"*** (Matthew 2:13). The Greek word translated ***stay*** is the small word meaning "to be." It is the root Greek word used for the "I am" of Christ. Joseph and his family are fleeing in the middle of the night. They are rushing to a foreign land. The culture is different; they will be in exile. The command of God was for them to just be there until He spoke to them again. How difficult this must have been! They were living out of a suitcase, in a temporary home, without a job, no friends, and wondering what is going to happen next. They are called upon to rest in exile for God will speak again. If we do not rest in the exile, will we be able to hear His voice? We are so busy trying to solve the problem. Anxiety fills our hearts to the point that it overshadows His speaking. The answer is for us to rest in the glory He has already given us. He will speak again, but we must rest.

# Matthew 2:20

# One More Time

Something about the fourth narrative is strangely important. While the details of this narrative may not be as startling as the others, the impact of the passage is just as valuable. As you read the other narratives you feel like you are standing on the edge of something really big. There is an evil plot which must be survived. Then in the fourth narrative it is as if things are over. Herod is dead. All has been conquered! We are ready to return to Nazareth and get back to the plan of God. In a real sense, this fourth narrative pulls the story theme together and brings conclusion.

In this narrative we discover phrases which have been used throughout the story. We have already discussed ***behold, an angel of the Lord appeared in a dream.*** This continuing statement appears three times in three different narratives as the evil attempts are made on the life of the Christ child. Now another continuing statement draws our attention. When the angel of the Lord appears to Joseph, he says, ***"Arise, take the young Child and His mother, and go to the land of***

***Israel, for those who sought the young Child's life are dead,"*** (Matthew 2:20).

The wise men, being guided by a star, come to the house where they find the Christ Child. Worship is their natural response. During the night God warns them in a dream. After giving gifts, they depart for their own country and do not return to Herod to report the location of the new born King. It is during this same period of time another warning comes to Joseph. ***Now when they had departed, behold, an angel of the Lord appeared to Joseph in a dream, saying, "Arise, take the young Child and His mother, flee to Egypt, and stay there until I bring you word; for Herod will seek the young Child to destroy Him,"*** (Matthew 2:13). Matthew uses the same kind of language and grammar he uses in the fourth narrative.

The angel of the Lord appeared to Joseph the first time in the first narrative. The pressing issue then was Mary and the birth of Christ. The conception of the Babe in her womb created a moral dilemma for Joseph. He came to the obvious conclusion that Mary had been unfaithful to him. However, the angel of the Lord appeared in a dream and gave him specific instructions. ***Then Joseph, being aroused from sleep, did as the angel of the Lord commanded him and took to him his wife*** (Matthew 1:24). This is a different kind of statement than the actual quotations in chapter two (Matthew 2:13 and 2:20). It is not a quote from the angel of the Lord, but the grammar structure of the sentence remains the same. We have three different occasions which Matthew presents this same emphasis.

The two other narratives (first and third) have this same emphasis, and we have gleaned this truth in our past studies. Now we want to view the same concepts through the statement in the fourth narrative. It has similar truth in the statement in this fourth narrative, but there is value in a fresh look.

**Initiative**

We must recognize at the outset, God has taken the initiative. Those who are familiar with these studies of the narratives may feel this has been emphasized enough. But this is not our emphasis. Matthew has written this into every section of his writings. He is guided by the Holy Spirit. He makes a strong attempt to remind us that this is not Joseph's plan. He does not determine the schedule, nor is he the source of the deliverance. From the beginning to the end, God is directing.

This truth is clear from the story theme, and from the angel of the Lord's instruction. He said to Joseph, ***"Arise, take the young Child and His mother, and go to the land of Israel, for those who sought the young Child's life are dead"*** (Matthew 2:20). The assumed subject is "you" which is an obvious reference to Joseph. The reason for the assumption is that the main verbs of the sentence are in the imperative mood. The sentence has a compound verb consisting of ***take*** and ***go.***

The angel of the Lord introduces his command to Joseph with the word ***Arise.*** It is a powerful word! It is used in connection with someone going from a sitting to a standing position, from sleeping to an awakening, from scattered to collected, from unfocused to concentrating, from death to life (resurrection) or from part to total. This is the word most frequently used for the resurrection of Christ from the dead. The angel of the Lord is not interested in Joseph turning over in bed and going back to sleep. It is a call to be alert and focused. The entire facility of Joseph's being is called into play. The Greek root word carries the idea of collecting one's faculties in order to focus on the activity at hand.

The startling thing about the word ***Arise*** is its tense. It is in the aorist tense. There is nothing like this in our English language. It is a total focus on the event itself. In the English we most often translate this in the past tense. Therefore, it could be translated "having been risen" or "being raised." This is not one of the main verbs, and it is certainly not an imperative (command) to Joseph. His focus is to be on ***take*** and ***go.*** He does not need to be concerned about being raised. The angel of the Lord is totally adequate to call the entire facility of Joseph's being into an alert focus on the needed activity of the moment.

This is verified by the fact the word ***Arise*** is in the passive voice. The subject is not responsible for the action of the verb. The angel of the Lord does not require Joseph to awaken himself. He does not ask him to set the alarm and get up at two o'clock in the morning. He does not require him to splash cold water on his face and come to alertness. The angel of the Lord does this to Joseph. There is a direct intervention from God into the life of Joseph. Will he respond to God's intervention?

We must understand that this is not an isolated case in these narratives. This is the normal pattern of the angel's action in encountering Joseph. The Greek word which is translated ***Arise*** is used five times in three of these narratives (Matthew 1:24; 2:13; 2:14; 2:20; 2:21). Each time it is in the aorist tense, and it is always in the passive voice. The activities happening in Joseph's life are initiated by the angel. Joseph does not have the plan. He is not rescuing the Christ Child. God is in charge, initiating His plan.

This concept is fundamental to the Christian faith. In theology we entitle it "Prevenient Grace." We do not come to God; He comes to us. We do not seek Him; He seeks us. Even our desires for happiness, love, purity, and forgiveness come from Him. Everything good which comes from us is initiated by Him. We are not and never will be the source. Christianity is a call not to "action" but to "RESPONSE." I fear we have developed a hybrid Christianity. We act out of our own discipline and knowledge. We produce a great religion, but do not know intimacy with Christ. This great religion is filled with duty, obligation, striving, struggling and pharisaical pride. It is as all other world religions. It is man's attempt to reach God. But our passage again reminds us this is not acceptable Christianity. The Christian faith is God's attempt to reach man. God calls for our response. We must shift our control to His control. The central issue is "source." Every action, thought and attitude must be judged by its source. Nothing produced by us is acceptable. God has come and awakened us! Will we respond?

In our passage, the element of time is important. Joseph and his family are exiled in Egypt. He has already responded to the angel by coming here. The instructions were to remain until he was told differently (Matthew 2:13). How difficult this must have been for this family. It meant days of uncertainty in which they must trust the call of God. When will their exile end? Joseph is not to return to Israel on his own. The safety of his family and the redemption of the world will be determined by his response.

The message strongly applies to us. What God did in the life of Joseph, He does in our lives. He calls us to respond, but we are busy "doing" for ourselves. We say we are "doing" in Him, but we each have our own plan and fight over our Christian tradition. This destroys what God wants to bring to pass. He calls us to "respond." We do not need to wait for Him to come to us. He has already awakened us! We must not turn aside from Him in favor of ourselves. Will we respond?

***Arise*** is a participle. In this case it acts like an adverb and gives content to the main verbs. We must see the action of ***take*** and ***go*** through the eyes of this word. We must interpret these commands determined by this participle. This great concept will color anything else stated in the command of the angel. We need to look at the commands.

## Intimacy

Here again is the angel of the Lord's statement. ***"Arise, take the young Child and His mother, and go to the land of Israel, for those who sought the young Child's life are dead"*** (Matthew 2:19). The first command of the angel of the Lord is to ***take.*** The angel of the Lord used this same identical word to command Joseph to bring the Child to Egypt (Matthew 2:13). The emphasis of the word is renewed.

We have studied this word before, so we will not need to spend much time on it. It is a deep word and its content is startling. It is a relational term. Other Greek words could have been used to emphasize the idea of transport. This is not a call for Joseph to load up the supplies, place Mary and the Child on the mule, walk the many miles back to the land of Israel and his duty will be done. The Amplified New Testament uses the word "tenderly" in connection with ***take.*** Deep relationship, care and concern are required by this word.

In the New Testament this word is used to refer to marriage relationship. The angel of the Lord commands Joseph in the first narrative. He says, ***"Joseph, son of David, do not be afraid to take to you Mary your wife, for that which is conceived in her is of the Holy Spirit,"*** (Matthew 1:20). By the use of the word in this statement, relationship is intended. It is the most intimate of relationships.

John writes in his account of the Gospels about the relationship between Jesus and His own people. ***He came to His own, and His own did not receive Him,*** (John 1:11). The Greek word translated ***receive*** is this same word. The disappointment is not in the food served, the offerings given, or the hospitality extended, but it is in the embrace. Jesus is certainly the example of this kind of embrace. He said to His disciples, ***"And if I go and prepare a place for you, I will come again and receive you to Myself;"*** (John 14:3). Jesus is not just making room for us in His house. He is not just seeing that we have proper provision. He embraces us. In the second coming, Jesus tells us, ***"Then two men will be in the field; one will be taken and the other left"*** (Matthew 24:40). The very description of Kingdom relationship is found in this word.

Now the angel of the Lord commands Joseph to this kind of relationship with Christ. Can you imagine the feelings Joseph must have had during those days? Jesus is not his natural Son. His whole life has been upset by this Christ Child. What is to keep Him from resenting this intrusion into his life? What obligation does he have in this matter except for the command of God? Because he is a righteous man, perhaps he will simply do his duty. He will at least see that the Christ Child is safe, but this is not the call of God. He is to take the Christ Child and embrace Him as if He were his own. In tenderness and great concern, Joseph is to father this Child.

Now let us view this action of relationship through the participle ***Arise.*** Obviously this is not an action in which Joseph is going to be adequate. The same God who awakened him in the middle of the night will also source the love needed to be an earthly father to Christ. Joseph must respond to resource beyond his own! The task which is before him is beyond imagination. He is playing a key role in the redemption of the world.

Somehow you must see this for your own life as well. God has called you to relationships in situations beyond your ability. You must embrace those who have intruded into your space. How are you to do this? You are to respond. You did not start this and you will not complete it. This is His doing and requires your response. Will you allow Him to accomplish this in you?

## Imperative

There is one other command given to Joseph. The angel of the Lord says, ***"Arise, take the young Child and His mother, and go to the land of Israel, for those who sought the young Child's life are dead"*** (Matthew 2:20). Joseph is to ***go.*** In the previous command (Matthew 2:13) Joseph was commanded to ***stay,*** but now the threat is over and the call is reversed.

The significance of this word ***go*** is not in its definition, but in its mood. As already suggested it is in the imperative mood. In this certain instance, there is tremendous theological significance to its usage. It is an expression of God's sovereign command. It is used often enough in the New Testament account to cause us to attach to it Divine importance.

There was a man who was paralyzed. His friends brought him to the house filled with people trying to get close to Jesus. They took him to the housetop ***and let him down with his bed through the tiling into the midst before Jesus*** (Luke 5:19). Jesus immediately forgave the man his sins which invoked negative response from the scribes and the Pharisees. Jesus explained to them it was as easy to forgive his sins as it was to make him walk. ***"But that you may know that the Son of Man has power on earth to forgive sins" – He said to the man who was paralyzed, "I say to you, arise, take up your bed, and go to your house,"*** (Luke 5:24). It looks as if there is a strong similarity between this statement of Jesus and the one delivered by the angel of the Lord, but there is not. The grammar and words are strongly different except for the word ***go.*** It is a command of Jesus not to simply leave His presence and go back to his house, but to walk in the power of what has just happened to him.

This same truth is found in the healing miracle of the nobleman's son. A nobleman came to Jesus desperate for Him to come and heal his son before he died. Jesus simply said to him, ***"Go your way; your son lives"*** (John 4:50). This was not a request for the man not to bother Jesus any more. Jesus was not announcing that the interview was over. This was a Divine command for the nobleman to go in the faith in which he came. Even though he could not see at that moment the result, he must continue in the same faith.

The same idea applies to our passage! Joseph is to ***go to the land of Israel.*** The emphasis is not simply to return or make another trip. God moved upon Joseph. He is to go in the power of that supply. He is to go in the strength of God's command and in the faith of God's guidance. The ***land of Israel*** is a broad term. It basically does not give Joseph any idea exactly where he is to settle in all of Palestine. But he is to go in the confidence of the presence and guidance he has already received. In this faith, God will make the way plain, and indeed he did (Matthew 2:22).

God calls us to ***go.*** Many of us have taken ownership of the call and designed ways to accomplish it as well as shaping the final destination. But in light of the word ***Arise*** and the impact of the Divine imperative ***go,*** we are to make our way carefully in the presence of the One who has called us. We are to respond moment by moment to the unfolding revelation and the constant supply of grace being given to us. The call is not ours and the journey is not ours. We have nothing but the response of the moment. Even the ability to respond is not ours. We simply embrace the moment, respond in His power and find him adequate at every turn. Christianity is ultimately a call to simply respond.

# Matthew 2:20

## More Seeking

We have been viewing a summary of the fourth Christmas narrative. Matthew takes the themes of the first three narratives and focuses our attention on them once again. There is the theme of Divine intervention where God is not an idle bystander to the drama of these narratives. He appears through the intervention of the angel of the Lord. Time after time God miraculously saves His redemption plan. There is a consistency in the message delivered by the angel. This message resounds throughout the narratives. It is God's attempt to tell us that He is our new Source. He has initiated the call and will empower us to accomplish this call.

Matthew highlights another central theme in this fourth narrative. The idea of "seeking" appears once again. The actual Greek word used in verse twenty is also used in verse thirteen. These two statements are made by the angel of the Lord and are definitely connected. The angel of the Lord describes the condition in Herod's life. It is also a state of "seeking." No one can view Herod without being aware of the drive which seems to be within him. There is an aggressive hunger that dominates his life. It did not just appear when Herod reached this circumstance in his life. The birth of the new King was only one more threat to his personal security. As we view the history of his life, it appears repeatedly. He murdered Jewish leaders and members of his own family. Herod is a seeker!

While this Greek word does not appear any other place in the narratives, the intent of the word does. It seems to be the tone of each of the four narratives. Everyone in the narratives is seeking. It permeates the life of Joseph and Mary. The wise men are definite examples of individuals who are driven to seek. The very statement of the prophecies in the narratives makes us aware of the seeking heart of the prophets. The angel of the Lord appears often enough to give us evidence of the quality of his seeking heart. Though Herod seeks the Christ Child because of His selfish insecurity, even he is a seeker. "Seeking" seems to be the characteristic of every life. It is not a matter of whether or not we will seek. We are all seekers. We do not have any choice on whether or not we will seek; we only have a choice on what we will seek. Something is going to dominate our lives; we will be driven by something. The issue is "What are we seeking?

## Divine Seeking

It is impossible to saturate in these four narratives without being deeply impressed with the seeking heart of God. He is definitely not seeking with a self-centered motive. His driving motive is the redemption of the world. More specifically it centers in your life. You are in the picture. The opening statement of the very first narrative is a seeking statement (Matthew 1:18). It spills out of the genealogy which expresses the heart of God. It highlights the hundreds of years involved in the planning, dreaming, and seeking of God. Matthew thunders into this key statement of the incarnation with such thrust that it will carry you through the rest of the book. What God is doing in Christ is seen as the high standard of seeking.

The seeking of God in the four narratives is seen in the constant intervention of the angel of the Lord. It bespeaks the high priority and desperate desire of God to bring about redemption for the ones He seeks. God involves Himself in the fulfillment of His plan. This is too important to delegate to another party. God takes the initiative in the various Divine interventions throughout the narratives. Do you not sense the high level of intense desire? Is this moment not the climax of the entire plan of an Old Testament? Has not God been moving everything to the hour when He would assume your flesh? Surely this is what the Apostle Paul was saying, ***But when the fullness of the time had come, God sent forth His Son, born of a woman, born under the law,*** (Galatians 4:4). It is the seeking heart of God.

This same passionate seeking rises to the surface repeatedly in the revelation of the Gospels. Jesus told a parable to illustrate it. It was lifted from the heart of their shepherding culture. At the close of the day the good Shepherd brought His sheep to the fold. As was His custom, He stood in the doorway as one by one the sheep passed by His inspection. He was looking for injury and was accounting their presence. Ninety-nine had successfully entered the fold. One was missing. Jesus said, ***"Does he not leave the ninety-nine and go to the mountains to seek the one that is straying?"*** (Matthew 18:12).

It is important to note, the word ***seek*** is a translation of the same Greek word used in our study text. All Bible scholars agree on the emphasis of this verse. The focus is on the anxiety of the good Shepherd. He cannot tolerate the thought of one lost sheep out on the mountainside alone. He is driven to risk His life to rescue the lost sheep. He must seek! It is a picture of the heart of God for Jesus continues, ***Even so it is not the will of your Father who is in heaven that one of these little ones should perish*** (Matthew 18:14).

This same emphasis appears in the strangest conversation. A woman has come to the well at an unusual time of the day to avoid the other women of the town. She encounters Christ. John says, ***He left Judea and departed again to Galilee. But He needed to go through Samaria*** (John 4:3-4). It would be more correct to say Christ encounters her! It is the seeking heart of God. During the conversation, in a discussion of worship, Jesus says, ***"But the hour is coming, and now is, when the true worshipers will worship the Father in spirit and truth; for the Father is seeking such to worship Him"*** (John 4:23). Jesus highlights the Father's seeking. It is a translation of the same Greek word as found in our study text. The Father's drive is for those who will move into the new covenant which will bring them to a state of heart passion for Him.

The passages in the New Testament are too numerous to express in our study. Surely we must acknowledge the seeking heart of God. Has not God always taken the initiative? Has He not persistently sought us with a passion that is relentless? We should be stricken with awe and wonder at the passionate heart of God. He will not let us go. There is no length He will not go to in order to bring us to Himself. No price is too much to pay in order to win us to His heart. It is the story of Christ's birth as well as the story of His death. It is the redemption of the seeking heart of God! This is the vivid picture of what seeking should be.

Sadly, there is another picture of seeking revealed by Matthew. The intensity of the seeking is the same as we have just discussed, but seems like an inaccurate statement because self-sacrificing is not involved in this seeking. This selfish seeking opposes God's seeking.

## Demonic Seeking

Matthew gives demonic seeking equal attention in these narratives. The angel of the Lord states this boldly in our passage, saying, ***"Arise, take the young Child and His mother, and go to the land of Israel, for those who sought the young Child's life are dead,"*** (Matthew 2:20). Demonic seeking is most vividly expressed through Herod. Certainly the angel of the Lord applied the strength of the word ***sought*** to Herod. In the night hour the angel of the Lord appeared to Joseph to encourage him to flee to Egypt with the Christ Child. The reason was plainly stated: ***"for Herod will seek*** (it is the same Greek word in both texts) ***the young Child to destroy Him,"*** (Matthew 2:13). No one could question the truth of this statement upon hearing the cries of mothers and fathers who have lost their baby boys. In the passion of his seeking, Herod declares an edict which ***put to death all the male children who were in Bethlehem and in all its districts, from two years old and under, according to the time which he had determined from the wise men*** (Matthew 2:16). There are no limits to the seeking. Whatever repulsive acts have to be committed, they will be done. There seems to be no end to the depth of sin in Herod's seeking. Everything seems to be justified in light of his desires.

The same emphasis is given at the close of the earthly life of Jesus. There were many occasions for the leaders of Israel to set aside their evil plot of crucifixion, but they would not. Rather they heightened their efforts. ***But when they sought*** (same Greek word as in our text) ***to lay hands on Him, they feared the multitudes, because they took Him for a prophet*** (Matthew 21:46). There activities ranged from hiring witnesses to lie to holding illegal trials in the midnight hour. ***Now the chief priests, the elders, and all the council sought*** (same Greek word as in our text) ***false testimony against Jesus to put Him to death,*** (Matthew 26:59). They did not hesitate to blackmail Pilate even though it bypassed the working hand of justice. We would not be shocked at these methods if we were speaking of the evil men who commit criminal acts. But these are the works of churchmen, men of high standing, and men who follow the Ten Commandments. In his Gospel account, Mark highlights the demonic nature of their seeking. ***After two days it was the Passover and the Feast of Unleavened Bread. And the chief priests and the scribes sought*** (same Greek word as in our text) ***how they might take Him by trickery and put Him to death*** (Mark 14:1).

The demonic seeking is certainly expressed through Judas, the betrayer. Judas took the initiative to approach the leaders of Israel with the idea of betrayal. In his approach to them, he demanded money. When Judas receives the thirty pieces of silver, Matthew writes, ***So from that time he sought*** (same Greek word as in our text) ***opportunity to betray Him*** (Matthew 26:16). There is no dispute this seeking was sourced by demonic influence. ***Then Satan entered Judas, surnamed Iscariot, who was numbered among the twelve. So he went his way and conferred with the chief priests and captains, how he might betray Him to them*** (Luke 22:3-4).

One of the strong truths of the crucifixion event is the reality of our own personal participation. It was our sins which brought about this event. We were there! How often have you been told, these men were stating your desires? It was your sins which were responsible for such a hideous crime as this cross. Your face was in the crowd and you were shaking your fist and yelling in the face of Christ. Is it not just as true in this Christmas scene? Is Herod's expression not representative of our own? It is almost too hideous to think. How could something so vile be present in me?

## Derived Seeking

I am absolutely committed to the truth of the Scriptures that you and I are in one scene or the other. That is a bold statement, but you are either linked with Divine seeking from the heart of God, or you are linked with the demonic seeking from the heart of Satan. I have tried to discover a third category. Perhaps we would call it "non-seeking." Could it be possible that a person might not care about either of these ways of seeking? I cannot find this category anywhere in the Scriptures. The very make-up of our nature as built by God contains the element of seeking. The conclusion is that we are all seeking.

We need to agree on the next step. There are only two realms of seeking. Either we are motivated and driven by the nature of God, or we are motivated and driven by the demonic nature. My immediate reaction was that I may not hunger and thirst after righteousness like I should, but I am certainly not evil, depraved or filthy. We must not identify the demonic nature with gross, repulsive sins. The greatest examples of this are the Pharisees and the leaders of Israel. Jesus was firm on His evaluation of their spiritual condition. They took great pride in the fact they were descendents of Abraham. Jesus said to them, ***"I know that you are Abraham's descendents, but you seek*** (same Greek word as used in our text) ***to kill Me, because My word has no place in you. I speak what I have seen with My Father, and you do what you have seen with your father,"*** (John 8:37-38). They argued with Him. But Jesus pointed out that if they were really the children of Abraham, they would do the ***works of Abraham*** (John 8:39). Why were they seeking to kill Him? It was because ***"You do the deeds of your father,"*** (John 8:41). How could this be when they are so religious? They have consistent prayer times and fast on a regular basis. They are faithful in tithing and church attendance. They headed the list of righteous people in their day. Who exactly is their father? Jesus boldly says, ***"You are of your father the devil,"*** (John 8:44). The most religious and righteous people of the day were seeking out of the demonic nature.

We must recognize the carnal nature as the demonic nature. It is the source of all sin. It causes us to be aggressive about anything but Jesus. The list is long. Our seeking is focused on materialism, old cars, athletics, sex, power, prestige, peer acceptance, glamour, fame, popularity, control, and the size and cost of our house. The list could go on and on! It would include anything except seeking Jesus. The demonic state is a focus on self. The issue is not about the focus or content of the deed. It is the source! Anything sourced out of self is demonic seeking, and it leads us away from Christ.

What does the Divine nature produce in us? In the Sermon on the Mount Jesus instructed us, ***"But seek*** (same Greek word as used in our text) ***first the kingdom of God and His righteousness, and all these things shall be added to you"*** (Matthew 6:33). Here is the focus of God's heart! The aggressive desire and passion of the heart of God is for righteousness. Everything else is secondary and incidental to the embrace of the Kingdom which is all about Him. Paul echoed this same truth when he wrote, ***If then you were raised with Christ, seek*** (same Greek word as used in our text) ***those things which are above, where Christ is, sitting at the right hand of God*** (Colossians 3:1).

There is a strong contrast between Divine seeking and demonic seeking in regard to results. Every one who has lived testifies that demonic seeking never finds. Satisfaction is never achieved. The wisest man in the world wrote an entire book on this very subject in which he concluded:

> ***"Vanity of vanities," says the Preacher,***
> ***"All is vanity."*** (Ecclesiastes 12:8)

He went on to say,

> ***Let us hear the conclusion of the whole matter:***
> ***Fear God and keep His commandments,***
> ***For this is man's all.***
> ***For God will bring every work into judgment.***
> ***Including every secret thing,***
> ***Whether good or evil.*** *(*Ecclesiastes 12:13-14)

Involved in the Divine seeking is a powerful promise which is supported by the sovereignty of God. Jesus said, ***"Ask, and it will be given to you; seek*** (same Greek word as used in our text), ***and you will find; knock, and it will be opened to you. For everyone who asks receives and he who seeks*** (same Greek word as used in our text) ***finds, and to him who knocks it will be opened"*** (Matthew 7:7-8).

Jesus pictured the intensity and the all consuming nature of a heart seeking Christ. He told several parables which highlight how focused Divine seeking is. The parables paint the picture in settings we can easily understand. He said, ***"Again, the kingdom of heaven is like a merchant seeking*** (same Greek word as used in our text) ***beautiful pearls,"*** (Matthew 13:45). When this merchant finds the one pearl of great price, he ***went and sold all that he had and bought it*** (Matthew 13:46).

Everyone is seeking! You are driven and focused on something. There are only two options. Will you give yourself to that which matters forever? Will you take on the heart of God? It is not a matter of discipline or reform; it is a matter of nature. Your seeking will be a direct result of your linkage!

# Matthew 2:21

# More Responding

Repetition is the best teacher. We know this is true because this has been repeated again and again. The statement proves its own point. Matthew carefully uses this teaching technique to establish in our minds the foundation for the Gospel message. In the fourth Christmas narrative (Matthew 2:19-23) he restates the great principles he has highlighted several times previously. We must grasp these foundational principles or we will miss the depth of Jesus' parables and the training of His miracles. We cannot comprehend the value of His death, resurrection and ascension, without understanding the basis for these events.

Matthew presents these great truths in story form. The four Christmas narratives are formulated around these principles. The fourth narrative pulls together the story and brings us to a temporary conclusion. The immediate threat of Herod the king's plot to murder the Christ Child is resolved. ***Herod was dead*** (Matthew 2:19). A renewed interaction takes place between Joseph and the angel of the Lord in the midnight hour. It is a repeat of what has been consistently happening in the other three narratives. The great truths of God's initiative and the sovereignty of His plan are again unfolded to us. We plainly see Joseph is not in charge of the plan. God's plan has reached out to include the response of man. What an opportunity!

As we previously studied, the grammar of the beginning of the fourth narrative (Matthew 2:19) is the same as the beginning of the second narrative (Matthew 2:1). In addition, the announcement of ***an angel of the Lord appeared in a dream to Joseph*** (Matthew 2:19) has now occurred several times. Matthew again records the instruction of this angel of the Lord. He takes the same grammar form, and Matthew uses the same phrases as in the previous appearances. The angel only changes the instruction to fit the circumstances of that moment. Matthew again highlights Joseph's response to the instruction. He distinctly repeats the phrases used (see Matthew 2:14). Matthew writes, ***Then he arose, took the young Child and His mother, and came into the land of Israel*** (Matthew 2:21).

God is establishing a new covenant. He will require a new kind of obedience. Matthew writes to give knowledge needed in the new day. The plan of God has come into the fullness of time. Radical changes will be instituted. The Gospel account soon reveals that the Jewish leadership will not make the adjustment. And it is not hard to see Herod's unwillingness to embrace the change. He becomes the counterpart at Christ's birth to the leadership of Israel at Christ's crucifixion. At the birth and at the death of Christ we are presented with the same challenge. Will we embrace an obedience which is sourced by God and only requires response, or will we remain in an obedience which is sourced by self and requires self-discipline? Will we live in the fullness of the Holy Spirit now indwelt within us or will we continue to live a life produced by self-resource? Will we be crucified with Christ and allow Him to live His life through us or will we continue to live our own life attempting to please Him? Will we allow Him to serve through us or will we continue to serve Him with our best ability? Will we allow Him to accomplish His living in us or will we continue to struggle, strive, and attempt to achieve the high standard our own hearts call us to?

Matthew presents Joseph as the transitional example into this new way of interacting with God. He sets the pattern which will be repeated by numerous individuals calling us to a new life with a new source. We can learn by knowing the details of his response.

## Immediately

Response must be immediate! Joseph obeyed (in terms of response) immediately. This is revealed by the grammar structure of the passage. There is a parallel between the angel of the Lord's statement and the explanation of Joseph's response. Let us review the grammar structure of the angel of the Lord's statement. The angel said, ***"Arise, take the young Child and His mother, and go to the land of Israel, for those who sought the young Child's life are dead,"*** (Matthew 2:20). The two main verbs of the sentence are ***take*** and ***go.*** They are in the imperative mood which makes them a command coming from God. The subject of the statement is assumed since it is a command. It is the assumed "you" which obviously refers to Joseph. Each of these main verbs is in the active voice. This means Joseph is to take responsibility for carrying out these commands.

The statement begins with the word ***Arise.*** This is also a verb, but it is in the participle mood. It acts as an adverb giving content to the main verbs. You must see the action of the main verbs through the lens of this participle. Since this word is a verb it also has voice. It is in the passive voice. The assumed subject (Joseph) is not responsible for the action of this verb. He is being acted upon by the angel of the Lord. Joseph does not initiate this encounter. The angel of the Lord comes to him. Joseph is asleep and this angel appears to him in a dream and awakens him. This is not Joseph's plan. He does not set an alarm clock, slap himself on his face, splash cold water on his head and set down at the table to design a way out of his dilemma. This is brought about by the intervention of an angel of the Lord. This intervention is so powerful it is going to give content to the main verbs. The only reason Joseph is able to ***take*** and ***go*** is because the angel of the Lord intervenes and empowers him. The focus of the entire statement is upon the interaction of God in the life of Joseph.

This now brings us to the study of our verse. ***Then he arose, took the young Child and His mother, and came into the land of Israel*** (Matthew 2:21). This sentence is presented in the same grammar form as the previous sentence (Matthew 2:20). The two main verbs are ***took*** and ***came.*** These are in the active voice which means the subject is responsible for the action. The main subject is ***he*** which is a pronoun referring to Joseph. But the sentence begins with the verb ***arose.*** It is exactly the same word in the same grammar form as ***Arise*** (Matthew 2:20). They are both in the aorist tense, passive voice, and participle mood. It acts as an adverb giving content to the main verb. Joseph is not responsible for its action but God is acting upon him. While he can choose to respond, take the Christ Child and go to Egypt, he has no choice on being aroused. God has acted upon him. Both in sleep and in being awake he is called into full attention and focus. God enables him to respond.

Let me emphasize this does not do away with the choice Joseph had to make. He could have rejected the message. He could have gone back to sleep. No doubt he had plans for his day or week. But he does not hesitate. He is awakened by God, brought to attention, and he responds immediately.

I have a deep desire not just to respond to God but to respond immediately. This seems to be crucial in regard to response. One sees this strongly in viewing the various times when the angel of the Lord brings an awakening to Joseph. When the call comes to flee to Egypt it is imperative it be immediate (Matthew 2:13). Any delay will jeopardize the safety of the Christ Child for Herod in his anger will cause the slaughter of the baby boys in Bethlehem and its surrounding districts. Timing is absolutely crucial in the plan of God. Running ahead out of our own desires or lagging behind out of our own neglect are both devastating. Keep in mind God's plan is never casual or incidental.

## Intimacy

The second element of his response is intimacy. Every response has as its focus the embracing of Christ. I realize this is a broad statement. One might think this only applies to the commands from an angel of the Lord. Do you think your treatment of your family, boss, next door neighbor or the waitress at the restaurant should have nothing to do with embracing Jesus. But look at this passage. ***Then he arose,***

***took the young Child and His mother, and came into the land of Israel*** (Matthew 2:21). The first response of Joseph is expressed in the fact that he ***took*** the young Child.

In our previous studies we have investigated the Greek word translated ***took.*** This is a relational term. The tone of ***took*** highlights the idea of embrace, concern, and care which all point to relationship. The Amplified New Testament places the word "tenderly" before the word ***took.*** This is an attempt to relate the attitude and feeling involved. Joseph was not the natural father of this Child. He has been forced into a relationship he did not foster. His plans were very simple. He intended to enter into marriage with Mary and have several children. He would work at the carpenter trade and they would live happily ever after. Now he has been forced into taking on the responsibility of a Child not his own. He realizes it is the will of God. How easy it would be for him to do only his duty. He could transport, feed and cloth the Child as necessary but have no feelings for Him. God takes him beyond his natural capacity. He embraces Christ with a love beyond human effort. The response Joseph makes will take him into intimacy with Christ.

We discovered in the first Christmas narrative (Matthew 1:18-25) the moral dilemma in Joseph's marriage. He believes Mary has been unfaithful to him for she is with child. He should have her stoned to death according to the Jewish law. He decides to simply run from the situation as fast and as far as possible by giving her a divorce. But the angel of the Lord appears to him in the night hour. The instruction is to embrace Mary in marriage. To embrace the marriage is to embrace the Christ Child. Christ is in the middle of Joseph's marriage. As Joseph faces what all of this means for their future, the angel of the Lord appears again (Matthew 2:13). He instructs Joseph to immediately flee to Egypt. To embrace the future is to embrace this Christ Child. The entire safety and destiny of Joseph's life is determined by the Christ Child and his response to Him. In this fourth narrative we discover Joseph's residence and thereby his friends, employment, and cultural environment are all determined by his response to the Christ Child. To respond to the call to locate in Nazareth is to embrace the Christ Child. Intimacy with Christ determines Joseph's entire life.

This same truth appears in the lives of the wise men. Every response has as its focus intimacy with Christ. In order to respond to the star which they have studied through their astrology, they must respond to intimacy with Christ. God has used their knowledge to bring them to this response. There is no question, if we seek truth and real knowledge we will naturally come to Christ. How they respond to their own finances is determined by their response to Christ. The great expense they encounter traveling with the large army for perhaps a year and a half is a result of their response to the new King's birth. Their gifts of gold, frankincense and myrrh are an expression of their response to Christ. Is there any area of their life which has not been affected by Him? Even the route they take back to their home is determined by their response to Christ.

In Herod the king's life we see his response to Christ in the negative form. This negative response to Christ brings an agitation (Matthew 2:3) which will dominate him to the end of the story. His relationship with the Church (Matthew 2:4), how he treats the wise men (Matthew 2:7-8), and the laws he decrees (Matthew 2:16) are all determined by his response to Christ. There is nothing in his life which is not affected by his response to Christ. It is the determining factor of his life. It ultimately brings him to death.

Responding to Christ is not one response among many. It is not the satisfying of one need so your attention can now be turned to the other great areas of life. To respond to Christ is the determining factor of all areas of life. To embrace Him brings you into intimacy which controls and influences every area of your living.

## Incomplete

I want to propose to you that every response to Christ is incomplete, and it is the other element of response we must consider. Every response Joseph makes to the call of God is complete within that specific call, but it is only a step in the direction and plan of God. One response always leads to another. The angel of the Lord appears to Joseph in the midst of his moral dilemma (Matthew 1:20). God calls Joseph to respond. Indeed he weds Mary and the birth of Christ is legitimized, fulfilling the plan of God. But Joseph is not going to be allowed to retire from responding. The call of God will come strongly again in the night hour (Matthew 2:13). The angel of the Lord instructs him to respond by fleeing to Egypt for the safety of this Christ Child. Now in this fourth narrative response is required again. The angel of the Lord appears in the night to call Joseph and his family back to the land of Israel (Matthew 2:20). Joseph again responds. Herod is dead so you would think it is all over. Does response ever come to an end?

The ***land of Israel*** is used here (Matthew 2:20) and in verse twenty-one, but nowhere else in the New Testament. It is a broad term which could have taken them any place in Palestine. No doubt Joseph's plan was to return to Bethlehem from which they had fled for safety. Most Bible scholars think they were in Egypt for only a period of three months. This family must have many friends and relatives in Bethlehem. They had been there for almost two years. No doubt Joseph had found work there and it would be waiting on him. Also there was the factor of being nearby Jerusalem, "the holy city." The temple was there and at the center of Jewish religious life. If all the angel of the Lord had told them about Jesus was true, would He not need to be at the heart of the Jewish religious movement?

But as they make their way to the ***land of Israel*** God requires another response (Matthew 2:22). Does responding ever come to an end? When will the last and final response be accomplished? Joseph takes his family into Galilee and settles back in Nazareth which fulfills prophecy (Matthew 2:23). One can quickly see from the passage and from our own lives that response is never complete. Relationships are built on the fluid flow of response. It is not about duty, obligation, or accomplishment, but it is about embrace, expansion and depth. The embrace of Christ is an on going relationship requirement and you never complete it.

Will you open yourself to the constant flow of changing, stretching, and responding? How else will we know the depth of His person? Can our hearts be satisfied with where we are in our embrace of Him? Do we not ***hunger and thirst for righteousness*** (Matthew 5:6)? Is there any place to stop in our search for the fullness of His heart? We must shun any sense of arrival. We must recognize what God has done in our lives as the preparation for what He wants to do. Let us continually embrace Him!

# Matthew 2:22-23

## Let's Do Business

Matthew tells the unfolding Christmas story in four narratives. He gives us the story through the eyes and experiences of Joseph. As we walk through the narratives we must place ourselves in the sandals of Joseph. The narratives cover a period of at least two, maybe three years. Joseph progresses and grows tremendously as he learns to depend upon the angel of the Lord for the very safety of his family.

There is some indication that Joseph may have been an older man and Mary was a young teenager. He had finalized the marriage contract with the parents of Mary. He had paid the endowment, and this couple had entered into the betrothal, normally a period of one year. This time gives all involved individuals time to realize the full extent of the decision they have made. Mary and Joseph have very little contact with each other during this year, but they are legally married to the extent of being called husband and wife (Matthew 1:19). To retract from this betrothal period takes a legal divorce (Matthew 1:19). Joseph was to spend this year getting ready for the marriage ceremony. He was to put the house in order and set aside the needed finances. He had wonderful plans and dreams, and he was busy about getting everything ready.

Can you imagine the stabbing pain he feels when word reaches him Mary is with child? He knew she went to visit her cousin Elizabeth (Luke 1:39, 40). This was not unusual, but why did she stay three months (Luke 1:56)? Her pregnancy was becoming evident when she returned home and the rumors began to spread. Put yourself in the place of Joseph. He could only come to one conclusion. Mary had been unfaithful to their betrothal. It was over! With a broken heart Joseph realizes everything they had planned and dreamed was over. He should have her stoned to death for such a sin, fulfilling the Jewish law. To proceed with their plans of marriage would be totally out of the question. What should he do? Nothing is right!

He decided not ***to make her a public example,*** but ***to put her away secretly*** (Matthew 1:19). But in the night hour ***an angel of the Lord appeared to him in a dream*** (Matthew 1:20). This was the first time anything like this had happened to him. It was startling! He was horrified by Mary's pregnancy, and now she was suddenly raised to a new and higher level. Mary had made no attempt to explain what had happened to her prior to her visit to Elizabeth. If she had explained, Joseph would not have believed her. She was depending entirely on the movement of God to defend her. Joseph began to realize he had the privilege of being involved in the fulfillment of God's tremendous dream.

This was the first of several appearances by the angel of the Lord. Great faith built in Joseph as he lived in this unfolding drama. Experiences of deliverance bring him to a high level of expectation. God sent wise men to provide the very finances for their exile into Egypt. A relationship develops between Joseph and his God, the kind he had only heard about from the Old Testament readings. He knew God spoke to men in the past for the sake of His plan. He had learned the stories of great deliverance by the hand of God in the lives of Daniel, the three Hebrew children and others. Now he is experiencing it! It is too much to comprehend. He must have looked at his own lowly state and doubted that he could be involved. Yet he was!

The angel of the Lord was very specific in his instructions. They were to go to Egypt and stay there until the angel appeared again and gave permission to return. How long would this be? Should he seek employment? Should they buy a house or simply rent an apartment? It is hard to wait. But finally the angel of the Lord appears again. It is safe to return to ***the land of Israel*** (Matthew 2:20).

This left a lot of options that Joseph and Mary undoubtedly discussed. They probably decided to return to Bethlehem. After all, they had lived there for nearly two years. Perhaps they could get their old house back and Joseph could reconnect with some of his old customers in his carpenter trade. There were friends who would receive them with open arms and help them get established again. If what the angel of the Lord said was true about their Son, this would be the best place to raise Jesus. He would be close to the temple in Jerusalem. The best schools with the best scholars were found there. If Jesus was to be any kind of leader making the right friends now would be important. Bethlehem was definitely the place to which they should return.

It must have been while they made the journey that they began to hear the latest news. Herod the King was dead and ***Archelaus was***

***reigning over Judea instead of his father Herod*** (Matthew 2:22). The accounts of the evil things he was doing were as bad as those of his father. Joseph ***was afraid to go there*** (Matthew 2:22). The angel of the Lord did not give them a specific city to which they should return. Had Joseph progressed in his relationship with God enough for him to ask? All the other times the angel appears to him, God takes the initiative. Even the first time when Joseph had to make a decision about his marriage, he had not sought an appearance or answer directly from God. But something has happened in these last few years. Can he not now in confidence seek the face of God and expect an answer? Now it would be different than all of the other times. Could Joseph be so bold?

The Greek word translated ***being warned*** (Matthew 2:22) reveals a different tone to the revelation from the angel of the Lord. It is used twice in these four narratives. It is used in regard to the angel of the Lord appearing to the wise men (Matthew 2:12). It presents the idea of "an answer to a request." It indicates God's response to the seeking of Joseph. The angel of the Lord gives his instruction. Joseph is at liberty to go where he decides. But he has come to depend on God because of his established relationship with Him. That gives him the confidence to seek further guidance. He wants God not only involved in his overall life, but in the daily details.

The Greek word translated ***being warned*** is an amazing word. It comes from the root word meaning to do business. It has to do with having a "business affair or dealings, manage a business especially in trade and money affairs." It is used in relationship to kings and magistrates who do business publicly or give audience to others. It refers to giving an answer to ambassadors or petitioners. Thus it came to mean to give warning, to give advice, or give a response or decision.

God conducts big business and Joseph is in the middle of it. All the way through Joseph's experience with God we begin to see a new pattern developing. We see the Spirit of God enable Joseph to respond to His call. God pulls Joseph into His heart and the fulfillment of His dream for all mankind. Can you imagine the staggering opportunity Joseph has to participate with God in the redemption of the world? God brings Joseph into the core of His business. Joseph plays a key roe in God's fulfillment of God's business. Joseph comes to the place where he can be involved in the formulation and details of the business plans.

As I studied this idea the word "partner" began to appear. Luke gives us insight into the linkage between Peter, James, and John. He refers to James and John as ***partners with Simon*** (Luke 5:10). In writing to the Church of Corinth Paul says, ***If anyone inquires about Titus, he is my partner and fellow worker concerning you*** (2 Corinthians 8:23). This word is only used ten times in the New Testament, but is used numerous other times with a prefix on it. It is the word which gives expression to the body of believers. It is the Greek word "koinonia." I am afraid there is no way to give you the depth of this concept. Often it is translated "fellowship." But in our thinking there are various levels to this involvement. We have casual fellowship with many people at church, but we are not linked with them. We certainly are not a part of their daily lives. We feel no "business involvement" as if we are linked in a great enterprise.

I am sure this must have been true in the life of Joseph. He was ***a just man*** (Matthew 1:19). The Greek word translated ***just*** focuses on behavior. An individual conforms to the accepted standard of behavior. In the case of Joseph it is the standard of the Jewish law. While this is significant, it is not "koinonia." Fellowship with God is not his experience in the beginning. While he may have had a sense of being involved in the Jewish enterprise, he no doubt lacked any awareness of personal fellowship in the plans of God. But the last two or three years have changed that. A whole new "partnership" is established. Can you imagine how Joseph feels? He is a simple peasant man who is intimately involved with God in His redemption of the world! What is happening with Joseph is the primary step to bring us all into "partnership."

Paul was writing to the church at Corinth. He was dealing with the issue of buying the cheap meat which had been offered to idols. He makes it very plain that idols are nothing (1 Corinthians 10:19). There is no life in them and they have no effect at all. This is also true with the meat being offered to them. It is simply meat. The issue goes far beyond the idol and the meat. He explains that the Gentiles make ***sacrifice to demons and not to God*** (1 Corinthians 10:20). He then pronounces the crucial issue***: I do not want you to have fellowship*** (partnership, koinonia) ***with demons. You cannot drink the cup of the Lord and the cup of demons; you cannot partake*** (synonym of koinonia) ***of the Lord's table and of the table of demons*** (1 Corinthians 10:20- 21).

When living in sin we think we do what we choose to do. After all it is our life. We respond to our body drives and what pleases our spirits. All the time we enter into "partnership" with demons! We are a part of Satan's enterprise. We are aggressive business partners fulfilling the dreams and desires of the Devil. In our own self-centered will, we are drawn into intimate fellowship with the demonic person. It is horrifying to consider.

The Apostle Peter gives us the opposite picture of "partnership." He begins his second epistle speaking of the Divine power of God. This power is the author of all things that pertain to life and godliness (2 Peter 1:3). It is through this power that ***precious promises*** have been put into place. Through these promises which express the very heart's desire of God ***you may be partakers*** (koinonia) ***of the divine nature, having escaped the corruption that is in the world through lust*** (2 Peter 1:4). We enter into a partnership with the very heart of God. His burning heart's enterprise becomes ours. We are in intimate fellowship with what makes Him who He is!

The writer of the Book of Hebrews presents this possibility to us. In so doing, he gives an illustration of how we can have actual union with God. He tells us of Christ. ***Inasmuch then as the children have partaken*** (form of koinonia) ***of flesh and blood, He Himself likewise shared in the same, that through death He might destroy him who had the power of death, that is, the devil,*** (Hebrews 2:14). A son has become a partner with the very nature of his father, so Jesus has become a partner with our humanity. The Greek word translated ***shared*** is a synonym of "koinonia." God has become flesh. Thus the incarnation is an illustration of the kind of partnership God offers to us. The Hebrew author tells us the reason why God has done this. He is destroying the devil, who has the power of death. One partnership is eliminated for the sake of another partnership.

The Bible only considers two kinds of partnerships. There are only two possibilities for your life. You are either going to be a partner with Satan, fulfilling his dreams, engaging in his enterprise, or you will be in partnership with Christ. You will be filled with God's nature, involved in His plans, knowing His heart or you will be possessed with demonic nature, accomplishing Satan's ends, embracing his heart. There is no third category. The concept of neutrality does not exist. You cannot even be half and half.

God pulls us into His very nature. We are not workers on the assembly line. We are sons in the main office. We are not errand boys accomplishing assigned tasks. We are business partners in the enterprise of God. Has the awesomeness of this gripped your heart? You can be a partaker (partner) in the nature of God. We have the status of sons and daughters. We are next of kin to the Trinity, and we are heirs of God. Beyond all the benefits of this position is the greatness of joining God in His heart's desire. He shares His vision with us. He resources us by His Spirit to join Him in the highest level of His dream.

Paul expressed this through the concept of grafting. ***And if some of the branches were broken off, and you, being a wild olive tree, were grafted in among them, and with them became a partaker*** (form of koinonia) ***of the root and fatness of the olive tree*** (Romans 11:17). Paul emphasizes the close participation of the engrafted branch in the total life of the cultivated olive tree. It is a partnership in a great enterprise. It is far beyond being "a part" or receiving benefits. It is actually experiencing the life giving sap of the tree. It is being a vital part of the great business of the tree. Without the branch the tree can not fulfill its natural desire. Oh, to be grafted into Christ in such a way. Is it possible to become such a partner of the Divine? We become the fulfillment of His very heart's desire!

Paul is strong on this mystical union with Christ. He says, ***God is faithful, by whom you were called into the fellowship*** (form of koinonia) ***of His Son, Jesus Christ our Lord*** (1 Corinthians 1:9). Our life is identified with Christ. We become partners in His death and resurrection. ***I have been crucified with Christ; it is no longer I who live, but Christ lives in me; and the life which I now live in the flesh I live by faith in the Son of God, who loved me and gave Himself for me*** (Galatians 2:20). The danger of this partnership seems to be in misunderstanding the union. Paul consistently clarifies the issue. ***And our hope for you is steadfast, because we know that as you are partakers*** (koinonia) ***of the sufferings, so also you will partake of the consolation*** (2 Corinthians 1:7). He has clearly stated the content of the suffering to which he refers. ***For as the sufferings of Christ abound in us, so our consolation also abounds through Christ*** (2 Corinthians 1:5).

To become a partner with Christ is to join Him in His life style. It is the life style of the cross! It is His enterprise, His business. But how else could it be? If we are grafted into the root, if we are partakers of the Divine nature, would not the fruit be His? If we are business partners in the enterprise of His heart, would we not be an extension of that redemption? To join Him in His resurrection is to join Him in the fellowship of His suffering. To join Him on the deep level of His heart's concern is to partner with Him in the accomplishment of that concern.

I want to share with Him on this level. My heart must be joined together with His. I am surrendering the right to live my own life. I want Him to live His life through me. Wherever this takes me, it will be fine. I must know intimacy with Him!

# Matthew 2:23

# The Nazareth Syndrome

Have you been in an evangelism seminar when the statistics of salvation were given? It is astounding how few people are saved after they become adults. The greatest opportunity of evangelism is in children. We have all heard the statement made by the Catholic Church which says if they can have a child for the first seven years, they will have him for life. Children are very impressionable. They learn by example and we influence them when we are not even aware of it. The medical profession is telling us that the mother's attitude and actions have a staggering influence on her unborn babe. I think if we truly understood these things, we would be far more careful when it comes to our children.

We want to investigate the early years in the life of Christ. Matthew gives us a description of the events and influences which affected His childhood. What was his childhood environment like? Did God the Father protect Him from the abusive, ungodly culture of His time period? We are given tremendous insight into these questions in the fourth narrative of the Christmas story (Matthew 2:19-23). The drama of the story revolves around a major decision made about where He will live when His family returns to Israel. Herod is dead (Matthew 2:19). There is no reason for Joseph and his family to be exiled in Egypt. They have been patiently awaiting the appearance of the Angel of the Lord bringing the announcement that they can return home. But where is home? The message of the angel refers only to ***the land of Israel*** (Matthew 2:20). Joseph and Mary are allowed to decide where they will raise the Christ Child.

According to Matthew's writing, God seems to be very interested in directing Joseph and Mary to settle in Nazareth. This couple is headed toward Bethlehem. It is the most logical place to raise the Messiah. It is close to Jerusalem with its superior schools, strong Jewish influence and cultural purity. But there is still danger from the government. This causes them to seek further guidance from God. He guides them back to Galilee. Nazareth was their natural choice. Matthew reminds us through prophecy that this was the plan of God. ***And he came and dwelt in a city called Nazareth, that it might be fulfilled which was spoken by the prophets, "He shall be called a Nazarene,"*** (Matthew 2:23).

If you were a concerned parent with many options to choose from, Nazareth would be the last place to settle. While it was a small town, the trading caravans of the world traveled through it. Every culture, language, and belief system of the world influences this city. It is reported to be the home base of the Roman garrison responsible for policing a major section of Galilee. The Gentile influence upon the citizens of Nazareth is significant. Would this really be the best place to raise the Christ Child?

Why would God choose this atmosphere as the place for the Christ Child to spend the most impressionable years of His life? This does not seem like the proper place when you think about it. If you are going to ask this question about Jesus' hometown, you will have to ask that same question about most aspects of Jesus' life. There seems to be a consistent pattern throughout the life of God's Son. What impresses me most is that this seems to be unplanned from Christ's view. It is a natural result of who He is! There seems to be something within Him which simply responds in a certain style. He did not decide based on discipline or training. His decision came from the basic motivation and source of His life. He responded to the Spirit of the Father living within Him. It was His style!

### A Call to a Style

The southern province of Judea was separated from the northern province of Galilee by the central province of Samaria. Galilee was a distance of eighty to one hundred miles from Judea. Judea was the heart of traditional Judaism. The environment was culturally pure with less Gentile presence and influence. The leaders of Israel were exerting their influence in the temple to keep the traditions steadfastly in place. The synagogues in far away Galilee would have made some cultural adjustments amounting to compromise. This would not be tolerated in Jerusalem.

All the inhabitants of Galilee were looked upon with contempt by the people of Judea. Galileans spoke a crude dialect, and even this was offensive to the residents of Judea. The Galileans were less educated and their environment was less cultivated. They were not acceptable to the Jewish faith because of their constant exposure to the heathen element.

As Jesus was just beginning His ministry, He chose eleven of His twelve disciples from Galilee and only one from Judea. His baptism by the Holy Spirit took place at the River Jordan near Jerusalem. John the Baptist gave clear testimony concerning Him when he said, ***"Behold the Lamb of God!"*** (John 1:36). Two disciples of John the Baptist who were from Galilee were present at the baptism. They began to follow Jesus and they quickly enlisted their friends from Galilee to follow ***"Jesus of Nazareth, the son of Joseph"*** (John 1:45). One of them, Nathaneal, hearing these men testify about Jesus, asked this question, ***"Can anything good come out of Nazareth?"*** (John 1:46). The Greek word translated ***good*** is used in an ethical sense.

While Nathaneal's opinion was the same as that expressed by many residents of Judea, it is significant that he was from Galilee. This Galilean was criticizing someone from Nazareth, a city of Galilee, insinuating Jesus was beneath him. This indicates that the inhabitants of Nazareth have a bad name among even their Galilean neighbors for being irreligious and loose in their morals. This idea is strengthened by the response of the people of Nazareth to the ministry of Jesus. According to Matthew, the people of Nazareth are so upset with Jesus they attempt to kill Him (Matthew 13:54-58). Luke writes of another incident where they simply run Him out of town (Luke 4:16-19). Their willfulness and unbelief keeps Jesus from performing miracles among them (Matthew 13:58). They strongly reject Him and compel Him to reside at Capernaum (Matthew 4:13).

Jerome, a church leader from the fourth century reported that "Nazarene" was a slang or idiomatic term for an individual from a very remote or obscure place. It was a term used like our contemporary words "hick" or "backwoodsmen." Again it clearly expresses the way the Jewish culture viewed the residents of Nazareth.

It is important we understand Jesus was not just raised in Nazareth, He was continually identified as one of them. While He was born in Bethlehem, He was never referred to as being from Bethlehem. Nazareth was the original home of both Joseph and Mary (Luke 2:39). When the angel Gabriel came to Mary with the announcement that she would be the mother of God's Son, it was in the city of Nazareth (Luke 1:26). We have discovered from the passage we are studying that Joseph brought Mary and Jesus back to Nazareth from Egypt (Matthew 2:23). Nazareth is called the native country of Jesus; though He was born in Bethlehem, he grew up in Nazareth from the time His family returned from Egypt until His manhood (Luke 4:16). He was known throughout His life as "The Nazarene." He taught in Nazareth's synagogue and was rejected as we have already noted (Matthew 13:54; Luke 4:16). ***JESUS OF NAZARETH, THE KING OF THE JEWS*** was inscribed on a sign placed over His cross (John 19:19). On the day of Pentecost, as Peter gave the explanation of the event to the people, he said, ***"Men of Israel, hear these words: Jesus of Nazareth, a Man attested by God to you by miracles, wonders, and signs which God did through Him in your midst,"*** (Acts 2:22). At the conversion experience of Saul of Tarsus, Jesus revealed Himself as ***"I am Jesus of Nazareth, whom you are persecuting"*** (Acts 22:8).

There is certainly enough evidence to convince us that this was not a token identification. It was not even an identification which was forced on Him by an ungodly world. From the thrust of prophecy to the very embrace of Christ Himself, His identification with Nazareth was on purpose and with reason. Jesus identified Himself with the lowest and most despised town of His day. There was absolutely no personal advantage for Him to have taken on this distinction. Why would He do so?

I do not want to be guilty of making too much of this fact. If we overemphasize Jesus' identification with Nazareth we might be tempted to base an entire doctrine upon it. But the issue is not really "Nazareth." This is but a single expression of the principle of His life and the style of the cross. There are numerous other expressions to be noticed. To Jesus, all expressions were without significance. It was simply the way He is! He is controlled and dictated to by the very expressions of God. Therefore, the significance is not in the expression, but in His nature. Oh, to be possessed with this same nature!

Are you not overwhelmed by the God of the universe who leaps off His throne, makes entrance into human flesh, and is birthed through peasant parents of Nazareth? What kind of heritage is this for a King? As if that is not degrading enough, His parents are required to go to Bethlehem just prior to His birth for the reason of taxation. This would have been an advantage if Joseph could have found proper accommodations. But only the worst of surroundings were good enough for Him. The new King was born in a stable only fit for cattle. Dusty straw replaced the silk bedding of most newborn kings. No royalty watched in admiration at His birth, only donkeys and cows. Those paying homage to Him were lowly shepherds. Where were the leaders of Israel who were daily expecting the Messiah to appear? Even when the pagans from the East arrived in Jerusalem to give them the announcement of His birth, those anticipating the Messiah's arrival did not take the time to go the five miles down the road to Bethlehem to visit Him. Does this not reek of the same sense of the Nazareth syndrome?

The temple of Jerusalem was off limits to the handicapped and needy. Even the Court of the Gentiles intended for them had been closed to their presence. After all, these types of people are far beneath the leaders of Israel and their acceptable crowd. The people in need might defile those who are whole. But they formed the multitude to which Jesus ministered. Matthew writes, ***Then the great multitudes came to Him, having with them the lame, blind, mute, maimed, and many others: and they laid them down at Jesus' feet, and He healed them. So the multitude marveled when they saw the mute speaking, the maimed made whole, the lame walking, and the blind seeing; and they glorified the God of Israel*** (Matthew 15:30-31). Does this not sound like the Nazareth syndrome?

Was this not the heart of His teaching as well? Two disciples tried to manipulate Jesus through their mother to acquire the right and left hands in the coming Kingdom. The other disciples hear their discussion and are very upset. Jesus uses the occasion to reveal the heart of the Kingdom to them. He says, ***"But whoever desires to become great among you, let him be your servant. And whoever desires to be first among you, let him be your slave – just as the Son of Man did not come to be served, but to serve, and to give His life a***

***ransom for many,"*** (Matthew 20:26-28). It is the teaching of the Kingdom of God reflected in the Nazareth syndrome!

The ironic part of all this is Jesus was going to die just as He was born! The soldiers take Him into the Praetorium and gather the entire garrison (six hundred to a thousand) around Him. They are relaxed in their home quarters. It is time to have some fun with this proposed King. They strip him of his clothes and place a discarded scarlet robe on Him. He is King of the throwaways. They twist a crown of thorns together and place it on His head. They crown Him King of the thorn bushes. They put a reed in His right hand, and it is His royal scepter as He rules over the reed weeds. They bow their knees before Him and mock Him saying, ***"Hail, King of the Jews!"*** (Matthew 27:29). They parade Him through the streets, making Him carry His cross. They nail Him to that cross, and He reigns as King from the cross throne. Has there ever been such a style for such a King? Is it not the Nazareth syndrome?

There is a pattern developing which is completely beyond any of the physical instruments used. It is the very nature of who Christ is! He never ever lives for Himself. He always pours out His life for others. He is constantly redemptive. He never protects or pulls for Himself. He always risks Himself for the sake of others. It is the style of Nazareth, the cross style. We should be gripped by this style above all others! Can we allow any self-seeking or profit making in the name of Christianity? How can the appearance of softness and ease ever attach itself to this lowly Nazarene?

The writer of the Book of Hebrews spends thirteen chapters convincing the Jews of his day that Jesus is far superior to anything they have experienced in their old traditions. As he thunders to the climax in chapter thirteen, he contrasts the animal sacrifices for sin with the provision of Christ (Hebrews 13:10-13). The animal sacrifices are offered in the sanctuary. Their blood is spilled in the temple, but their flesh is burned outside the camp. In like manner, Christ offered His blood and suffered outside the gate. The Hebrew author's concluding statement is, ***Therefore let us go forth to Him, outside the camp, bearing His reproach*** (Hebrews 13:13).

This symbolism is definitely related to the cross. The Greek word which is translated ***reproach*** is the noun form of the verb used to describe the actions at the cross. ***Even the robbers who were crucified with Him reviled*** (reproach) ***Him with the same thing*** (Matthew 27:44). Jesus highlights this in the beginning of His ministry in the Sermon on the Mount. ***"Blessed are you when they revile and persecute you,"*** (Matthew 5:11). Can you read the New Testament without being deeply gripped with the call to join Him in His sufferings? The cry of the Apostle Paul's heart was ***that I may know Him and the power of His resurrection, and the fellowship of His sufferings, being conformed to death,*** (Philippians 3:10). He described Christianity to the Church at Corinth as ***always carrying about in the body the dying of the Lord Jesus, that the life of Jesus also may be manifested in our body*** (2 Corinthians 4:10). Is this not the expression of the Nazareth syndrome?

What would it mean in our lives to bear His ***reproach*** and ***dying?*** Our tendency is to make a list of activities which will constitute "reproach activities." We can find the least respected town in our area and move there, or at least go and live in the slum of our present town.

We can renounce all materialism and live the life style of a modest hermit. But whatever activities we might place on our list will only be activities. The Nazareth syndrome is not about Nazareth at all. It is about the nature of God being manifested in the life of Christ. The life style of Christ was not a list to which He constantly referred to be sure He was doing the right thing. He was filled with the very nature of His Father and He spontaneously acted in the style of the cross. In any circumstance, Jesus simply knew what to do. It always looked like the cross.

Is this not the cry of your heart? Is it possible to become so filled with the nature of God that we live out that nature? Do we know Him in intimacy until He is our life, and we express His style. It is an identification with His person to the point of death to our own personhood. I am giving up the right to live my own life with its self-manifestation. I want Christ to manifest His cross style through me. The total focus of my life will be on Him. He will be the total resource for my living. When others can see the cross style in and through me, it will be the obvious result of His being. Any self effort to produce on my own will simply taint its quality and scream of hypocrisy. It is the call from His birth and His death. It is the Nazareth syndrome!

# Matthew 2:23

# The Cross Style of Nazareth

The threat of the Assyrian monarch was no small matter. This monarchy was going to take Israel into captivity and dominate her. From His compassionate heart, God sent prophets to prepare the people. The reason for the exile was sin, but God had only forgiveness for His people. Prophecies were stated clearly, ringing of reconciliation and restoration. Isaiah was one of those prophets.

Isaiah did not belittle Assyria or undermine her great strength. He represented the Assyrian monarch and his army as a great dense and flourishing forest with all its glory and grandeur (Isaiah 10). Who could possibly defeat this power? He uses words like "high stature" to describe the towering power of this conquering army. Yes, Israel will be taken into captivity, but it will not be the end of the story. The Lord God Jehovah is greater than the ***thickets of the forest*** (Isaiah 10:34). Isaiah cries out, ***"And Lebanon will fall by the Mighty One,"*** (Isaiah 10:34). This once magnificent, vast spreading forest will fall and decay. It will be cut down with ***iron*** (Isaiah 10:34). In fact, Ezekiel, the prophet, attested to how the mighty Assyrians ceased to be a nation.

As Isaiah continues into the next chapter with his prophecy, he establishes an amazing contrast. He speaks not of a great nation, multitudes, or massive armies. He speaks of a single Person (Isaiah 11). While the Assyrians were at first magnificent and like a vast spreading forest, they will fall into total decay. This Person is pictured as the little sprout of a decayed tree. Yet, this Branch will rise, expand, and flourish. Isaiah is speaking of Jesus, who cannot be stopped.

In his prophecy, Isaiah speaks of Christ coming from ***the stem of Jesse*** (Isaiah 11:1). He refers to the great heritage and lineage of King David. God made specific promises to King David. All Jews were trained in the knowledge of these great promises. These promises caused hope to rise within them. On the occasion of the outpouring of the Holy Spirit, Peter preached to the people of Jerusalem. In speaking of David, he said, ***"Therefore, being a prophet, and knowing that God had sworn with an oath to him that of the fruit of his body, according to the flesh, He would raise up the Christ to sit on his throne,"*** (Acts 2:30). Could this ever be forgotten?

God promised that One was coming from the lineage of King David, and He would establish and rule on the throne of Judah for ever and ever. The very first test of anyone proposing to be the Messiah was his heritage. He must be able to prove his ancestors were of the line of King David. But the prophecy seemed so far removed and even lost. The ancestral line of King David had fallen into decay. When Jesus was born, His mother, though she was of that line was poor, obscure and unknown. From all appearance, the glory of the family had departed.

Yet, from the long-decayed root in the ground there would spring forth a Sprout that would restore the family to more than its ancient glory.

Many Bible scholars believe there is a direct reference to this fact in our passage (Matthew 2:23). They see a direct parallel to the Greek word translated ***Nazarene*** (Matthew 2:23) and the Hebrew word translated ***Branch*** (Isaiah 11:1). These scholars consider that Matthew was creating a linkage between this fourth narrative and the prophecy of Isaiah. Jesus was a ***Nazarene,*** a ***Branch*** or a Sprout from a decayed, dead root.

The Scriptures constantly draw us back to this concept. Victory and life do not come from the massive and magnificent forest, but from the dead, decayed root. What appears to be defeat and humiliation gives birth to victory and exaltation. Life is in the midst of death. Could this be the single truth of the Kingdom of God? If you investigate the crucifixion of Christ, life is found in the midst of death. If you come to the incarnation, life is in the midst of death. The crucifixion screams at us in the incarnation. Everything found in the life of Christ between these great events does nothing but reveal this concept. Life is in the midst of death!

We must state this concept clearly. The only way to live is to die. Remember the words of Christ. ***"For whoever desires to save his life will lose it, but whoever loses his life for My sake will find it,"*** (Matthew 16:25). Christ continually displayed this in His life. He never ever thought about Himself, but was always pouring His life out for others. Now we discover this principle was in His birth. He is a Sprout, a ***Branch,*** coming from the decay of a dead root. What a picture of the incarnation! What a picture of the crucifixion!

Again Isaiah is a prophet through whom God pronounced such a concept hundreds of years before the birth of Christ.

> ***There shall come forth a Rod***
> ***from the stem of Jesse,***
> ***And a Branch shall grow out***
> ***of his roots*** (Isaiah 11:1).

He not only stated the basic principle, but he also gave us insight into how it would be lived out. The concept sounds spiritual and theological. One could debate it for hours, but what does it really mean? How will it look in real life? What does it have to do with my daily life or my employment? Isaiah writes,

> ***The Spirit of the Lord shall rest upon Him,***
> ***The Spirit of wisdom and understanding,***
> ***The Spirit of counsel and might,***
> ***The Spirit of knowledge and of the fear***
> ***of the Lord*** (Isaiah 11:2).

Isaiah foretells of the baptism by the Holy Spirit upon the ***Branch***. The life of the Messiah is going to be one of total dependency upon the Spirit of God. He will not live out of Himself, but He will live out of the source of God. The human nature of Jesus both required and received in abundance the sourcing, sanctifying, and enlightening influences of the Holy Spirit. This enabling was not in Him transient or occasional as it had been in some individuals in the Old Testament. It was not limited to specific areas for life such as leadership, but it dominated the entirety of His life. There will be no resistance to the

***"The Spirit of the Lord shall rest upon Him,"*** (Isaiah 11:2). The primary meaning of the Hebrew word translated ***shall rest*** is "to rest, to settle down and remain."

The flow of the Holy Spirit is manifold. It affects the entire complex nature of man. Isaiah saw three pairs of distinct blessings flowing from the sourcing of the Holy Spirit. The first pair relates to the intellectual life, having to do with ***wisdom and understanding.*** The second pair focuses on the practical life touching ***counsel and might.*** The third pair relates to His direct relation to God which is ***knowledge and the fear of the Lord.*** We will now look at the first pair.

## WISDOM and UNDERSTANDING

We live in the information generation. We are information junkies, and in every field of endeavor it is a constant struggle just to keep current with the new data. Wisdom and understanding are not an accumulation of facts. In the Old Testament, the source of all wisdom is God, who is holy, righteous and just. His wisdom is always expressed within the context of His omnipotence and omniscience. Wisdom is a Divine attribute (Job 12:13). God numbered the clouds (Job 38:37), founded the earth (Proverbs 3:19), and made the world (Jeremiah 10:12) by His wisdom. Man, left to his own speculation, is totally void of all wisdom. God alone must provide this wisdom for man's moral and ethical life (Proverbs 2:6; Job 11:6).

The focus of the Old Testament wisdom is that the human will was dominated by its reality. In the realm of practical matters, man was to be subject to the Divine plan and cause. Hebrew wisdom was not theoretical or speculative. It was practical and based on the revelation of God as man lived in relationship with Him.

Now coupled with ***wisdom*** is another member of the same family which is ***understanding.*** The background idea of the verb form is to "discern." The Hebrew word used by Isaiah is a feminine noun meaning "understanding, comprehension, discernment or righteous action." In the Old Testament the act of turning away from evil was said to be understanding (Job 28:28). It was based on a proper prior discernment of what was evil.

It is easy to see how these two concepts are interrelated. Isaiah boldly says the Sprout from the dead root is going to be completely submissive to the ***wisdom and understanding*** of the Spirit of God. The Holy Spirit will be such a strong controlling factor in the life of Jesus; He will be a demonstration of the Divine discernment of evil. He will shun everything which even hints of unrighteousness. As He experiences the control of the nature of God, He will be naturally repelled from all things evil. Thus, there will be spontaneous, instinctive expression of God's ***wisdom and understanding*** in practical life. If anyone desires to see how the ***wisdom and understanding*** of God are actually lived out in life, look at Jesus!

Is it possible for the same exact Holy Spirit to indwell you and me? Can I experience such intimacy with the nature of God? Can the same expression of God's attributes be seen in me? Could I have a natural repulsion of all things which are evil? If this is possible can we settle for anything less? We will never consider partial or acceptable levels of interaction. Our lives will crave the fullness of the Spirit of

Jesus. The fullness of the Holy Spirit will be complete or not at all! Jesus set the standard for us.

## COUNSEL and MIGHT

There is a second pair of blessings flowing from the Holy Spirit. It might be well to consult a previous statement by Isaiah concerning the coming Messiah. He writes,

> ***For unto us a Child is born,***
> ***Unto us a Son is given;***
> ***And the government will be upon His shoulder.***
> ***And His name will be called***
> ***Wonderful, Counselor, Mighty God,***
> ***Everlasting Father, Prince of Peace*** (Isaiah 9:6).

Isaiah gives us the source of these great qualities which we share through Christ. The concept of ***counsel*** is far more than giving advice or guidance. The Hebrew word translated into the Greek word points to the inward predisposition or bent from which an action comes. It is strongly attached to the concept of purpose, to have in mind, or to intend. It denotes the unconscious willing or inner decision. Isaiah must have been shouting when he spoke these words. The Christ Child who is to come would have the weight of the government of the world on His shoulders. He will be One whose plans, purposes, designs, and decrees for His people are produced by the Spirit of God.

It is important to note that ***might*** is linked with ***counsel.*** The Hebrew word translated ***might*** is commonly associated with warfare. It has to do with the strength and vitality of the successful warrior. The purpose and designs of God are placed in the inner heart of Christ by the Holy Spirit. Christ is supplied with the strength and might of God by the same Spirit in order to bring to reality all God has dreamed.

Is Jesus the prototype of all sons of God to come? Is it too big a dream to think you and I can be filled with the Spirit of God and live in ***counsel and might?*** Oh, to have the very disposition of God controlling my every emotion and thought! Can the heart of God's desires be spontaneous within me? Will this not place Christianity on a unique level of living? Christian living will move beyond discipline, attempts, and struggles. It will be the new covenant as promised by God. ***But this is the covenant that I will make with the house of Israel after those days, says the Lord; I will put My law in their minds, and write it on their hearts; and I will be their God, and they shall be My people*** (Jeremiah 31:33).

This will not be religious ceremony or rule keeping. It will be the wild experience of intimacy with God! We will actually share the nature of God! As Jesus was the expression of the disposition and heart of God, so we will express the desires of Jesus. Can you comprehend how intimate that will be? We will not just know things about God. We will not just perform certain activities which we are told will be pleasing to Him. We will actually be drawn into the heart and nature of God. We will be one with His very being!

## KNOWLEDGE and FEAR OF THE LORD

This is the third pair of blessings. The Hebrew word translated ***knowledge*** comes from the root word meaning "to know." It is the same word used to express the most intimate relationship in marriage.

This word goes beyond information or data. It takes you into actually knowing the Person. This was given to Jesus through the Holy Spirit. The reason He could state His oneness with the Father is because of what He shared by the Holy Spirit. No wonder Jesus said, ***"And this is eternal life, that they may know You, the only true God, and Jesus Christ, whom You have sent,"*** (John 17:3). This is the accomplishment of the Holy Spirit from within.

Closely related to this concept is ***the fear of the Lord.*** In the Old Testament this is viewed as a positive quality. Embracing Him in ***knowledge*** will naturally bring this to pass. It relates to the awesome feeling of living in the presence of greatness. It is an expression of constant awareness that you have the privilege of joining the heart and nature of the One who is far beyond you. It can never be merited or achieved, but is graciously bestowed upon you. You will daily pinch yourself to be sure you are not dreaming. How can you be so privileged to have stumbled into an intimate relationship with One so great and to know Him in such intimacy? This is the expression of the life of Christ.

When one stands aside to view the great truths connected to the Sprout coming from a dead root, they are definitely tied together. Jesus is the prototype to usher in a whole new breed of humanity. He will be the prototype of the person the new covenant will produce. He will be an individual sourced by the Spirit of God. He will have ***wisdom and understanding.*** The Divine attribute of ***wisdom*** contained within the nature of God will flow through this individual which will give him a discernment concerning evil. He will be able to sense the slightest move toward unrighteousness. He will have the predisposition of the nature of God ***(counsel)*** and the ability ***(might)*** to respond to this guidance. He will live in such intimacy ***(knowledge)*** of the person of God that the atmosphere of wonder ***(fear of the Lord)*** at what he is experiencing in this embrace of oneness will be a constant expression in his life.

Does this sound like Jesus? Is it not a description of Christ as He was empowered by the Holy Spirit? Did He not come to establish this possibility for you and me as well? Does this description define your life?

Want further
resources
to help you
grow?